VILLAGE NOTABLES IN NINETEENTH-CENTURY FRANCE

SUNY SERIES IN EUROPEAN SOCIAL HISTORY
Leo A. Loubère
General Editor

VILLAGE NOTABLES

IN NINETEENTH-CENTURY FRANCE

Priests, Mayors, Schoolmasters

BARNETT SINGER

STATE UNIVERSITY OF NEW YORK PRESS
ALBANY

Published by
State University of New York Press, Albany

© 1983 State University of New York

For information, address State University of New York
Press, State University Plaza, Albany, N.Y., 12246

Library of Congress Cataloging in Publication Data

Singer, Barnett.
    Village notables in nineteenth century France.

    (SUNY series in European social history)
    Bibliography
    Includes index.
        1. Middle classes — France — History — 19th
century. 2. France — Rural conditions. I. Title.
II. Series: SUNY series on European social
history.
HT690.P8S55   305.5 '53   82-3195
ISBN 0-87395-629-X   AACR2
ISBN 0-87395-630-3 (pbk.)

Contents

Preface

According to George Orwell, it is always an excruciating thing to write a book, and I can only agree. The scholar who manages to complete a manuscript finds himself in great debt to a number of people and realizes that without them he would have been lost.

John Cairns of the University of Toronto first "turned me on" to village schoolmasters as a subject for a lengthy M.A. paper. I then fleshed out the subject for a doctoral dissertation under David Pinkney of the University of Washington, whose excellent editorial skills and counsel help give Chapter Six of this book what felicity of style and content it may have.

When I completed my final oral examination and was awarded the Ph.D. in 1971, one of the examiners said, in essence: "Why not go on to the other figures of significance in French villages (i.e., mayors and priests)?" Why not indeed?

It proved quite difficult to do. The French scholars who considered my application for a Canada Council research grant said the subject had to be done but that it would be elusive. That grant in 1977, as well as Canada Council doctoral fellowships in 1969-1970 and 1970-1971, helped give me the archival basis I needed for this work. I was also sent to France as a professor in the Northwest Interinstitutional Program for the spring of 1974, which permitted me to dip into the archives of Vaucluse at Avignon. A summer research trip of 1976 took me to other departments. Without the help of the marvelous officials in over a dozen archives, including the Archives Nationales, this study could not have been completed.

Partly due to the influence of David Pinkney, who reproaches North Americans for trying to match the French at their game, I have not succumbed here to what I sometimes call the historian's mania for comprehensiveness. The more one sees, the more distinctions one makes—that goes without saying; but it was not my intention to make this book a morass of petty distinctions in which the reader simply wallows. Explanatory fertility can get out of control.

The French *thèses* have been consulted, but I have had more aid and influences from this side of the Atlantic. I would especially mention Edward Gargan of Wisconsin and Eugen Weber of the University of California at Los Angeles, both of whom have worked extensively in this field. The studies of Judith Silver and John Merriman also had an extensive influence on my own work. I must give special thanks to Professor Jacques Léonard of the Université de Haute-Bretagne, Rennes, who helped me with documentation; but the errors of judgment and fact that may doubtless be found here are due only to the author.

Last but not least, I must thank Kristin Hansen Singer, Julia Scully, and a number of secretaries, especially June Belton, for their indispensable aid.

CHAPTER ONE

Introduction

This book treats not the *grands notables* of André Tudesq, but the village notables of nineteenth century France — priests, mayors, and schoolmasters (especially of the Third Republic). It tells who they were, where they came from, what they thought, what influence they had in local society, how they competed with each other for village hegemony or enhanced status, and what problems they endured. It is about a world that is no more, already in transition toward modernity, or at least the kind of modernity we have so far experienced. On the positive side such notables are seen as local guides and as "easers" of transition; on the negative, as repressive "lids" on the would-be emancipated and sometimes creators themselves of unnecessary disorder in rural areas.

Obviously such a study lies under the huge shadow now cast upon all research in nineteenth century French social history by Eugen Weber's *Peasants into Frenchmen* (1976). Specialists in this field know the book well. Weber's book was an original attempt to show that much of rural France before 1870 was not really "France" at all, as historians have traditionally understood that concept; but rather a congeries of isolated villages unconnected to the national scene, bearing their own patois, folklore, and artisan industries; and concentrating on purely local concerns. Weber has shown how peasants became "Frenchmen" under the Third Republic through agencies like the schools and not least through a dramatic rise in the standard of living.

Such a short summary, intended for nonspecialists, does not begin to indicate how revolutionary *Peasants into Frenchmen* has been in our field. At a variety of points, my own book either sustains or qualifies Weber's conclusions, or else takes off from some of his copious data. As the woods used to crackle with birds and game, so our footnotes must now — there is no avoiding it — be full of Weber.

How do I go beyond him? I think I do so by attributing more of an ac-

1

tive role to rural notables than he does and by stressing the in-betweeness of their function in rural society. The ambivalence of their position can be gleaned from the thicket of Weber's own details, but he does not really highlight the theme. Yet throughout his book we see such notables fulfill ing functions that often contradict each other. One function may aid the village or the preservation of its idiosyncrasies, another may serve to enhance centralization and hasten the destruction of local norms. Here we find one priest who speaks the local dialect, uses it in church, protects it, is proud of it; and there another who knows only French, or who cares to use only that language. We find a mayor who can josh with pals in the "home" language—the language of the *pays*, of soul, if you will, but who can also speak French to outsiders and read the city newspaper and communicate with important authorities above him. Even with teachers of the pre-1914 Third Republic, it is important to note that these were not solely black-coated missionaries, intent on colonizing the countryside, but rather people who were generally drawn from the *pays* or from nearby and who cared deeply for their area, all the while purveying outside knowledge and values that helped erode its traditions. In brief, all three notables discussed were both agents of the retrograde and agents of change.

For those interested in what we might call the second Weber thesis, this notion of ambivalence or in-betweeness is an important qualifier. It permits us to see *no* village of the nineteenth century as a perfectly cutoff entity, perfectly virginal, untouched by national trends. Because of the existence of these in-betweeners or mediators, certain reciprocal transitions had to be made. The point could be proven without a great deal of evidence: the Church itself used liturgy and catechisms that were relatively standardized. As for another Weberian matter of some importance—the putative lack of national patriotism before 1880 at the local level—I find that mayors especially could rouse such patriotism to a far greater degree than Weber will grant and that peasants were well aware of the new nationalist or outside influences. Yet these mayors are *also* seen defending local rights and traditions—often concentrated upon rival notables and local topics of petty proportions.

Because of that pettiness this subject is one the French sometimes brush away with one characteristic statement—"Ah oui, tout ça c'est le Clochemerle de la France. . ." (Gabriel Chevallier's novel *Clochemerle* (1933) is a saucy send-up of French village life.) This is not always the most serious or dignified kind of history one can do. The weird pretensions of our black-coated guides were already being questioned in the nineteenth century, particularly the role of priests, but most certainly without all the irony moderns now bring to the subject. We, after all, live in an era when just about all the fictive veils have been lifted, when almost all imagery has been looted of its magical effect upon the imagination, when the ideas themselves that made the clothes now no longer exist except as shells.

One side of us can see the mayor in his municipal sash giving a certain coherence to his village, a certain legitimacy—I make the point many times below. But then one sees the Clochemerlian aspect—the senseless *taquinerie* between priests and mayors or schoolmasters and priests, the showiness and vain pretensions of people far removed from the Schneiders or Thiers, and one wonders whether he is not making an ocean out of a puddle. One of my students, in a seminar that concentrated on Weber's book, told me that his picture of rural mayors came from certain American movies about the liberation of France. Some all-American type, grimy from battle, would be met with his troops at the village by a little fellow loaded down with medals as though he were *not* just the mayor of a tiny town but had single-handedly won World War II. Here, then, is the droll side of this subject, the one that could provoke any Groucho-like propensities an historian might possess. My chapter on struggles between mayors and priests should especially impress upon the reader the essential pettiness of some activities in which these local figures engaged.

The serious side, though, is never far behind—the influence they had, the values they dispensed, their importance in any view of French rural history. We now know the great lineaments of the world that made them possible. Even if we stop short of Weber, failing to credit every bleakness he attributes to much of rural France before, say, 1870, we still must call this a largely dependent world, a world deprived of mass media, mobility, or the economic independence that would also have permitted independence from the local "guides," the local notables who had their position because of the nature of rural society as a whole. There were, after all, many forms of dependence: the caprices of weather, the killing routines in the fields or at the artisan's bench, the iron certitudes of oral wisdom; the sumptuary molds; the superstitions. Isolation, geographical ignorance, and linguistic atomization also contributed to the problem. The rural Frenchman was bound by a fear of strangers and a fear of officials; by the narrowness of daily diet (actual and mental) and by the country smells that kept him in his station; by illnesses and illiteracy. Prohibitions and constraints came from many quarters: there was the "lid" of the family, with its imposed orthodoxies and silences; the inferior status of women; the necessity of immersing oneself in a trade; political immaturity; and the lack of varied opportunity—all to some degree bound together, some changing here, some there. Whether one agrees with Weber's argument in whole, or even in small part, one understands the *necessary* relationship of local notables to the character of nineteenth century rural France as a whole, before modern media and conveniences made them obsolete.

It is of course necessary to distinguish among the many classes of rural people. Joan Scott's glassmakers were frequently born in the country; did they simply shed their rural habits by working at Carmaux? Even in the country, attitudes had to be different among *fermiers, laboureurs, manoeuviers*, sharecroppers, and day laborers, although Paul Bois argues for their "moral homogeneity." Winegrowers had an independent outlook all their own. Then there were rural areas which had significant links to the city, such as the Stéphanois, where peasants supplemented incomes by weaving for urban merchants. These links to the city became stronger as the century went on. Fairs in all regions threw country people into contact with city people. In some areas peasants migrated seasonally to become masons or miners, then returned to their villages.[1]

For all that, one *can* make generalizations on the state of rural France in the nineteenth century—or on those who submitted to the reign of the notables. Lack of leisure is crucial. For the average rural person, whether a skilled artisan or a common day laborer, there was little time to break loose, except on designated days, and even then it was difficult to "loafe and invite the soul." The concept of spare time weighed upon a minority only. And it is obviously leisure that permits release from bonds and the questioning of ossified categories. It is also a knowledge of history that does so, and this most peasants, at least, did not possess. The peasant view of history is usually that it always was and always will be as it is now. Things will stay the same. Even though one might look at designated authorities and grow anticlerical or detest this or that mayor, rarely did one go to the root of an institution.

Peasants, it has been variously pointed out, are generally resigned creatures. Weber, among many others, has amassed detail on this attitude for nineteenth century France, and comparative detail from other countries highlights the point. In travel memoirs of nineteenth century Russia, for example, the same resignation, only more pronounced, is detected in serfs—if a horse breaks his leg it is the fault of house spirits or the Witch of the West; if a man dies, if a fire destroys a village, it is God's will.

Leisure, then, generates the values that might have overcome the reign of the notables. So does the diffusion of ideas and ideals, especially with the growth of mass media. As Weber teaches so well, the ordinary rural person lacked even a language of revolt. The forms remain intact until one gazes in the mirror and asks, "Who am I?" and—more important—"What can I be?" Such a right was reserved for the Rastignacs of the better classes, blessed with abstract consciousness. Language alone could generate true critical values; and rural dialects, as we know from Claude Duneton and others, were too concrete to permit rivalry with the normative monopoly enjoyed by notables. (The same concreteness of modern

Hebrew, says Arthur Koestler, hampers it as a viable language of modernity.)

Within this nineteenth century set of givens, *animal laborans* just hadn't much time for talk itself. His wisdom was better kept proverbial — hand-me-down wisdom from that seemingly immemorial past of family and community. It was E. M. Forster, I believe, who noted that he could not tell what he thought until he said it. The repression of speech, a product of custom and of necessity, favored the notables.

Forms of sexual repression are also noted below in the chapter on "The Lid," which notables kept fastened over such eruptive spirits as people did possess. One cannot simply blame the nineteenth century and its custodians of morality for such an ethos. Even for the better classes there were certain restraints that need no mention here. But it is true that sexuality (or uninhibited amusements) and liberation do go together.

What also gave the notables importance was the fact that they incarnated specialism — not so much of knowledge, but of status. They had a social image, and this, in a world of concrete signs, of externals, was crucial. It meant that they possessed what we might call "ritual monopoly," and that they had no great competition for hegemony except among themselves. Not only did they supervise the norms, they personified the values, which were then reciprocally reinforced by people who admired the local, the real, the legitimate. It worked both ways.

Notables were members of the Napoleonic hierarchies and received added legitimacy from that fact. They were situated on the ladder of the Interior ministry-perfect-subprefect, or the ministry of Cults-archbiship-bishop-curé-lane, or in the hierarchy of the *académie*.[2] Because of their connections with these superiors they brought at least something of an urbane context to the villages, and Weber certainly underestimates peasants when he divorces them completely from such urbane contexts. Correctly, he represents prefects or bishops as superior in social origins. But I have seen perhaps a thousand letters written by peasants to these officials, either taxing the local notable with some defect or praising his virtue. Peasants were never quite as ignorant of the outside or upper world as Weber supposes. They knew whence notables derived some of their legitimacy; and like any child who sees a parent writhe beneath his or her own parents' authority, they could spot the flaws in the armor and the obvious sources of hesitation.

Some of this book has to do, then, with these hierarchies and relationships. Notables lived in two worlds, two parallel existences, and it would be impossible for me to discuss them only in the village milieu. For that matter, it is impossible to discuss the village itself only in the village context.

The social origins of notables are also a source of the ambivalence of their positions. To be brief, a good many notables were of fresh issue, either from the peasantry itself, or from something pretty close. It would not be unfair to characterize some of them as half-peasants themselves. And this begs the question already broached. When in fact does a peasant stop being a peasant? When someone builds a road to his town? When he begins to read the newspaper for himself? I am not quarreling with Weber's basic viewpoint on this matter, or the delineation of a major sea change in attitudes; what I am suggesting, however, is the ancillary notion of residual peasantry, something one can hold onto even in the city. *A plus forte raison*, nineteenth century village notables often retained more than a little of the peasant background. Most were certainly not bourgeois. I discuss the point most fully with regard to Third Republic teachers, but it might be even more applicable to mayors. Mayors were one of the boys, yet they could usually read, and some travelled to the regional capitals. They were important *traits d'unions* but well anchored in one place too.

Now it may be that I am projecting some of my own ambivalence upon the subject; yet I also see this as an aid to comprehension. Too often we see the past in one way *or* another. For example, to say that the rural nineteenth century was illiberal and puritanical (by our standards) is partly true: but is it the whole story? It's half the story at best. Local notables I discuss were in many instances repressive, authoritarian, full of indecent puffery. But what I also try to get at is the pleasures of service, to others, the positive joy men have had in hierarchy, disciplines, and signs of legitimate power, or even semilegitimate power. *There* is M. le Maire; *there* is M. le curé, even with his authority questioned.

In our period of what we might call "The Whole Earth School" of French historiography, such ambivalent biases as historians have are not often presented. Perhaps it is right that we conceal our ideological cards, and what lies behind our motivations; but what I detect today is a curious nostalgia for Crane Brinton's little things, for the little people of history and the restrictions they endured. We curse those restrictions, but like moths attracted to a lamp, we seem overly fascinated with them. It may be that now, after all the restrictions seem to have been erased, we actually find ourselves paradoxically more repressed than public acknowledgment can decently permit. Or perhaps some who do feel liberated may suspect that the new freedom is not precisely what it was cracked up to be. By traditional criteria, we are almost all emancipated in the West today. Yet there may be an unstated nostalgia for hierarchy, and even — this is purely a guess — for illiteracy.

Of course the notables were themselves hampered by moral norms and I devote a good deal of space to this subject, for it illustrates larger *mentalités*. They had to respect the very limits they themselves gave to ordinary life. In Roger Thabault's world as shown in his excellent village study³, all people endow the simplest matters with meaning and relationship to their life: Amusements are not vague, but part of an ordered world. The casualty of such a world is of course the sensitive, disorderly romantic like Mme Bovary; quite rightly, she rebels against such a world. For her, and the genius Flaubert, notables were self-important bores, and we cannot say that Flaubert was wrong from his point of view.

But a man like Thabault knew village life better than Flaubert did (for all his powers of observation); and where Flaubert snickers artistically at the *lumières* of country cognoscenti, Thabault sees the real worth in each gain that came to the countryside, and understands the religion of progress and the solemnities of the backwater embodied by notables. The grave installation of a telegraph office by M. le Maire can stand as one of the most emotional pages in his *Mon Village*.

As for me, I suppose I find most poignant the final period about 1880-1914, crucial for both Weber and Thabault, who see it as the period of real loosening in the countryside. That it was. The postman now walks to work and holds a newspaper and has opinions and wants his son to get a scholarship and go on to secondary school. The prospects seem infinite.

Elsewhere, I have signalled this as a period of shaky equilibrium, which even its own inhabitants could not understand as such.⁴ I suggested it as a frail moment in French history. To me it is rather like a butterfly slowly sucking himself down out of the cocoon, ennobling himself in the tension wrought between the old constriction and the infinite horizons he finds outside. This I think Weber, for all his wisdom, fails to highlight. It is the beginning of the end of the notables, but they are still there. There is both hierarchy *and* progress, things look fine ahead, but M. le Maire and M. le Curé, not to mention the *instituteur*, are still here behind.⁵ Perhaps the evening work bees (*veillées*) are dying out, but there is a local brass band, and local pride coexists with the larger view of an ever-developing France, and the easier life. Stations in life, uniforms, beards, black coats, sashes, cassocks: these things still do have their importance. The notables are part of an older world, and yet in some cases part of the new.

Call this then a historian's own confession of preliminary ambivalence. Perhaps it will help explain why I see the era of local notables, and their very positions, in such an ambiguous light. But these notables of course had their own differences, and the following pages show that. And they can be set within chronological limits: most of the chapters do end with the *fin-de-siècle* perspective.

Finally, after all these philosophical justifications, perhaps more important here are the portraits themselves, showing just who these local figures were. Their *mentalités*, their financial positions, their origins, their daily difficulties are significant in themselves, for they shed light on all rural history in the period.

CHAPTER TWO

Portrait of the Nineteenth-Century Rural Priest

Works on nineteenth century priests are not lacking — we have several written by eminent scholars; and in the two most revolutionary works to appear in recent French historiography (by Weber and Zeldin) priests are also afforded significant treatment. Add to this output the many tomes in religious sociology, the diocesan histories, the great French *thèses* in the field, and you have an imposing amount of secondary work to begin with.[1] Necessarily I frequently employ it here. But I think there is still room for archival aperçus, especially on the psychology of priests and on areas like their sex life that no one has treated — on *mentalités*; and so, drawing heavily on sample diocesan and departmental as well as the national archives, and also sampling parish monographs, memoirs, and novels, I have felt ready to say something about this difficult group, heeding Oscar Wilde's dictum that he who would be exhaustive generally ends up by exhausting his listeners.

When we talk about the priest as local notable, we do so knowing that this depended on the region and its general tenor, and, as Victor Hugo would stress, the moment. The priest at least had to respect tendencies around him; in the Touraine and Berry, for much of the nineteenth century, that meant a "conformisme saisonnier"; in Brittany, unusual devotion to local saints, cults of the dead, pardons, pilgrimages; in the Lyonnais "a sober and individual piety"; in Flanders "a religion of the family and community, robust and simple. . . ." But the progressive slippage of religion everywhere makes even these generalizations suspect. Moreover, the curé was suspended not only between national and local, but more fundamentally, between heaven and earth — the very phrase used by Denis

Diderot to describe the curé's ambiguous situation. For Jean-Jacques Rousseau, the ideal country priest was a "minister of goodness", another hazy term. In day-to-day situations the curé had some of the jack-of-all-trades about him, a characteristic also of the Third Republic teacher; he could be something of a lawyer, a source of information and a go-between. Even that most gluttonous of priest-eaters, Voltaire, saw some merit in this earthly part of his vocation.[2] But the priest was also pre-Freudian psychologist, a doctor of souls, as the pages of the novelist Georges Bernanos show. If priests could rarely get as close to parishioners as psychologists can to their patients, and if the long buttoned gown they wore kept them always somewhat above and outside, nonetheless in the most respected of curés there was that element of confidant.

Did priests have more sway before the French Revolution than after? In general I would agree with those who say they did. After the Revolution there were fewer priests, and they were now employees of the State and more subservient to the bishop (who appointed them to parishes). Moreover, as the nineteenth century wore on, secular views obviously gained many converts. In the words of Roger Magraw, "the nineteenth century French clergy were never able to shed their dreams of a return to an idealized ancien régime. . . ." With villagers now harder to handle, looking backward could do them plain harm. Even seasoned priests must have felt sometimes like taking ideological lessons anew, courses in the art of persuasion, especially in hastily evolving regions such as the post-1830 Midi. Already a priest had complained in 1781 that a parish is "a multitude composed of all conditions, of all kinds of minds and characters. . ."[3] — rich and poor, superstitious and sceptical, immoral and prudish, patois-speaking and French purist.

Professor Weber has shown the persistence of priests as numinous father figures in the early nineteenth century and then their demise at the hands of potent rivals.[4] The crosses that guarded the fields had been symbolic of the priest's ascendancy; both were guardians in a superstitious world. Of course religion, or at least superstitious feeling, never entirely dies. Could the curé ever lose *all* his influence? Weren't convinced anticlericals sometimes confessed in the end? It is important, at least, to denote the psychological appeal a man in black had, and how that appeal transcends limited chronological boundaries. Doubtless, the priest was most needed by those who were prey to an insecure rural life: the old, the young, the infirm, and the nonscientific peasant. Dependent women were especially vulnerable to his appeal, even a bit erotically; many priests must have responded to such needs. Flaubert's Abbé Bournisien, indifferent to the gangrenous Hippolyte in *Madame Bovary*, can have been little more than a caricature.

Were priests hard workers? Not in the sense that peasants were. They were mind workers in a civilization where that kind of work was still rare and somewhat despised. Flaubert had a delightful, if contemptuous term for this—*des assis* (the seated). Yet they often rose as early as 5:30 a.m., had religious services to perform, visits, social affairs, charity, and meetings with welfare and parish councils. They kept parish records, performed marriages, burials, baptisms, and communions. They taught catechism, looked in on schools, looked in at the château, sometimes kept themselves abreast of local politics. And they watched over societies like the Congregation of the Children of Mary—(in *Clochemerle* one of its pious young members unfortunately gets pregnant); and supervised processions, before these were banned under the Third Republic.

Priests in processions were symbolic figures, enhanced by their mystique and charged, where their influence still remained, with being "significant others." These processions were grand, of course, in clerical areas like the West, where the garlanded church and candles and strutting bishop all left deep impressions in most parishes as late as 1870; but they were sometimes as impressive in less clerical areas as well. Emile Zola recalled the luminous character of Fête-Dieus in the Provençal town where he grew up—church bells claiming the sleepy afternoon, curé at the head of the procession, churchwardens in sandals, mayor in sash.[5]

One has to be impressionistic to portray adequately the priests' effect, as Flaubert paints it in the case of the young Emma. Here the priest holds the young girl in a kind of trance. One of the best passages on this primitive, prerational, or extra-rational influence is by Clemenceau, incredible as that sounds. It shows that good satirists half-love what they satirize.

> The crowd runs up, and the painted statues, and the paper flowers in gilded vases, the sparkling costumes, the display of the sacrifice, all this barbarous pomp that makes us smile, charms the primitive vision; and the shrill melodies of the breathless harmonium make the nerves more sleepy by eternal connection with the earth, vibrating deliciously.[6]

As the century progressed, priests were occupied with more and more extracurricular work: Action Catholique, Jeunesse Ouvrière, Jeunesse Catholique, Cercle Saint-Pierre. The mundane character of this work contributed to their loss of influence. Being seen frequently, and on such terms, stripped one of prerational charisma. With the rise of a competing power, the secular school movement, these societies had to fight the good Catholic fight, not just provide sociable outlets. Perhaps growing clericalism impeded the transmission of authentic Catholicism. Politics led

one curé of Gironde to form a public real estate company in 1896, composed of himself and five other notables; another to initiate a bread-making
society (*société de panification*) in 1900, which created more divisions in an
already divided commune.[7] But this takes us ahead of the game. Already
there existed a whole galaxy of lay Catholic organizations, such as the
Société de St. Vincent de Paul, with which the priest must be in close contact. But even without these special societies, village priests could be loaded down, especially in strong Catholic áreas. The Bishop of Luçon, for example, noted in a report of 1846 that his priests of the Vendée were in
general overworked.[8].

Building activity was one of those activities that kept them occupied,
and we need more work on the positive action of curés in pushing their
villages to repair or complete churches (the nineteenth century was in
many ways a caretaker century, especially between Napoleon and 1848);
and on their influence in places where entirely new churches were erected.
Those churches, simpler than earlier ones and incorporating architectural
traditions, are still worthy additions to the local landscape of France.
Their tiny spires, uncluttered façades, accordionlike apertures make them
accessible; they rarely detract from any town or village. Much of the correspondence on or by priests, and many village quarrels in the nineteenth
century relate to church-building. Let us not overestimate the purity of
motivation here. Many curés were interested in working on churches
precisely in order to gain leverage over inhabitants or councils, or to humble a recalcitrant mayor. We also know that the church was a village
showcase. It was the only meeting hall in many towns. Markets and water-
ing places were usually located in the immediate vicinity.[9] In short, the
curé hoped to share the church's prestige. Still, the results are more important than the motivations, and we can fairly say that by stimulating church
work priests were also stimulating sources of local pride in community,
which is no negligible thing. But all the time the great rival, the State, was
gaining, with its great school-building programs, its townhalls, and
tree-planting bonanzas at the grass roots. That was the way the wind was
blowing.

The need to repair churches was acute in places where the Revolution
had been destructive. At Escaudes (Gironde) the priest fought for twenty-
odd years to improve a devastated church, struggling both against
local notables and religious indifference of the Landais. In 1790 saints'
statues, wood carvings, and other ornamentation had been mutilated
there, and the church, which went back to the eleventh century, was now
dilapidated.[10] Certain priests could literally kill themselves on fruitless
building or repair campaigns, like the Abbé Courbezon of Ferdinand
Fabre's novel, *Ma Vocation*. Here, the physical church is a man's
self-destructive monomania, his crucifix.

The nineteenth century was also the century of the controversial Viollet-le-Duc, and not surprisingly some observers cast a jaundiced eye upon all restorers of that time, including priests. Others deplore a decline in taste, or slavish imitation in the new edifices. Abbé Pierre Brun, in a survey of Girondin churches, notes the inelegance, the banality of many nineteenth century churches. Like Drieu La Rochelle, a twentieth century writer, he seems to link this to general decadence. (Why can't *we* erect Gothic cathedrals anymore?) In another book he disserts on successful art as self-forgetfulness, holy idealism. The nineteenth century, he says, having lost most of this idealism, shows in its architecture the triumph of "a certain conformist and comfortable Christianity."[11] But the author sensibly points to other influencing trends, such as the decline of noble support for churches and of skilled artisans. Given such problems, priests did not do badly, even if their motivations were not always pure. How one views priests depends on one's view of religion. A village schoolmaster fighting in the frontier era of the laic school, and against a curé who had built an *école libre* (private school) to fight the good fight (along with repaired church and free clothes) against the Republic might see this building enterprise in a different light. Each side stacked the deck of rationalizations in its favor. Thus when we read summaries of priestly lives by other priests, we know we are in part getting romanticized history.

Still, let me succumb a little and summarize one such career. This concerns the curé of Seichamps in Lorraine, who died by the altar, in 1894. Born at a small village of a parish that was known as a hothouse for budding priests and nuns, he was raised in a Christian family, and pushed onward by the curé. He took orders in 1861. Subsequently he became vicar for two years at one church, then curé of the poor parish of Lorey, poetically set by the grape-enclustered Moselle banks (unpoetic in its bareness). His parish had only a tumbledown church, no bells, no windows, no sacristy, and no house for the priest. Soon, he had one built and got a sacristy, ornaments, and three bell towers, from which sounds tolled over the lovely valley. He then restored the chapel in a neighboring village. After eighteen years at Lorey the curé took on the post of Seichamps, with even more extensive and costly repairs to do. Though frugal, he was always giving away part of his salary to God and the poor and wearing himself out in visits to parishioners. "Le bon curé" of Seichamps died poor, and thirty-five priests attended the funeral.[12]

We now know that priests, mayors, or schoolmasters often cared more for their immediate village than their superiors did, and that their own love of place might mean a subversive attitude toward prefect and bishop. In 1873 a mayor of the Mâconnais praised an old curé for his connection to the area, writing: "He is an excellent priest, busying himself a lot with his

Ministry and making himself loved and esteemed by all Parishioners; he will be replaced with difficulty." The man had been born in that area, had parents living there, and loved the village, but his bishop nominated him for another commune and the prefecture went along. At another village in the *pays* a curé, recommended by the subprefect for a better post, was praised for having won the sympathy of everyone during his eighteen-year stint, and for creating a mutual aid society and cloth-weaving workshop.[13] One might examine a few of the local monographs written by hundreds of priests, and that now rest in archival reading rooms beside those of schoolmasters or mayors. Or note the involvement of priests in important archeological digs, such as at Vaison-la-Romaine, or their untutored interest in science. One priest versed in speleology, for example, first located and studied one of the important caves of southwest France (Niaux), famous for its paleolithic drawings.

Like lay teachers praised in reactionary villages of the 1890s, curés who earned the grudging admiration of formerly hostile mayors or councils could be considered bona fide notables. At a village of the Périgord in 1869 a priest was up for another post, and the mayor deeply regretted it. The curé had given gifts to the commune, continually prayed for the emperor, been prudent in bruitous municipal elections, and, through his energy and against opposition, had restored the magnificent church. He had survived attacks by some on the municipal council, and had also received money for schools and adult courses. Even his former enemies regretted his imminent departure. Several years later a priest who was also sick of local strife transferred out of a village of the Creuse after twenty-six years there. All the municipal councillors, mayor included, burst into tears, declaring that *he* had made them love religion, had raised their children well, had helped them in need, and that he must be allowed to stay. It is not known whether the appeal worked.[14]

Phrases used by prefects in recommendations or in grants of assistance also reveal clerical notability. One, for instance, on a retired priest of Gironde (1874): "Always, he deserved the esteem and sympathy of those who knew him. . . . Without resources he now has 'considération générale.' " Another in Dordogne praises a curé "cherished by his commune" (1836).[15] Generally, these recommendations can be assumed to be based on actual village opinion. We could multiply examples, but there is really no way of quantifying such evidence. The case is the same with obituaries. Pierre Simoni's study of local notables' obituaries from *one* periodical makes an attempt at quantification. Simoni has representative examples of cultured curés whose reputation radiated through their department—big fish in small ponds. Thus a man who became archpriest at Apt (Vaucluse), dead in 1900, had been a distinguished poet (at this level), historian, and writer of hagiography—"le Fénélon aptésien."[16] Or take those celebrated local culturati mentioned in newspaper editorials, like one of Gironde, who died in 1902. The obituary of *La Petite Gironde* (January 10, 1902) sketches his rise through various village posts, from vicar to curé to *professeur* and *archiviste*, correspondant of various academies, member of the Academy of Sciences and Arts of Bordeaux, and of most societies in that town, author of erudite works, and a person of a likeable and tolerant character: "His death is a real loss both for Bordelais letters and clergy of the area."

A final index of notability might be longevity at a post, though the more intelligent priests often migrated up to cantonal capitals and towns. Still, if a priest lasted a long time at one place, and if parish documents show no imbroglios there, then one can safely infer a degree of notability. Bernard Guillemin, in his work on Bordeaux, clearly links the two, giving us examples of one curé who remained at a village 52 years and another for 47. Abbé Maillot remained 41 years at Lhuitre during the nineteenth century, a commune of less than 1,000 souls. Several times he rejected offers of more prestigious posts, earning the respect of his parishioners. At his death he left his money to the parish council for church repairs and his clothes to the welfare council (*bureau de bienfaisance*.)[17]

As local notables, priests often had relations with *grands notables*, and it is perhaps artificial in this summary to make them more autonomous than they sometimes were. Dependency on *grands notables* was an old theme. According to Austin Gough (in the West that he studies) this dependency was intensified by the mid-nineteenth century; nobles were particularly arrogant to priests, who were made to feel their social inferiority, by not being asked to sit down, and so on. Gough's evidence is unfortunately scanty.[18] Literary evidence on such relations may also be suspect, but its incidence shows how important these internotable connections were considered. Later, we will note how priests would think of bishops as their fathers. In Stendhal's *The Red and the Black*, old Abbé Chélan tells the young Julien Sorel not only to flatter bishops in that way, but other notables like mayors, subprefects and local nobles (*châtelains*.) The theme of priests bowing to high to high notables is elaborated by Honoré de Balzac, for example in *The Curé of Tours*. Zola saw the priest, as did Georges Clemenceau, as a hireling of the rich. Here, anticlericalism exploited the theme for all it was worth. Chevallier's *Clochemerle* takes it into the twentieth century. And then we have fascinating portraits of the priest as humiliated retainer, upon which one could theorize at some length. Priests were used by squires as "vicarious consumers" to increase their prestige (as in Thorstein Veblen's view), or as obedient parrots, or enhancers of the faded dignities, or poor country cousins.

We have at least two novels on priests placed in such circumstances: one is Octave Feuillet's *L'Historie de Sybille* (1862), where a country priest of lower-class origins is attracted to the great families of the area, becomes a parvenu retainer at the chateau, and loses his soul in the process. A second novel, by Prosper Mérimée (*L'Abbé Aubarn*), demonstrates the variant of priest allied with rich ladies of the area—ladies like the married Julie of Rousseau's *La Nouvelle Héloïse*. Here, in Noirmoutiers, the lady almost takes over the priest. She wants him to be always at her beck and call, and to service her soon-perishing interests in Latin or botany. Priests were also in contact with noble or well-to-do ladies for the distribution of welfare and in private school campaigns. Moreover, noble women were generally more pious than men. And if they had the depth of suppression of a Mme de Renâl (Stendhal's heroine), as well as eyes of hurt, suffering kindliness, so much the better.[19]

Rival notables might also be found on the parish council, though plain peasants also took such posts. The nine-man parish council (*fabrique*) was first made compulsory in parishes with over 5,000 inhabitants by the law of 30 December, 1809. Five men were to be nominated by the bishop and four by the prefects, and therein lay one source of trouble: curés often had no homogeneous committee to deal with in the ever-present business of repairs and acquisitions.[20] And, since the mayor was also a member, this intensified conflicts with that notable also (reserved for another chapter).

Parish councillers might be submissive or recalcitrant. Like the old relationship of nobles and king, it depended on the character of each. A poor man's Philip the Fair might hold the council entirely under his thumb, as happened in a village of Ain in the early 1840s. Acquiring property illegally, this priest received their approval because the council, according to the bishop, "is composed only of simple peasants." A correspondence on the priestly domination of parish councils continues there until the 1880s. At many villages priests would simply prevent difficult councils from being called, until higher authorities intervened. Still, these often sided with or pardoned curés, refusing to diminish their authority in the councils. The prefect of the Tarn in 1843 related the episcopal attitude on one such conflict there: though the priest has erred one must uphold him, otherwise the bishop "fears that such a precedent will result in putting a priest's nomination at the discretion of the parish council." In a dispute at a village of Aveyron in 1857, prefect and bishop both agreed on the curé's bad character, but said that the parish council should first be dissolved before the priest was transferred. Some parish councillors were as arbitrary as priests, refusing to repair churches that were leaking or to buy necessary supplies. Councils could squabble about the silliest things—forty-one francs worth of manure for one priest's garden being perhaps the best example. (That manure was raising lovely cauliflowers.)[21] Thwarted council members often resigned in disgust. Of course, many councils got along perfectly well with their priest and matched his zeal in church building and provisions; they are scarcely noticeable in our documents.

Where did priests come from; who were they? Geographical origins varied, and it is not my intention to attempt a detailed map for all of France here. Quite obviously Catholic areas sent an overflow of priests into surrounding areas—Brittany feeding the West and North, Rouergue parts of the South. Such internal migration would be more important in periods when suitable clerical candidates were lacking—the Napoleonic period, for example, which saw a "concert of lamentations" on the lack of good priests; or the period after 1870, when the *instituteur* comes to full power. Equally interesting is the variation in rural versus urban recruitment. In the diocese of Bourges, especially before 1850, many so-called "country curés" hailed from towns, with Bourges itself in the period 1815–1840 providing 16 percent of vocations. But from the mid-century the pendulum swung back toward country villages as centers of recruitment. We find the same pattern in the diocese of Bordeaux and over a longer period. From 1837 to 1882, on priests whose origins are known, 28.5 percent of vocations came from metropolitan Bordeaux. Yet in the diocese of Rouen the evolution went from country to town, with peasant recruitment by 1890 down 50 percent from what it was under the July Monarchy, and "petits salariés," most of whom would be found in towns, picking up much of the slack.[22]

Foreign candidatures, those from outside diocese or department, can rarely have passed 20 percent of the diocesan total. For example, 15 percent is the normal figure for the Cher during the nineteenth century.[23] Especially after 1815 seminaries in each department "processed" local priests. As noted, areas lacking priests after 1870 would have to import from elsewhere, but that period is abnormal and will be discussed separately.

Social origins are of course related to geographical ones, although I would argue my own arbitrariness in neatly dividing urban from rural in the nineteenth century (does "rural", for example, simply mean villages under 2,000?). I would similarly wonder whether a peasant is always so different from a village artisan. Zeldin oversimplifies when he says that after the Revolution priests were "usually of peasant origin", using their church post to get further up the ladder of life. The latter view would be true in many cases, but the former not. In Alain Corbin's Haute-Vienne only 6.6 percent of the parents of 103 priests from 1835 to 1836 were *cultivateurs*; 45 percent were artisans. Zeldin says the drift moves toward shopkeepers, clerks, and artisans, these classes providing almost 60 percent of recruitment in 1950. But of course an artisan in 1950 is scarcely the same thing as an artisan of 1850, or at least in most cases.[24]

Certainly, the priesthood must have seemed a step up for poor, ambitious boys, even for that "dog of a reader" Julien Sorel (not really so poor). In an area like Bretonnant Brittany, priests learned a French that set them above the people, making of them *messieurs*.[25] If they had no taste for the priesthood, the seminary offered them the literacy to become a *notaire* or tutor (few probably so lucky in their posts as pale Sorel). Jean Jacques Rousseau was once directed toward the priesthood by a French count, but then went on to a more lofty métier. Generally, before 1850 most priests came from modest circumstances, or worse. In answer to an important circular of 1835, the bishop of Nîmes noted: "Most of those whose destiny is the Ecclesiastical Estate come from the least comfortable class of society." The archbishop of Toulouse, responding to the same circular, said that young churchmen are "almost always today without money. . . ." And the bishop of Poitiers noted that "almost the totality of those who embrace the Ecclesiastical Estate are from the lower classes" ("la classe peu aisée"). Like Zeldin, I would speculate that priests came from backgrounds that were economically more stable as time went on. Terminology, of course, is a problem, especially in the hazy term "peuple". A muckraking abbé, for instance, noted in 1873 that the clergy is mostly from the "peuple."[26] I suppose Gérard Cholvy's "modest milieus" is the most comprehensive category, and the one he credits 80 percent of priests in Hérault (1846-1878) as coming from. Very few priests in Hérault came from the poorest and most illiterate sectors of the population.

We can also generalize that priests around France usually came from larger families. Hard statistics on this are lacking before 1914, but the formula "Christian and large family" ("famille chrétienne et nombreuse") was frequently seen on career forms dealing with priests. After 1920 a precise statistical sample from the Hérault, hardly a hotbed of clericalism, shows that over a thirty-five year period priests came from families averaging 3.2 children; the figure was higher in a number of other departments.[27]

Among curés, character differences must have been as variable as in the general population. Nor can historians easily probe their *inner* differences or variations, following Pascal's view that no man is more different from another than from himself at different times. Type-casting may be hazardous, but still there were distinct types, just as there were among monarchs. The analogy with monarchs is again not a bad one to use. Certain untenured priests (*desservants*) may have had character troubles because they found themselves in the shadow of old curés they hoped to supplant, wishing that these long-lived George IIIs and Louis

Quatorzes might go away. Or, coming to a new parish or branch, they may have found certain predecessors very hard to follow. In a local study of a parish post in Lorraine, the priests from 1815 to 1857 are middling and nondescript. Later Joseph Müths (1857-1876) sits well with everyone, and is a great builder; then Auguste Adam (1876-1902), perhaps in part because of the Republic, is bellicose and argumentative. This study says of Adam: "Very authoritarian and of a rather rough manner of speaking, he terrorized the children, to each of whom he had given a nickname." The next man, Edmond Gabriel (1902-1933) is again well-esteemed and nicknamed "the builder."[28]

The constraints of parish life also caused character difficulties. For example, my study of the diocese of Bordeaux indicates a bias against the young priests new to their posts; whether he has merit or not, says one petitioner (supported by 100 signatures), he will not have our full confidence. At difficult villages—and in the progressively irreligious nineteenth century there were many—priests had to be abnormally tactful. Bishops and prefectoral authorities concurred on this necessity, if from frequently differing perspectives. A fellow being considered for the post of Notre-Dame de Vitré (Ille-et-Vilaine) after twenty-five years at a previous one is praised by the subprefect for his "sweetness of character", the "moderation of his opinions". Another man recommended by the bishop for a branch at St. Malo is "of a very mild and conciliating character." These were desiderata. But the priest, as previously detailed, was also lidder of the would-be emancipated, and this was no easy position to assume. Above others, he must not be *too* much above. Sometimes he must demonstrate affinities for the area. A curé, writing to his superior, summarized the requirement for the new occupant of a difficult Bordelais village in 1865 by saying the priest must be from the diocese, or at least familiar with local patois. He must have a conciliating disposition, yet be firm enough to hold his own in an area of religious ignorance and doubtful morals. That many priests were prone to feelings of isolation is certain.[29] That many rued their own stiffness we can only guess. That a kind of madness might ensue only rarely emerges from the documents, but must have been more frequent than we know.

The problem here was the clash of rationality and religion. In the extreme puritan impulse, for example, or in the fundamental tenets and sacraments of Catholicism itself there is really no rationality at all. In the nineteenth century overly pious priests could be seen as aberrational; whereas in the Middle Ages a fellow preaching to the birds becomes a saint, will be reverently painted through the Renaissance. Contrast St. Francis with a mendicant *desservant* of a village of Cher in 1869, who says "strange" things, writes strange letters, and is roundly criticized for it.

Noting that the man is "original and singular" the archbishop of Bourges yet considers him "a priest of indubitable piety." But a religious explanation could cut little ice with secular authority, or with increasingly secular-minded parishioners. They simply saw such a man as mad. A curé at Montesquieu's La Brède, once excellent, became tired of his job after thirty years there. He grew paranoid, started insulting people right and left, and was finally replaced. Then he began yelling at his successor in mass, and trying to push him from the altar, he was taken away by police, vowing to return to celebrate the St. Jean bonfire for children. The official terminology? "Moral fatigue."[30] Not, perhaps, lack of compensation for religious zeal?

The major character defects of priests were their rigidity (often seen by historians as a reason for anticlericalism) and their self-righteousness. These qualities were very often encountered in their correspondence, which could be florid, emotional, even hysterical, frequently punctuated by exclamation marks and underlining. Here is the curé of Soulignac (no pun intended) in a letter to a mayor with whom he had differences:

> I conclude by telling you Mr. the Mayor that in the twenty-seven years that I have been a priest I have had no other compass than my *conscience* and no other goal than [doing] good. neither pride, nor whim, nor vanity has made me act beyond these motives, in other words, *never* would I ally myself with men who are inspired by these poisoned sources. . . .[31]

I have seen other letters with sentences that go on for a page or more before terminating. As for the arbitrary curé, he might refuse first communions, choice of god-parent, or the celebration of hasty marriages. This kind of priest, for two of the above reasons, among others, alienated a whole village in the Dordogne in the 1840s and was transferred. Anticlericalism was easily intensified by such clerics. An abrasive priest, overly sensitive and rigid, could push an area that wanted religion into outright hostility. This was the case of one at Sablons (Gironde) who had bounced around from post to post, written letters that the archbishop considered tearing up, alienated children from catechism, and provoked, from the mayor of Sablons, the following testimony in 1860: "Religion, Monseigneur, is tumbling under the care of this person who is unworthy of serving as an example; it will take a long time to cure this illness, even with the care of the best or most intelligent pastor." A much older priest of that diocese aroused contempt by his manifest incompetence. Aged seventy-five he was plagued by a bad leg and deafness, and as a result of the latter problem made people shout their confessions in church, giving away secrets in the process.[32] This incompetence, as much as arbitrariness, produced a similar result.

Another kind of priest was the morally lax one, or at least the kind who liked to enjoy life as much as direct it: the good eater, drinker, or hunter. Bishops were especially hard on this type. Their guides for priests told them not to fish or hunt too much. Clemenceau, depicting an eighteenth-century priest (supposedly his ancestor), says the man was a faithful out-doorsman, whereas a present-day (late nineteenth century) counterpart says: "Today, our lords, the bishops, would stifle this fancy in short order. In the eighteenth century they were more indulgent." Another homey curé made trouble for his less lapsed successor, who complained tearfully to the archbishop about the problem. The priest he succeeded at this post in 1863 hunted and fished all day, played cards, and drank white wine with the old-timers at night. The new priest, unable to follow suit, soon received a post more congenial to a firmer nature. Rival notables, of course, would often be happy to have a relaxed priest by their side. This was especially true of harried Third Republic teachers. One, commenting on what should have been a difficult "laicization" of a Breton girls' school in 1902, noted that the priest mercifully kept silent in the pulpit, and uttered no protest. As a man of peace, he was more interested in "waging war" on rabbits and hares than inflaming the Church-State conflict at the grass roots.[33]

Did violent priests have more inner frustrations than peaceful ones? Were they more prone to conflict with rival notables? (Much clerical violence, as will be seen in a later chapter, was directed at mayors.) Was verbal display related to the nineteenth century crisis as a whole, or perhaps to suppressed sexuality? With Professors Weber and Freud respectively, I think we could safely answer "both". Alain Corbin traces clerical outbursts mainly to fears of modernity, citing many examples of thundering from the pulpit, such as one sees so often in documents, and the use of bad language — an abbé, for instance, calls a child "son of a bitch, son of beggars. . . ." for not knowing his catechism. Corbin then discusses clerical injunctions against dancing (prominently treated also in Marcilhacy's book on the Orléanais) or fear of railways. He also cites their hatred of superstitions like the "good fountain" and *reinage* (bidding for the right to be king or queen for a day). Corbin's thesis demonstrates the paradox that clerical antipathy to retrograde practices was precisely the reason, or one important one, for dechristianization and the advent of modernity in the Limousin. Yves-Marie Hilaire, however, sees priests becoming more violent in the diocese of Arras due to an ultramontane compaign directed from above after 1848.[34]

As for *physical* violence, priests were expressly forbidden such an outlet, and it is rare to see examples of it. The few priests who were physically violent had trouble with superiors and especially after 1870 with the regional press, which hopped on these incidents to further the laic cause. One such incident involved a curé who saw military recruits drinking, and pushed one through a window pane in disgust. *Lyon Républicain* (November 11, 1894) gave this a prominent spread, entitled: "Un Prêtre Idiot!" In 1900 a priest grabbed the throat of a maid working for a retired rector that the mayor had been "protecting." On an earlier occasion this priest had received a sentence of court costs and three days hard labor for his violence. The priest was transferred out of the village soon after. A curé at Marcilly (Saône-et-Loire) had ruined an already bad reputation in 1862 when he got in a drunken slugging fight with his nephew. You hear of a *desservant* growing violent after drinking four or five litres of wine with a sharecropper at Rosnay (Vendée) in 1866.[35] In fact these seem to be the archival exceptions, and what is more the rule are priests expostulating, yelling, cursing, or insulting mayor and government at mass.

Clerical violence, moralism, even fatherliness must also be linked—though how much we'll never know—to the sexual problems or sublimations associated with celibacy.[36] Celibacy cannot be properly discussed by the secular historian. He can only note from a distance the concepts of marriage with Christ or the Church, test of vocation, or freedom in discipline (a theme again of *La Nouvelle Heloïse*). At most he can slap upon celibacy indecent modern labels like "value-expressive function", or trace the attitude of awe that once made sexuality a truly numinous adjunct of the religious kingdom itself. The secular historian will remember that puritanism and renunciation have inhered in every religion, sometimes with greater force than at other times. He may find interesting the notions of power ascribed to celibates by Balzac; for example, the virginal Eugénie Grandet who possessed far greater depth and mysterious charisma than would otherwise have been the case, or the old abbé Janvier of *Le Médecin de campagne*, thoroughly placid within himself.

G. K. Chesterton once said that it takes much courage to spout a truism, but I don't think one needs courage to notice this central fact about the priest, that he was a single man, perhaps a repressed man, a conceivably masturbating man for some of his life. Often he would be consoled by renunciatory faith, something one without it cannot easily understand. But he must have found himself in need of other outlets from time to time. These might be vicarious (salacious confessions, mainly) or less vicarious, leading us to the delicate problem of relations with females and sexual advances (*attentats à la pudeur*). Archives tell us very little about this.

Bear in mind that both villagers and administration were inclined to hush up sexual problems in the moralistic nineteenth century. Investigative reports on priestly transgressions — more quaintly, *écarts* — seem to exist only in cases that could not be dealt with privately, or which were too openly known to suppress. Admission of such a problem might compromise church authority in the village. Until the Third Republic, secular authorities had no reason to score points, since public order was their desire too. Moreover, it was no simple matter to dismiss a lapsed priest, for the process involved different courts, some in competition, and might drag in mayor, local police, prefectoral authorities, Paris ministeries, bishops, archbishops and, on occasion, the Pope himself. In a royal ordinance of 1814, supporting a bishop's revocation of his priest, it was noted that wrongs must be "very real for us to take a measure that is that rigorous." (This priest had had a mistress for two years and allegedly made two women pregnant.) Concerning another curé up for revocation, the Minister of Cults would write (1852): "But you know, Monseigneur, that the dismissal of a priest is a very serious measure which should be reserved for extreme cases, that is, for the cases where there is a public scandal." To avoid these problems, bishops might try to pressure the priests in question to resign, since a resignation did not require the approval of secular authority. Priests, however, might remain defiantly in office, or attach multiple conditions to their resignation. One who resigned at Beaumont (Dordogne) in 1839 warned his bishop that the new curé had better keep the story secret or else he would make trouble for him. In general, tenured curés could make more trouble than the *desservants* or *vicaires*. Sometimes one finds a priest entirely justified in doing so, for he might be dealing with an unfair superior. This was the case when the bishop of Valence pressured a supposedly immoral cleric to resign in the 1850s, and the priest protested with an expansive epistle to the Minister of Cults. Supporting him, the prefect noted that this bishop was already known for severity and disequilibrium, and after an acrimonious exchange between bishop and prefect, the curé was finally reinstated.[37]

A simple transfer was the usual method of nipping the bud of possible scandals. Priests who compromised themselves by speaking to too many women, or who seemed too close to their female servants (often the subject of folk songs) could set people talking. It was better to send them elsewhere. One in the Limousin was transferred for painting female portraits. Canonical law often forbade servants to be under forty — presumably that was an age of abandonment. But authorities could munificently forget past offences in certain cases and wipe the proverbial slate. A priest known to have been intimate with a young *institutrice* was simply transferred from Côte d'Or across France to Oise in 1890. He respected the Republic, a plus, and had the good opinion of his new parishioners, who did not know his past.[38]

Then there were those who simply took off when the scandalous details became known in a village. A police report in Ille-et-Vilaine, 1847, notes a man on the run for having allegedly tried to seduce several women, taking borrowed money, and breaking up homes. A subprefectoral report of 1895 in Puy-de-Dôme, mentions a *vicaire* who had gone off with an eighteen year old girl, rumored to be pregnant and in possession of 3000 francs taken from her father. A most Clochemerlish or Boccaccian cleric at La Hérelle (Oise) resigned and left the commune in 1861, supposedly to seek treatment for syphillis. The man was a known drinker, with a housemaid of bad reputation ("*mauvaise vie*"). He had had sexual relations with at least three women of the locality—the wives of a blacksmith, road-mender, and field guard—and then, wanting to break with the first lady, he provoked a jealous confession of incriminating evidence. Still, some of the villagers regretted his departure. Another priest in that department furtively sold his furniture and dressed like a bourgeois to flee to Paris and meet a woman with whom he had been intimate. This flight to Varennes was confirmed sadly by bishop to prefect, who said the priest had earlier petitioned to leave for the colonies.[39]

What of more serious affairs involving children? My root feeling is that such cases would be even less publicized than the former kind, but we have little secondary work to guide us here. Austin Gough does say that there were many incidents in Poitou of the July Monarchy period, partly due to forced recruitment of poor candidates, but he holds back specifics.[40] Let me give two examples from the department of Saône-et-Loire in the late nineteenth century. The later one, from the period of Emile Combes (early 1900s), is instructive because, after repeated sexual advances by the curé toward different children, and in neither an area nor a time noted for clerical bias, parents kept their suspicions quiet. It was only when a child was expelled from catechism that his father complained to the *instituteur* about this "other" problem, and asked advice. It came out that the curé had been rubbing against a half-dozen children from behind. One mother now called him a "dirty pig", and neighboring communes then heard of the "filthiness ("*cochonneries*") of the curé of Fley." In an earlier series of incidents at Malay in 1874, the priest was not only brought to justice and found guilty, but his actions were exploited by anticlericals in the republican press. Here the matter had involved seven sons of farmers aged seven to eleven. The police report is explicit: one child was given fifty centimes to keep quiet, another made to hold the curé's "creature" ("*bête*").[41] The *Alliance républicaine de Saône-et-Loire*, a Mâcon daily, ran a prominent article on this, April 2,

1874, and spoke of another recent outrage (by a sixty-nine year old priest), declaring that such affairs could only further the republican movement in the area.

It is hard to know whether republicans were usually this prompt to rejoice at such revelations. I have found a propagandistic column called "The Clerical Year" in *L'Union républicaine* (Libourne), January 11, 1880. The paper's editor was Jules Steeg, one of the great laic war-horses and a very puritanical one as well. Taking facts from Paris' *Petite République*, the paper compiled a list of noteworthy clerical incidents over the last year: an abbé at Laval was condemned to six months in prison for assaults on three girls; another was condemned by a court of the Rhône to twelve years hard labor for assaults on young boys, and so on—a half-dozen per month. Most incidents involved clerical violence or quarrels with the mayor, or priests who hunted without permit. The list in this issue stopped in the preceding February, but then promised more.

In fact, we simply cannot know the actual incidence of sexual attacks in the nineteenth century. If one can't quantify such matters, some say, it is preferable to drop them. But I do think we should neither overestimate nor underestimate this problem of clerical outlets. At least we can chart characteristic responses to such incidents and thereby learn about *mentalités*. Many curés, it appears, were let off easily, and perhaps more in the clerical areas. Two incidents from the Vendée in the 1830s are instructive. One priest, while preparing girls for a first communion at St. Sigismond, had several place their fingers in their organs. Taken before the public prosecutor he was found guilty, but given no punishment. A year later the curé of St. Christophe du Ligneron was accused of drinking and talking off color to young girls. A petition was sent by the mayor and many inhabitants to the bishop, who promised to transfer the man, but there was no evidence that such action was taken. Another priest of Vaucluse was convicted for sexual advances to a girl at communion, but the sentence was light. Perhaps these incidents were not of the first seriousness. One that was, in Puy-de-Dôme for 1896, induced a poor "curé-desservant" to hang himself in his cell; and we have the last letter the fifty-two year old man wrote to his nephews, fulminating against the mayor and others who had found him out. Already suspected of relations with several women, he had then assaulted sexually two young girls, whose fathers complained to authorities.[42]

What also hampers us from better understanding this problem is the metaphorical, hazy way it was often dealt with in correspondence. For example, a curé of Gironde, commenting on an incoming priest up for a post in the department, noted "Suspicions and complaints" that he had occasioned in the Lyon area. There were doubts on his sense of decency ("*pudeur*") with young boys. But nothing concrete was elicited. Or else one reads correspondence prior to a clerical transfer, and realizes it might involve a moral problem, but it is impossible to tell for sure. Curés under attack might compound the problem with their apologetic, long-winded prose: "I declare this," says one accused (of something) in 1863, "because your Eminence's heart, so good and paternal, must have been grievously saddened by it. . . . But I come in all candor, humility and with a child's sincerity to affirm at the feet of your Eminence [my innocence]." Yet two years later the same "enfant" was transferred out of the diocese, so some fire must have accompanied this smoky correspondence, of what nature we still cannot tell. Then there were suspicious situations, village ambiguities that were not easy to resolve even then. At a village in Oise, 1859, the daughter of an old, incompetent schoolmaster becomes pregnant. Both the father and the mayor suspect the curé, who reddens when confronted, and as much as confesses to relations. Yet the girl, it turns out, has *also* been seeing two other young men in the area. The priest, having lost "considération" there, may be transferred, but the archival evidence peters out at this point.[43] Were all villages simply puritanical in atmosphere? Some of the delightful stories in Clemenceau's volume on the Vendée, hardly a "modern" area, cast doubt on this. Once the whole picture of village sexuality and attitudes to it are more amply clarified by other historians, we may begin to understand the behavior of priests better as well.[44]

Partly, of course, this is the realm for the more specialized psycho-historian. Once again, the amateur blunders in and makes his own crude attempts to understand. Going beyond the sexual problem, he may then identify major psychological strains in clerical characters. There are a few that stand out. For one thing priests, like mayors, quite obviously considered themselves fathers to their flocks. Marcilhacy, among so many others, emphasizes that as fathers spurned, some could become old Goriots, only more violent, while others brooded inwardly. Modernization is one of the key issues involved. In the earlier part of the century in traditional areas priests could still supervise healing, miracles, weather-taming, exorcisms, and fortune-telling, not to mention religious solace, and get away with it. At mass and in confessional they were indeed Fathers, before peasants learned self-sufficiency, or had it visited upon them. But with religious decline, particularly in areas prone to anticlericalism like the Limousin, one has cases such as Corbin reports as early as 1829 — a priest complaining: "They hooted from the fields the women who went to the Holy Mass. . .they ridiculed me in every manner possible."[45] This aspect of "ridiculed-father" is doubtless one of the psychoanalytical bases of clerical violence and of overly rigid behavior.

Quite opposite to this, or perhaps because of it, one finds in many priests a wish to be son, a sort of servile dependency. Cut off from their own family, either geographically or intellectually, and without wife or children, priests used superiors to fill the gap. The following are two examples from the Vendée. The first *desservant*, more moderate, wrote to his bishop in 1842: "I am happy to have a Father as tender as you, to discharge my heart and announce to you my chagrins. . . ." (These chagrins partly stemmed from a quarrel with the mayor.) A second curé wrote more passionately to the prefect, hoping to avoid a transfer. The letter, which shows signs of derangement, illustrates a *mentalité* more pervasive than is noted by historians. This curé at Napoléon wrote his prefect as follows:

> Today I come to throw myself at your feet, bursting into tears, and begging you. . .to obtain me this pardon, from Monseigneur Baroche, as promptly as possible; for I am dying from despair! I can't sleep, either at night or in the day!. . .
> You are a father, Monsieur Prefect, and it is to you as a paternal supporter that I address myself. Placed at the head of our department, you represent *the Emperor who is the Father of his subjects*. . . Can a father abandon his child, whatever wrongs that child may have committed? No!"[46]

Three more representative examples, from Gironde, will further illustrate this outlook. The first is most interesting because it shows guilt or *fear* of being a child. The curé of Mouliets in 1863 thanks the archbishop for procuring him a 200 franc supplement, without which he would have no dignity; for that would "accustom the population to seeing the priest at the mercy of a council, treated like a little boy. . . ." More maudlin is a priest to his archbishop, saying that it is "sweet for a child to find himself near a father tenderly loved. He likes to converse with him and tell him his troubles, his joys, and. . .open his heart to him." Another curé, a skittish one, has been the brunt of gossip due to violent language and an attraction to ladies. He assures his superior that "It is while trembling with tears in my eyes that I write you these lines. I understood a little too late that I profoundly saddened your heart of Father and Pontiff. . . ." Other priests would sign their letters "Your devoted child" or with some variant of the latter.[47]

Bishops as father-figures? Psychiatrists even? But they could be stern, unyielding ones, too. After the Revolution, some became almost absolute sovereigns in their sees.[48] Older (usually over fifty) conservative, sometimes excessive in their expectations, bishops did not like their authority brooked. If some curé saw them as fathers it was because they, on their side, encouraged such dependency. That dependency was also due to lack of education—education producing consciousness, as bishops understood very well. Bishops were from a better class than priests (in most cases), and generally spoke a more polished French. In 1835 the government tried to provide more outlets for higher education of clerics, and its circular was met with a hail of episcopal protest. Partly, this was a protest against the State; it also expressed a fear of having priests' eyes opened too much, particularly in the big towns where they would study. As the bishop of Rodez wrote best in answer to that circular, "I add that in the country where they have conserved the simplicity of morals, the modesty of most of these pupils will recede before the ambitious pretensions they will have to garner. . .going far away at great costs, making them want to occupy [positions of] dignity. . . ."[49] This word "dignités" seems to me very important—it was what so much of the nineteenth century was about. Prostitutes may have worn the queen's jewels in Flaubert's revolution of 1848, but bishops did not want to cede *their* refinements to humble priests.

I have already mentioned the pomp of episcopal visits to various parishes. These must also have impressed upon priests their own subordination and inferiority. As late as the 1880s in a moderate Catholic area, the bishop was met at a typical village by the mayor, municipal council, parish council, an escort of firemen, a society of archers, and by fifty-four chosen confirmands.[50] The church ornaments must be in top shape; the priest must have suitable answers to many possible questions the bishop might pose.

Bishops had a key lever of authority over priests—where they would live and preach. Many priests, demanding better conditions, something closer to home or to a railway line, or with more security, found bishops totally insensitive. The latter took pride in asserting the authority of decision. In 1849 a prize cantonal post came vacant because of a death, and the bishop of Arras, confronted with at least ten demands, pointedly awarded it to a priest who had not even applied. This was an object lesson on knowing one's place.[51]

What we call clerical conservatism, or an inability to flow with the time, must have originated in many cases with episcopal authority. We have seen it in the diocese of Arras, with the instigation of Ultra-montane attitudes there. In 1835 in another area a priest humbly asked if he might make a change in a service, aware of the significant "counsel that you give so often to priests, not to change, without good reasons, established customs in their parish."[52] But on the positive side bishops might be in the forefront of diocesan building campaigns.

Priests *had* to have good relations with these superiors. Who else would normally protect them in squabbles with villagers, mayor, prefecture? So resentments must have been buried, and we have no waves of forthright criticism of higher clergy such as had issued forth in the late Middle Ages or in late eighteenth century France.[53] What criticism existed came mainly from religious intellectuals like Lamennais.

Instead, small bubbles of protest may be noted. Certain priests, for example, were tired of the rigid hierarchy imposed upon them. Some *desservants*, who had not yet become curés, and perhaps never would, wanted their status upgraded. "Desservant" had a lowly ring to it, even though many were called in their villages or by superiors "curé-desservants." (I sometimes use the words interchangeably here.) One of Côte d'Or, perhaps emboldened by the Revolution of 1848, wrote the Minister of Cults asking that they abolish the word "desservant" altogether — "being improper, unpopular, spurned by the Clergy and by the People. . . ." It often took an absurdly long time for promotion. In 1830, for example, almost 33 percent of tenured curés were over sixty.[54]

The hierarchy began at vicar, roughly like a young teaching "stagiaire" under the Third Republic, except that some vicars would grow old in that inferior position. Then came "desservants" in their branch parishes (*succursales*); then curés, supposedly found only in the real parishes of cantonal capitals ("*chefs-lieux*"). Thanks, however, to the constant erection of parishes during the century, full-fledged curés were found in more places than that. In 1814 there were roughly 29,000 parishes, of which but 3,000 or so were "*cures*". By the Second Empire there were 35,000, with 10 percent full parishes; by 1869 there were 42,000 parishes. This jump under the Second Empire reflects the clerical prosperity of the Falloux era, when the total number of priests grew by 20 per cent, from 47,000 in 1853 to 56,000 in 1869, and many vergers and assistants were added to the payroll. Recruitment, according to Edward Gargan, was definitely related to politics, above all else. A plunge in the 1830s, for instance, had reflected uncertainty after the July Revolution. (My own view is that it was also a plain lull after the boom of the 1820s.)[55]

Then there were the classes. We have many demands in the files for a move up, from fourth to third, or third to second, just as schoolmasters of the Third Republic wanted to mount their class-based salary scale.[56] And at the top were the exclusive archpriests (*archiprêtres*) of the episcopal towns.

Tenured curés were the apple of insecure eyes, and it is to be expected that democratization of tenure, or *inamovibilité*, was a subject of protest. Before the Revolution, most priests had enjoyed such tenure; after the Concordat, only a minority, one-tenth of the contingent, did. (This permitted Napoleon enhanced control of the order.) So there was a certain "golden ageism" involved here; but also a critique of hierarchy and softness above. In 1839 C. and A. Allignol attained a good deal of notice with their bitter *De l'Etat actuel du clergé en France et en particulier des curés ruraux appelés desservants*, a significant title. That work pointedly criticized conservative bishops. Another young priest, considering his post as "an only spouse", hated the bishop for transferring him around so often—a much later theme of Vance Packard's *Nation of Strangers*: "To move, run from residence to residence like tax collectors or employees of the excise office, to always change country, sheep, and fold! Other streets, another church, another altar, another bedroom, another dawn!"[57] Attempts at reform failed miserably in 1848. In 1873 Abbé * * * wrote his *La Question de l'inamovibilité canonique*, attacking the archbishop of Rennes in particular and attracting much attention in France, at a time when bishops were staving off a new request by Jules Simon for more tenured posts. The author deplores "a situation that places our material and moral existence completely at the mercy of their discretionary power, and condemns us, at the age of infirmity and old age, to go and beg for a piece of bread dipped in bitterness at the door of their palaces!"[58] Rhetorical? Overblown? No doubt. Justified? Certainly in part. Tenure, as one would expect, could lead to significant abuses, with deaf or blind curés hanging on into their eighties. Finally in 1910 the pope granted *desservants* the possibility of tenure; but only after a century of stifled discontents.

Priests also complained of overwork and lack of assistants. When money problems were acute, bishops might use one priest for several villages, and on important holidays combine the services of several villages into one. (This was called *binage*.[59]) But the main fact is that it was not lucrative to complain, for bishops held all the cards. When a country priest of the Beauvaisie spoke out and wrote disapprovingly of episcopal policies (1869-1870), he was not only taken out of the priesthood altogether and excommunicated, but excoriated in the press by all the archpriests of Beauvais, who defended a prelate they called their father.[60]

Did priests have the tools of literacy with which to fight back? Certainly their correspondence indicates they did, but a spirited scholarly debate on the intellectual level of nineteenth century priests still goes on. In one article Harry Paul argues for a better-educated priest than we knew, while historians like Gordon Wright have considered priests on the whole ill-educated.[61] Perhaps wrongly, I range myself in-between. It is true that young boys who were quite skillful at Latin, along with being pious, were impelled along the path of priesthood. But it is also true that education given by incompetent or narrow-minded superiors might easily drum out what intellectual curiosity these boys had once possessed.[62] Put the young Henri Fabre in such schools and we should never have had his great discoveries on insects. But other scientists of worth did have a Catholic education.

Priests were at least minimally literate, an advantage in French society before the 1880s. Many wrote for local journals of learned societies or for the regional newspapers, sometimes polemically. By around 1900 there were regularly typed parish bulletins in most parishes, as vehicles for their views. Handwriting, too, improved over the century, rivaling that of lay school teachers. Priests for that reason made good secretaries. Then there were educational facilities to look in on, if not to run. Under the Second Empire especially, *écoles libres* had multiplied, and so did the use of brothers and sisters in public schools. It was a period of security for priests, if comparatively short-lived, with many lay teachers under their thumb. Of course, the education they supervised was generally worse than their own had been. Still, many officials, even hostile ones, praised the instruction or intelligence of local priests, who might use this instruction, to be sure, as a weapon against mayor or teacher.[63] They might appreciate the priest's literary or oratorical style, even when it was sometimes unnecessarily verbose, florid, exaggerated.

Some historians like to point to higher intellectual activity in priests before 1789 than after—Zeldin, for example, using evidence that out of forty Périgordien subscribers to the *Encylopédie*, twenty-four were curés.[64] In an age when there were some 200,000 priests, how convinced can we be by such evidence? We can certainly generalize that the Revolution, in the short run, brought a drop in qualified, therefore educated priests. The diocese of Bourges, 1802, was probably typical. Most priests there, because of Revolutionary ordinations, were "not very educated" (*"peu instruits"*), many without a smidgeon of Latin or even fundamental notions of catechism.[65] The great takeoff in seminary building came after 1815, and especially during the 1820s. One of the consequences was a newer, more intolerant type of priest, frequently contrasted to the kindly old bumbler, who was less educated along machine-straight lines. The contrast between such priests is presented by Stendhal in *The Red and the Black*, by Balzac (Abbé Troubert versus "the curé of Tours"), and by prefects too. Béranger's *Mon Curé* (1819) and Raban's *Curé de village* (1833) clearly idealized the older type, the "good," childish country priest. Priests who now emerged from seminaries in areas like the Yonne were very different—some almost Jansenist in tendency.[66]

Petits séminaires, as Zeldin rightly notes, were ghettoes—rigidly routine in the daily alternation of prayers, meals, Latin instruction, and other activities. Then came the *grands séminaires*, deficient in science or mathematics, but strong on pious austerity. Sulpicians or Lazarists ran these places on a pre-1789 model. Rules and regulations stayed invariable and old-fashioned, while the world outside (and its regimes) moved elsewhere. Instruction was not in the least Socratic. The language used was

Latin, the method the same as catechism. If priests became incurious, if they became the absolutists Professor Brugerette accuses them of being, or if they had trouble fitting in with their evolving century, their seminary training had a lot to do with this.[67] Of course I speak here from an un-Catholic, lay-historical point of view. True Catholics might argue that once one chips away at the scaffolding of tradition the whole building comes down. This, for example, is the way Mr. Chesterton saw matters.[68] Chesterton, however, was no priest. But priests themselves began to question the "system" after 1870, in a period of general decline, when they were "insecure in their social status, uncertain about their presence in the world, poorly compensated, haunted by reservations concerning their training and comprehension of modernity. . . ." Some priests by the 1890s demanded equivalents of *grandes écoles* to give them more adequate, modern training.[69] Many simply chafed.

By 1870 or so there can have been few utterly ignorant country priests left. At the same time there were few who had the uneducated but inspired drive of the famous curé of Ars, who was made a saint.[70] Very different from that man was the priest who now ran gymnastic societies or orchestras, fought the teacher on his own secular terrain, or else the type who became a scholar and activist along the lines of Abbé Lémire. Lémire (1853–1928) showed by his career what a priest could learn, do, and overcome. Of peasant background, Lémire worked his way through parish priesthood to *collège* teacher to newspaper contributor to well-known and iconoclastic Christian Democrat, becoming a mayor after 1914. Another in Cher, of similarly modest origins, became an astronomer of renown by his own efforts, and a regional celebrity.[71]

Priests in some areas were now hard put to stay afloat. The sheer difficulties of the profession, the hostility of the Republic, and the availability of attractive alternatives is reflected in the problems of recruitment encountered in the late nineteenth century. Mingled with that problem was the lack of money for church repairs and for parish councils. The archbishop of Reims in 1888 complained of both these problems. He said municipal councils were withholding money, also that he hadn't enough priests for all the branches in his diocese, and that some villages must do without them. In 1893 the bishop of Autun emphasized to the prefect "how numerous are parishes deprived of a curé." And the archbishop of Avignon in 1879 pleaded to keep a priest in a village where he was disliked, because of lack of replacements.[72] To be fair, communes were sometimes without priests because local council or mayor could not tolerate the bishop's choice, and the priest, in turn, would "go on strike". This was the case in a village of Ardèche in 1895, after the municipal council became embroiled with a new appointee.[73] The bishop might penalize the commune by placing no priest there for a year or more. But the main point is that priests were on the curve downward in this period.

Decline in recruitment is a difficult problem to summarize adequately. The number of ordinations peaked in 1868, kept falling until 1877, then held, and then declined again after 1905, when priests were no longer paid by the State. Many bishops noted this decline, both in ordinations and in the general quality of recruits. Yet as Pierre Barral points out of the Isère, that department had more than its share of recruits in this period — a glut until the Separation, which most everywhere signalled further slippage.[74] Edward Gargan, leaning again toward the political, accounts for such drops by events like the Dreyfus Affair. In anticlerical areas, where Catholics needed priests badly to hold back the waves, clergy drastically diminished in number. In 1904 the diocese of Limoges had only 8.6 priests per 10,000 inhabitants, versus Catholic Rennes, with more than double that number (19.2). The gap grew worse in the twentieth century.[75] We may also say that more *older* priests held posts after 1900 than earlier. Just after the Revolution and during the Empire old priests and lack of priests had correlated statistically in many dioceses. From around 1820 things picked up in both categories and continued to do so at least until 1850. In the diocese of Nantes a clear trend of aging began after 1860. There, the percentage of priests over sixty was roughly 40 percent more in the period 1865-1869 than from 1850-1853. Old age bulges were also due to abnormally high recruitment in the 1820s. Nonetheless, the situation also worsened because of the crisis in recruitment. And in anticlericalized dioceses like Aix, typical of many others, the average age of priests by 1926 would be just over fifty-two. The trend there had begun in the last half of the nineteenth century (35 percent of priests in 1870 already over fifty-six.). But, because of poor recruitment between 1901 and 1914, priests are younger again today.[76]

Evidence of priestly poverty was all around in the late nineteenth century, though one can, I think, make too much of these money problems. Peasants wiped out by phylloxera were obviously worse off then priests, and so were unionless workers or the railway barmen who worked nineteen hour days. To say, as Weber says, that through the nineteenth century "priests were in an impossible [financial] position" is an overstatement for that world.[77] Priests in Catholic areas like Brittany supplemented income with gifts. Everywhere they had houses (*presbytères*) that were quite comfortable on the average, and had no seeds, outfits, or pleasures to spend on, no family to sustain, except on occasion elderly parents. (One priest of the Gironde in 1865 was crushed from having to support his parents, and demanded a better post.) For most of the nineteenth century, salaries were supposed to begin at about 700 francs, with a top point of no more than

1200 francs, except in certain strongly Catholic areas. But priests also "exploited" for burials, marriages, and other functions, like pew hire, and the collections at services brought in revenue too, not to mention "gifts" and supplements for old age. In turn this stimulated anticlericalism. Priests were accused of having hidden income ("ressources occultes"). But free gifts declined, and a hostile government, or at least majority, after 1875 made the situation worse.[78]

Evidence of poverty after 1870 is not difficult to unearth. At an extreme, we learn of an old, almost blind priest (1872) scraping by on 150 francs a year.[79] And from a well-known collection of letters written by curés we have many tales of woe worthy of Bernanos. A typical letter is from the curé Berthier of Comps.

> My parish is situated on the banks of the Gardon where it flows into the Rhône. This means that it is often exposed to floods. My church has suffered a lot from this fact of geography. . . . At whatever price, it is necessary to remedy this situation. But how? The commune is very poor, and furthermore, the municipal council is hostile, and charity is far from generous.

This is a familiar story. Another letter written by the curé of Fontenay-les-Bris (Seine-et-Oise) shows the feeling priests had of no longer being needed — "le refus des tutelles," as the French say:

> Ah, yes! Sir, it is hard for a priest to live amidst a population that wishes to hear nothing of religious things, that flees you, that only loves and cares for the material! It is hard [on me] to see one's church empty on Sunday, to find oneself spurned by the dying, to very rarely give confession. . . ."[80]

There are many such statements by priests on the lack of respect accorded the order as a whole. Weber and Zeldin have examples to suffice. Parish councils might also be hostile, or were now divided on white/blue lines. At a village of Lot, where in the 1890s the president of the parish council asked for dissolution, all work on the church was halted, for two factions had deadlocked proceedings. At Marcilhac, the whole council resigned because the *desservant* would not furnish his private accounts and receipts. Independent-minded priests were less tolerated now. At several villages of Gironde the priest had to haggle with the parish council for every penny of repairs, and these struggles took a lot of energy. Money problems, as much as saving souls, had become a cardinal concern. Maybe such problems had always taken a good deal of energy and concern, even where the local population had a more generous character. In 1874 a lightning fire destroyed part of the church at Lhuître and a major project of restoration was necessary. The priest there went from door-to-door for contributions and then, despite growing ill health, to Paris. In all, he raised some 25,000 francs, but died soon after.[81]

On the whole there was now more competition for the funds available from both public and private purses. Many villagers now preferred to spend their money on lay schools; to priests the irony was galling. Schools, as Jacques Ozouf remarked, now covered France as churches formerly had.[82] There were now many more applications for the State to take over care of local monuments.[83]

In Catholic areas, however, priests could still be formers of opinion, rather than lowly beggars of funds. Writing on the Vendée at the time of the Separation, France Duclos notes: "Very believing and practicing, the Bocage inhabitant accepts as an article of faith each word leaving the mouth of the priest. . . ."[84] As late as the 1890s one still had many teachers in Brittany forced to administer catechism for appearance sake. In processions like the Fête-Dieu, banned elsewhere, mayors could be seen marching, sometimes out of conviction, sometimes to keep the peace. This was the case at Plertuit in the region of St. Malo in 1888, where a tailor complained about the mayor's clericalism but the subprefect said it was good politics. Catechisms in the West were also more political and anti-laic than elsewhere.[85]

But there is evidence that people even in the West of France were now less tolerant of bumbling or incompetent clergymen than ever before. In Hervé Bazin's novels you get this note of sedition—of intolerance toward old priests grown fat from occupational stability. We have other evidence of impatience with lax priests. In 1895 there are complaints about the Abbé Jolivet, who is hardly ever found at his post in a village of Ille-et-Vilaine. Sometimes, it is said, he leaves Monday and does not return until Saturday, preferring to hunt, which he does without a permit. He administers only a handful of baptisms a year, and is rarely available for counsel. The mayor, backed by the populace, complains vehemently, and the archbishop suspends this priest's salary as a punishment, before transferring him elsewhere. Another priest of the department refuses burials, gives three-minute services at funerals, has his servant do catechisms, and spends much time raising pheasants or bicycling in the country. In 1894 a petition signed by 150 inhabitants of this small village demands that the archbishop send him elsewhere.[86]

There are complaints as well about priests taking monetary advantage of their position. A "republican" in 1890 writes an anonymous letter to the prefect, talking of several curés in his area of the West charging too much for communion and other services. "They love money so much, our

clericals (*"cléricaux"*), the curé has refused us all bell-ringing and chan-
ting—one has to give him 100 sou pieces or no ceremonies. . . ."[87] The twist
in the West is that people often complain to secular authorities *not* because
of overly zealous priests, but because priests are not religious enough—they
don't protect the sacred. We have also seen how curés in the Limousin
hastened the advent of modernity by attacking superstition. Here, too,
they continued to attack superstition, but where it did persist, it showed a
kind of peasant resistance in clerical areas. In parts of the Vendée by the
turn of the century belief in ghosts, were-wolves, or haunted fountains still
existed. Charivaris, which the Church had always fought, were still
popular.[88]

All in all, however, even the West was no longer intact; and if this was
the case there, it was much more true of less Catholic areas. In areas like
the Beauce the priest could muster little respect. The South, despite important local variations, also saw large swaths of indifference to religion.
In 1892 Monseigneur de Cabrières, bishop of Montpellier for twenty years,
noted: "I am struck by the progress that indifference—an absolute and
almost disdainful indifference—is making in our *pays*. Even in the countryside they are leaving the churches. . . ." The result, for Cholvy, is that
"the good curé of the end of the century becomes a prisoner of the parish
milieu." Many now paid *him* the humiliating compliment of indifference.
This was the case in Bonnières, where even the Bretons soon fell into line
and by-passed both church and priest. There was no need even for anticlericalsim there.[89] Where, in fact, did the main anticlericals of 1900
come from? Clemenceau, Briand, Waldeck-Rousseau were from the West,
and Combes had studied there.

Responding to pressures after 1870 priests grew increasingly political,
but this is best dealt with in connection with the chapter on struggles with
mayors. Still we may note here an increasing incidence of political
preaching from the pulpit, obviously stimulated by the issue of the laic,
"godless" public school; and of priests actively intervening during elections, putting up or ripping down posters for candidates. Some devoted
whole sermons to denunciation of republican electoral lists. Certainly such
actions would vary according to area and the characters of individual
priests. But it should be recognized that an undercurrent of Legitimist
feeling and thought among curés had persisted right through to the end of
the century.[90]

However there were new movements which they supported. Adherents
were found for Christian democracy and socialism; on the other hand
many more sympathized with the conservative, clerical militancy of the
Assumptionists. Many priests took or read *La Croix* (and its various provincial editions), *Le Pèlerin*, or *La Libre Parole* of Drumont. They also wrote

for them. Antisemitism among priests was rife in the Dreyfus era, a stain somewhat purged by the actions of certain priests in World War II.[91] But that takes us out of our century and beyond our period of notability.

Perhaps certain older trends did persist in some places after 1914. The more I immerse myself in this subject, the more I have misgivings about the very notion of trends, or all-knowing reasons we cite for such developments. Let me give an example: in an interview I conducted with a lady from the region of Castres, she mentioned her village of Guitalens, where her father was mayor, and another less than twenty kilometers distant, where his cousin was mayor. Thus she knew both villages well. In the 1920s the curés at both these villages were sons of the area, both acquainted with patois, both veterans (in different capacities) of World War I. The villages—hers was Guitalens, the other Viterbes—were similar in size, outlook, and geographical situation. Yet the priests couldn't have been more different. According to her, the curé of Viterbes was an "absolutely charming" man, loved by everyone there, secretary to the mayor, always cheery, so trustful and open that he left his house unlocked and permitted villagers to go inside at all hours, leave their packages there, eat from his table. Both lay schoolmistress and the mayor had excellent relations with this priest. He was heavily consulted.

In Guitalens, however, no one liked the priest, for he had a singular, "particular" character. In the streets he wouldn't even say hello to parishioners, pretending to read in his breviary. His sermons, "very personal" in tone, threatened sharecroppers and others with hell-fire for working Sundays, put out ill-disguised snickerings about widows or made-up women (everyone knew whom he meant), and dragged in political notions. His religion was entirely one of fear. Add to that a good dose of pedantry, and one has, from her portrait, a most unappetizing character. When he cited Homer or Racine or Masillon, which he often did in sermons, he made sure to emphasize that "you, uneducated rabble, would not know such a person as I do." In fact, she says that he was not very intelligent. Her father, the mayor, had little to do with him.[92] In two contiguous villages enough of these details could be summoned to destroy any airtight thesis or explanation.

Not that one must conclude in agnostic fashion. There are indicators, and there are rough transitions. In essence, old regimes pass. But I do fear we will never adequately realize what priests once were, just as no one who has not lived the philosophy of laicity (even vulgarized) can really understand the pre-1914 schoolmaster. For these were, in varying degrees, ideological notables. And ideology (or religion) is a universe in itself, in which one must be immersed to comprehend it. It is the *mentalité* of the old curé-notable that most eludes the modern, secular historian, yet which may also fascinate him most among those discussed here.

CHAPTER THREE

Portrait of the
Nineteenth-Century Rural Mayor

"It seems to me," remarked Louis Girard at a conference in 1975, "that we have not done enough with the history of the mayors."[1] If Girard is correct—and I suspect he is—it is because mayors were in-betweeners, as noted in the first chapter, and also because the character of their position, or any collective makeup they might have, is not easy to discern. Here I use both quantitative and qualitative data to make my attempt. But with mayors we have the same problem as with curés—how to generalize on their outlook or *mentalité*.

The lady who gave me the data on those two contrasting curés for the last chapter had, as I noted, a father and a cousin who were mayors of nearby villages. Surely these would provide a random pair. Yet here the characters were remarkably similar. Both were large landowners (*propriétaires*) presiding over sharecroppers' feasts at big tables under the trees, respected and consulted by all the villagers, at home both in familiar patois and prefecture French, above, and yet a part, of their village. The only significant difference she could find—if indeed it is significant—was the fact that her father participated rarely in communal drinking at the café or in other such diversions. The cousin, on the other hand, was an "enragé des boules," and necessarily looser with his charges at leisure time.

It is certain that mayors, like many priests, had a paternal bent and in some cases, a downright cantankerous or authoritarian personality. I remember walking one Sunday with the mayor of a cantonal capital, before dining at his fine house. Watching him tip his hat and scrupulously vouchsafe small smiles to passers-by, I had the impression of a Machiavellian little monarch in perfect control of his gestures. On the phone at home he contemptuously refused the local schoolmistress' demand for a telephone in her school. Barthélemy Piéchut, the mayor of Clochemerle, is certainly this type, too. He is obviously a caricature based upon a wealth of examples. Moreover, mayors *were* their town halls (*mairies*)—like the medieval popes, they were denizens of something at the center of their world. Noble mayors, especially, considered the *mairie* as part of their patrimony and prestige, but all mayors identified to some degree with their physical surroundings. The town hall contained archives, making mayors custodians of the past. And their own houses were frequently finer than those of the average person in the commune—that at Nègre's St. Eulalie in 1860 was the best in town. Sometimes villagers built an opulent place in honor of their mayor.[3] Since mayors were often consulted at home this created an enhanced impression. Any mayor with an autarchic bent was thus encouraged by his circumstances to play such a role and exercise his sway over villagers.

Weber sees nineteenth century communes, especially before the 1880s or so, as citadels. To the extent that he is correct, mayors were made more important by this fact. He mentions one who literally ruled his commune for over fifty years, permitting no tax collectors to enter the village, dispensing all justice by himself. Admittedly, that area was more than usually backward. In the same region a young mayor ruled "his little Republic" of 1848 with as much sense of legitimacy as the provisional government had in Paris. A generalized prefectoral report on 701 communes of Oise in 1873 noted among mayors "a certain spirit of independence and defiance, difficult to analyze". A justice of the peace forgave a southern mayor for overriding his prefect and preserving a monopoly for local café owners, saying that this was usual behavior by mayors, who consider themselves "masters of the commune". Even an enlightened mayor, Dr. Pouzet (1841-71) of Thabault's village, "would not have dreamed of comparing them [the villagers] to himself."[4]

Paradoxically, the links of the mayor with the central government helped guarantee him a village position. To begin with, he was appointed by the prefect of each department. His relations with these officials, as well as with deputies, became important and lucrative. He was a distributor of such portions of the government pork barrel as he could receive, making for a certain atmosphere of feudalism. Such a mayor attracted local retainers who gave allegiance, even servility, in order to get something in return. As Clemenceau noted in a story on Vendean politics, it all ends up as a "question of clientele."[5] At festivals mayors supervised the distribution of bread and, as will be seen, often procured amusements like fireworks. It was the policy of Augustus at a local level. (Such a role was also possible because mayors were often president of the local welfare bureaus.)[6] But beyond material distribution the pre-1880 mayors of many French villages were also *ideological* middle-men or outlets. Reading a lone copy of a newspaper to peasants or artisans, they could channel a specific version of the outside world to the grassroots, politically edit, supervise, and shape the censored version of a macrocosmic reality. In the village they gave letters of recommendation, aided people in deciphering documents, petitioned for the entry of free students into public schools, and helped the sick—all of these activities which gave them a certain authority.[7]

So village dependency was almost axiomatic, even where enlightened mayors like Thabault's Dr. Pouzet held office. Weak mayors there were; but these often delegated their authority to a "sub-notable" like the village schoolmaster, who might be authoritarian. Still, how many crusty, balky, recalcitrant rural mayors there must have been! These were the types who made trouble for schoolmasters, dragging their feet on school or home repairs, who refused to give villagers the documents they required, or who procrastinated on the payment of workers.[8] Then there were mayoral pretensions such as the snootiness engendered by a position on the councils, and other such perquisites. Mayors, rather like Homais, might name their children the equivalent of today's Jasons or Tanyas (such snobberies now spread wider). Thus a mayor of Auvergne in the 1830s called his daughter Marie Léonide Zélie Jenny Dufresne, revealing a fashionable hint of Anglomania in his choice. In the same period the mayor of Lhuître had children named Josephine, Ambroise, and Adelphine.[9]

The *mairie* might also be the property not only of the immediate occupant, but of his family and descendants. We might even speculate that the sort of glaciation seen during the eighteenth century in elites like *parlementaires* spread downward later on to offices like the rural mayoralty. This was especially true of small villages, of noble-dominated regions, and of ones which specialized in one crop such as viticulture. Several village studies show the control of the *mairie* by one or two families for 100 years. As shown in Table 1, Corcelle-les-Arts (Beaune), one vine-owning family dominated both *mairie* and council.

In Charnat, two family names monopolized the *mairie* for forty-five years between 1800 and 1880. In Plodémet, a republican dynasty, the Le Bails controlled the *mairie* (as well as deputy and senatorial posts) from 1870 to 1952, with the exception of only two years. At Bouillancy (Oise), the Courtier family predominated throughout the first half of the nineteenth century, with one mayor appropriately named Charlemagne Courtier.[10] There were areas where this almost tribal hegemony of families was obviously strongest—Corsica or the Landes of the Southwest (before it began to grow modern amid the planted pines). Tony Judt finds a good

Table 1.   Mayors of Corcelles–les–Arts 1843–1953

1843–1864	Auguste M.
1864–1881	Pierre M. (nephew of Auguste)
1881–1884	Bénigne G. (nephew of Auguste)
1884–1888	Pierre R. (nephew of Auguste)
1888–1892	Pierre V. (no relation)
1892–1919	Louis G. (nephew of Auguste and brother of Bénigne)
1919–1925	Alfred G. (son of Louis)
1925–1929	Victor V. (nephew of Pierre V.)
1929–1945	Alfred G.
1946–1953	Armand J. (son-in-law of Alfred G.)

(Source: Laurent Lévi-Strauss, "Pouvoir municipal et parenté dans un village Bourguignon," *Annales* 30 (1975), 149–151.)

deal of it in the Var, especially in the more backward parts. Prefects were forced to choose mayors from certain preponderant clans of such areas, rather than alienate the key notables of the region.

In fast-developing towns, however, new blood could have an easier time entering the *mairie* — as was the case at Bonnières-sur-Seine. To that village came Paulin Courtaux in the 1840s, and he became its mayor from 1848-1870, spanning the whole of the Second Empire. Mismanagement of finances ended his rule. Other emigrants — Michaux, father and son — were to be mayors, the son "a veritable one-man agricultural and industrial revolution."[11]

How long did mayors remain in office, on the average? Given the alternation of regimes and prefects in the nineteenth century, one cannot answer with any reasonable certainty. Reasons for longevity of tenure were often plain freakish, and it was not atypical for a mayor to be elected four different times and yet rule a total of over twenty years, as at Henri Marc's Chenôve. A prefectoral document of 1874 from the department of Lot tells us how long current mayors had been in office there, and we find that even with the change of regime in 1870, some had quite long periods of un-broken tenure. Of eighteen mayors, the one with the longest record in of-fice was a man at Luzech, there as mayor since 1844 — forty years. The man had survived both 1870 and 1848. The person who lasted over fifty straight years was a rarity indeed; most mayors were turned out, then returned. But from this document of Lot, the average number of consecutive years in office (to 1874) was 10.2 years.[12]

Mayors, I would speculate, rarely acceded to their posts before the age of forty, not that there is anything earthshaking about such a supposition. The average age of twenty new candidates proposed by the sub-prefect for villages of the Lesparre district (Gironde) in 1840 was fifty-three. In a district of the Southwest, for 1835, about 60 percent of mayors in office were under fifty. But probably not by much, in some cases. Sampling one district of Puy-de-Dôme for 1852, I found the average age of mayors in office as 49.9 years; twenty-five was the youngest, seventy-two the oldest, but most were over forty. In another district, Riom, for 1837, I find the average age strikingly similar, forty-nine.[13]

Moving to income, there has been to my knowledge no precise study of mayoral wealth, which is surprising, for the archives contain many prefectoral forms that note their revenues. That mayors were in general above average in wealth has always been a kind of common knowledge. Village studies frequently confirm it. In a village of Alsace (population 300), the mayor in 1836 hailed from one of the four wealthiest families of farmers. In a village of Languedoc, whose mayors are traced from the mid-nineteenth century to 1940, all mayors were well-off village notables: two wealthy wine-growers, one doctor, and finally a teacher who owned good property as well. These are types who were called "not Maître."[14] Wealth, or at least financial stability, was one of the things prefects looked for in mayors, in addition to social position, aptitude, morality, and a modicum of literacy. The *propriétaires* my interviewee mentioned derived as much notability from their wealth as from their character.

What prefectoral charts do show us, however, is the great *range* in mayoral incomes. From the financial standpoint, this was a very heterogeneous class of men. On a form for the Riom area, 1837 (already cited), thirty men were proposed as mayors, most of them renewals. The lowest income of any incumbent or new candidate was 400 francs per annum; the highest 15,000 francs; and the average annual income of the thirty was 2,798 francs. For first assistants to the mayor (*adjoints*, some of whom would themselves become mayors), the figures are 200, 1,800, and an average income of 861 francs per annum, considerably lower than that of mayors. This is partly because some exceedingly wealthy mayors inflated the median; but it also shows that assistants who remained assistants remained at that level in part because they were relatively deficient in the money department. Income, in the concrete rural world, and especially income derived from land, was a strong correlative of status.[15]

Taking the same district for the year 1878, under a very different regime, we find the average income for mayors increased to 3,426 francs per annum and that of assistants to 3,208 francs, even more startling. I have also found a document, for Riom, that gives *total* fortune ("fortune personnelle") for ten villages of one canton in 1855. Here, mayors attained an average of 117,600 francs (with one at 400,000 obviously inflating our sample), and assistants 22,000. Moving to other parts of France, in an *ar-*

rondissement of wine-growing Gironde, 1840, the average income for mayors was predictably higher than in the Massif Central: 4,690 francs for ten incumbent mayors, 4,240 for first prospective candidates, 3,250 for the second prospective candidates. For new mayors to be nominated in the department of Moselle, in 1833, the average annual income of mayors presently in office was 4,920 francs, with the highest 25,000 and the lowest 1,200. In a sample of twenty villages of Lot, 1874, the average income of mayors was 4,941 francs.[16] Sometimes such data was summarized or given qualitatively in the margins, and there the phrases I have seen were invariably "riche", "aisance", "fortune considerable", and the like. "Sans fortune" was very rare, and one supposes that due to a lack of candidates such mayors must have been *pis allers*, chosen despite a real handicap. Mayors needed to have a certain financial independence — in the eyes of the government it was equated with political independence. Status was enhanced by the fact that the mayor had money elsewhere and did not need it in a non-paying office. This was pure Veblen — the virtuous ability to pay; but it also conformed to the French ideal of living nobly, one not yet moribund in the nineteenth century.

Moving to occupations or class, most rural mayors of the nineteenth century were in some way connected to the land, which is again logical, and does not need great explanation. One reason is the fact that lawyers or doctors or soldiers or *notaires*, occupational categories from which mayors were less frequently drawn, generally lived in cantonal capitals, sub-prefectures, or other towns. Moreover, prefects seemed to prefer the landed interest, especially before the republican revolution of the late 1870s. They were especially suspicious of inn-keepers (*aubergistes*) whom one finds active in radical movements at various times during the century. In Gironde, a blacksmith was passed over in favor of a big land-owner because the former man would be indebted to those who employed him. In the early seventies, the prefect of Oise seemed concerned that certain wine and spirits merchants should not accede to the mayoral positions, for because of increasing alcoholism in Normandy they were gaining too much influence over clients — and emphatically the wrong kind.[17] Such biases worked in favor of landed "gentry". They were sometimes chosen because no one else was right for the post.

Statistics we have probably even underestimate the proportion of such men in local politics, for many so-called merchants or industrialists also owned land in the nineteenth century. But it is not only that category that makes estimates difficult; it is also ones like farm bailiff (*régisseurs*), tax collector, land measurer (*géomètre*), or "ex-mayor" and "ex-*adjoint*" that appear on forms and which may also disguise land ownership. Thus when André Tudesq notes that 41 percent of mayors in the Landes of 1835 were *propriétaires*, he almost certainly cites a figure that is too low.[18] Sometimes *propriétaire* is lumped with *cultivateur* (*propriétaire–cultivateur*) on charts I have seen; and other times the terms are completely separated, as in Marguerite Le Saux' summaries for Haute-Vienne, 1865 and 1884. Notice how the landed categories show a slight increase toward the latter part of the century, in an area not noticeably backward:

Table 2. *Mayors of districts of Bellac and Limoges*

	1865	1884
Propriétaires	88	89
Cultivateurs	3	10
Professions libérales et indépendantes	31	14
Commerçants et artisans	3	8
Diverses	1	6
Non precisées	4	

Source: Marguerite Le Saux, *L'Evolution religieuse du monde rural dans 3 cantons de la Haute-Vienne. . .du milieu du XIXe siècle a la Première Guerre Mondiale* (unpublished thesis, Faculté de Poitiers. 1971, p. 49.)

Le Saux obviously included towns here — hence the high proportion of professionals. On a chart proposing mayors (many of them incumbents) for one district of Gironde, 1830, I find that of the fifty top condidates for fifty villages, 76 percent were *propriétaires* (no *cultivateurs* given here); and in the remainder several are "ex-mayors" or land surveyors. The true figure is probably over 80 percent. In the district of Beauvais for 1871, 80 percent of mayors proposed were either *propriétaires* or *cultivateurs*. On my charts for Riom district, the proportions are nearly 70 percent for 1837, and just over 83 percent for 1878. (I found 13 percent doctors in 1837, abnormally high.)[19]

Now in towns of 5,000 or over the situation was obviously different. Moreover, some "rural" mayors migrated to the larger towns for the winter, as did the poor nobles Arthur Young found languishing at Lamballe in 1788. But mayors of those towns were drawn in larger proportion from commerce and the professions than from the land. Take a sub-prefecture of Oise, 1831: there the mayor is a *propriétaire*, but the first assistant is a *notaire*, the second a wholesale merchant (*négociant*), and of the remaining councillors, four are in commerce, eight in the professions, and four are *propriétaires*. In 1848, the mayor is a lawyer, and even though more artisans and shop-keepers are included among councillors, the preponderance again is professional and commercial.[20] This leads me to a peripheral hypothesis, but one I can't substantiate: some mayors and councillors of towns over 3,000 or so were Freemasons in the nineteenth century and stimulated anticlericalism by connections in those clubs and societies. Having examined occupation charts of provincial Freemasons, I find that in the main they come from the rural bourgeoisie—the class of Homais; but unfortunately, the designation "mayor" is never used, only the original occupation. We know that certain mayors of sub-prefectures were in correspondence with lodge members. Certainly their ideas on hierarchy—initiation, oaths, dignities, rites, solumn punishments—might appeal to some mayors. Even a few mayors of normally isolated villages must have known about or been influenced by freemasonry because of their class and position. The documents, however, do not throw enough light on this.[21]

To draw up an occupational and financial chart for mayors in all of France would take more time and effort than is necessary. We should at least note, before passing, the existence of local variations, for example, the importance of men involved in the manufacture or dealing of spirits in Normandy; or that of sea captains or men involved in fisheries in Brittany.[22] In the main, however, land, and landed wealth predominated, especially before 1880, but even after.

Along with sufficient material resources, mayors must also possess sufficient mental resources, namely, the ability to read and write, or some observable hints of normal intelligence. Still, many mayors allowed themselves to be dominated by councillors, priests, or schoolmasters because of limited or nonexistent literacy. Tudesq says it was difficult to locate mayors with a proper degree of instruction in the Southwest of the 1830s. I have found many letters by mayors that are full of spelling errors, though very few I could not understand. On one of the prefectoral charts cited, for the district of Ambert, 1855, comments on mayoral literacy are appended; some tell us little, but for the thirty-eight mayors whose literacy can be ascertained, we find only one who is well-educated ("fort instruit"). In the medium category ("instruit", "suffisant", or "capable"), we have 57.9 percent of the total, and in the poor category ("peu instruit," or "only knows how to sign") are the rest—39.5 percent of the total.[23]

Prospective mayors should also have stable characters. Still, one finds more latitude extended to drunks and philanderers among them than to the moral notables (i.e. priests and teachers). Being married also seems to have been the usual status among mayors. Of four nominated for mayor and two for assistant mayor at Clermont (Oise) in 1848, all were married. "Vieux garçons"—somehow, "bachelors" does not convey enough—would not have the moral weight for such an office, according to rural prejudices. Moreover, the mayor's wife gave advice, attended funerals, and was generally important to his position. One prejudice, however, that neither populace nor administration possessed was what we might call senomania. In fact, France has always been partial to its older politicians. "If they're good, keep them as long as possible" seemed to be the prefectoral motto on older mayors. At a village of Oise in 1860 the administration was sorry to receive the resignation of an eighty year old mayor and his eighty-one year old assistant, both suffering from infirmities, but "venerable oldsters, enjoying universal esteem."[24]

The mayor must also go along with his regime, or at least appear to do so. How ready the prefect was to purge his mayor depended on the position of the regime, and will be dealt with later. It is safe to say that most mayors, like most prefects for that matter, were political weathervanes. But better the man should guarantee a certain village stability than that he should adhere to orthodoxy. On one prefectoral form of 1870 one sees formulae like "highly thought of man of order", "esteemed conservative", "moderate republican—well established", "without opinions—well established". In each case the adjectives probably carry more importance than the noun. The perfect candidate for mayor must have a variety of desirable traits, or come closest in the limited talent pool that was the nineteenth century rural world. Such a man was proposed as a replacement in a village of Haute-Garonne in 1854. He was a councillor, property owner, ex-soldier, a man "very attached" to the government, well esteemed by the villagers, and well-off financially.[25] This was the ideal candidate; needless to say, ideal candidates were not always that easy to procure.

In the process of choosing a mayor, prefects sought recommendations from various sources, preeminently ex-mayors and justices of the peace, and from sub-prefects, who also gathered information from those already mentioned. Mayors themselves had a lot of sway in the choice of their own successors and could thus found dynasties of protégés or family relations. But their choice was often echoed by the council and by village opinion in places where the new nominee was an obvious person for the job. For instance, departing mayors at five villages of Cher in the early 1860s designated successors who were all accepted by the prefecture. One was the father-in-law of a mayor who was near death; two were assistants to the mayor and also close friends of the departing officer.[26] When appropriate candidates were not so obvious, the cantonal justices of the peace did the work of gathering information on imperfect men. They then sent their lists to sub-prefects, so that those "prefectoral" lists we have bearing occupational and monetary data were often, though not always, their doing initially. These reports can be valuable qualitative sources on men who ultimately became mayors. One in Cher had a model farm, "distinguished" manners, intelligence, and popularity. His only drawback was that he lived near the village only during the good season and went to town for the winter. But he became the new mayor. Deputies also made recommendations, as did priests, *conseillers-généraux*, and cantonal police commissioners. One of the latter from Bourges chose as new mayor of Vouzeron in 1861 a doctor, age twenty-nine, worth "no less than" 600,000 francs, and son-in-law of an influential councillor. The commissioner had canvassed villagers, who said the man was shy but esteemed; and the doctor became sole candidate on the prefectoral form.[27]

Sometimes, of course, it was politically advantageous to choose a lesser ability; but my impression was that the prefecture generally searched out the best candidates. Normally one should recruit (after 1830) from within the municipal council, but councillors might flee from such a position as from the plague. The sub-prefect of a district of Cher, 1865, had a problem with one village, where some of the councillors were dishonorable and the rest illiterate. At another near Toulouse, the sub-prefect was stuck with a semi-literate person who would luckily rule an unimportant commune. Sometimes we see on forms "the only one possible". A justice in Oise groaned at the lack of candidates in the council of his own cantonal capital, where it was either capacity, or fidelity to the regime that was lacking. In that department, part of hard-drinking Normandy, many inebriates were kept on while the search for suitable replacements continued. At the "problem village" of Beaudéduit, one mayor (1860) was a drunk who flaunted a mistress, and of ten councillors there, four were constantly under the influence. Meetings were held at the cabaret. The sub-prefect of Saint Amand gives us good detail on nine problem villages of Cher in 1868. At one, five councillors refused the mayoral chair and the other six were illiterate; at another, the sub-prefect disliked the whole council and wanted the ex-mayor back, but was afraid of the effect this might have on imminent government elections. It is interesting also to find a capsule portrait of each member of a council where none of them filled the bill. At one such village, 1875, the best candidate was a private bodyguard, which might be incompatible with being mayor, and he was also known for intemperance. Of the others, almost all were illiterate (a problem soon to be solved by Jules Ferry), and the only one who wasn't lived too far away. Several, besides being illiterate, were weak, open to bad influences, or mercurial, according to the report.[28]

In her fine work treating these aspects of local history, Judith Silver reports on communes fundamentally split between rival clusters of notables, making any choice of mayor a political Charybdis or Scylla. She notes increasing local self-sufficiency, even a cantankerous sense of independence wrought by notables acting in antipathy to the prefecture during the 1860s; and how struggles for the mayoralty determined political configurations in the area. At Naveil in 1865 the subprefect designated an ex-*instituteur*, now councillor for the post of mayor, on the assistant's advice; while another councillor recommended a M. Peguillet, against the majority opinion of the council. The former man had been a longtime secretary to the mayor, the latter a newcomer without a popular base. But the councillor who supported that newcomer had influence with the prefecture, and the subprefect was forced to appoint him, which created two rival camps in the commune for the next several years.[29] If anything, this shows again that relations with the prefecture still counted for a good deal in village politics, that they facilitated discord. Such detail again qualifies Weber's view of isolated citadels at the grassroots. Thanks to intermediary figures like mayors and councillors, villagers learned about politics, especailly under the Second Empire.

Some mayors exploited sources of independence to the full. They had power over prefects because of the allegiance or aid they gave to government candidates. Since it was reciprocal, such a relationship was very different from the one between teacher and *académie*, or priest and episcopacy. This is why prefects had to be rather lenient when it came to mayors' "écarts" in morality (not to mention the difficulty of finding adequate replacements). For instance, the mayor of Vinzelles under the Second Empire was known for his scandalous sexual habits—living with a married woman and showing off girl friends who complained about his infidelities; but since he had helped in government elections and was generally devoted to the government, the prefect would not dare censure him for it. Moreover, mayors had the last word in the appointment of rural functionaries, and could use that prerogative to build up local support and a power base against the higher authorities. So the mayor stood between prefecture and villagers, had a foot in both camps, and if he played his cards right, could turn this to his advantage, as an indispensable middleman.[30]

Especially under the Second Empire the government used its village mayors to guarantee or influence votes at the local level. Deputies, as much as prefects, owed many favors of the pork-barrel variety (so charmingly described by Sherman Kent) and officials who were not paid off felt free to show their displeasure. At one of Silver's villages, a mayor and his assistant resigned because the mayor could not get a legal case waived, both of which had been promised by the deputy. These officials probably reassumed office after a suitable delay. The government would also (as a payoff) divert railway lines—even if uneconomical—toward friendly towns.[31] So mayors might have quite a few people under their influence, or pressure; while reciprocally, such "pocket boroughs" could appeal to all regimes before the Third Republic.

I doubt, however, that one will ever ascertain the full extent of abuses at election times. As with sexual data on curés, electoral files in archives must indicate only the tip of an iceberg. At a village of Haute-Garonne there were a whole series of complaints on a mayor in the 1850s, a tarmaker who allegedly pressured his workers into certain votes, dangling illegal hunting rights before them as well. Nothing was done. Some mayors distributed free drinks, especially in Brittany, or had friendly café owners do so; some simply gave out money. Others kept people off lists, or like Falstaffian army captains inserted fictitious names on the rolls. Functionaries might be threatened with dismissal if they didn't vote correctly. Mayors also used field guards or other hirelings to pressure illiterates into voting correctly.[32]

In some cases, then, we are dealing with semifeudal kinds of relationships involving mayor-"lords" and clients. Mayors who had sharecroppers under them always had a ready coterie of well-nigh blind support. Tavern owners also used their own businesses as a power base, which is why prefects discouraged them as candidates and preferred independent property owners. Mayors who owned taverns predictably aroused the jealousy of other liquor dispensers, sometimes justified, sometimes not. At one village of Puy-de-Dôme it was clear that the mayor was getting customers at his bar by virtue of his office; at another the charges of competitors were probably also accurate, but were intensified by resentment of a poor outsider who had arrived penniless and grown wealthy there. The second mayor had been an indigent schoolmaster, and now as mayor and tavern owner, as well as land owner, was one of the wealthiest men of the commune. Part of the protest concerned the mayor's field guard, who spent his salary at the mayor's tavern and was often found drunk, while the fields were left open to poachers. In this case the prefecture seemed to be protecting the mayor.[33]

Given the attitude of authorities, often interested in returning their personnel at all costs, the extent of guilt in such cases is hard to determine. As with electoral abuses, it is also difficult to know how much graft and embezzlement went on at the local level in the nineteenth century. We do have a good source on mismanagement of funds (or what the French call *gestions occultes*) for departments like Puy-de-Dôme. Primitive old notebooks exhale their dust; investigations, one realizes immediately, might have taken more trouble than they were worth. Only rarely was a big fish caught. For example: the mayor of one village, confronted in 1829 with charges of skimming, said he had hands that were pure and clean. But accusations kept pouring in that he had made money on repairs, on marriages, on the bread tax, or from local butchers. Finally he was sentenced to one to ten years for having taken at least 8,000 francs illegally.[34]

Faced with such charges mayors had to produce many receipts, some of which can still be found in the files—payments to people like masons or storekeepers. A very large report was prepared in 1852 on a mayor who, during sixteen years in office, had been allegedly taking money off the top on repairs. The *percepteur's* conclusion is twenty pages long, and very detailed on each part of the budget; there is no conclusion. On the whole many investigations seem to have been hardly worth the effort. After another laborious, detailed report was made, a mayor who had taken money on bell tower repairs was required to pay back the miniscule sum of 138 francs and 76 centimes. Mayors also had roads built that were not really needed, or squirreled away money intended for keeping roads in good repair.[35] There are many other examples in this field and in the series as a whole; but again, investigations rarely yielded concrete results or restitutions.

The prefectoral policy on suspensions and revocations of mayors is also hard to ascertain from the evidence we have. Covert political or personal considerations frequently formed a part of decisions, yet these are not always readily apparent. (Prefects as noted, were as much political weather vanes of the century as mayors. Dissimulation was one of their necessary attributes.) One can at least mention typical causes of punishment. Focussing on a rich file for Haute-Garonne of the Second Empire, we have the mayor of one village dismissed from office for a whole spate of offences: avoidance of land taxes, land-grabbing, rewards to friends, the use of his tavern for political influence, and, most scandalously, the harboring of his uncle, an escaped convict, who even took over business at the *mairie* for a time.[36] In the same year two other mayors of the area were dismissed from office for fleeing their communes when an epidemic struck. Mayors, like ship captains, must remain at the helm until the end; they must show that they cared. A mayor who was violent toward his assistant and publicaly accused him of stealing was suspended for it. Mayors who had personal money troubles, thereby losing their independence, might also be suspended or dismissed.[37] I have chosen only a few typical illustrations from many kinds in this file.

Moral offences form another significant category, but mayors usually had to do more than just drink or philander in order to be significantly punished. One "père de famille" in Gironde, a skirt-chaser, *also* took money from repair funds, and it was recommended in 1825 that he be replaced. A year earlier we find a mayor of Oise revoked, not only because of his evident fondness for liquor and women, but because of an inability to control his council, mismanagement of personal affairs, and failure to aid the courts in prosecuting one of his friends. Many years later we have an Auvergnat magistrate who got into a drunk slugging fight, but was also brought to trial for graft and the falsification of birth certificates. It is rare to find a mayor's drinking problem listed as sole reason for punishment.

The following is an example of a moral lesson by the administration: the mayor's assistant in a village of Lorraine, located flat drunk in a ditch with his face covered in blood and mud, offered his own resignation (after recovery); but the prefect obtained a revocation instead "so that a useful example could be given to functionairies invested with municipal powers." [38]

There were, of course, many political revocations, especially after changes of regimes. This is almost axiomatic. Whereas, for example, only seventeen mayors were removed for political reasons during the placid period of 1837-1840, many more fell from power in the turbulent first months of 1848. Municipal elections showed much more turnover than in normal times. In the Department of Haute-Vienne 34 percent of mayors had been replaced by others after the first two months of the Revolution. By the summer "renewal" about half of mayors around France were newcomers. There were, however, significant regional variations. In Basses-Alpes only 31 percent of mayors and deputy mayors returned to their positions; whereas in more conservative-Catholic Côtes-du-Nord 62 percent were retained, and in Seine-et-Oise 85 percent.

Political dismissals, in other words, increased in a period of flux and reflected a general fluidity on the political scene. Hatchet jobs continued through 1850 and 1851. In the former year 265 mayors and assistant mayors were dismissed, for a variety of reasons. Many socialists, or demisocialists (or secret socialists), were dropped; it was a "hecatomb of mayors." [39] But then under the Second Empire mayors regained their security, and overtly political dismissals grew rare again.

Perhaps equally interesting is the political protection that was afforded to guilty, yet indispensable mayors. In this category was a mayor who was found by the sub-prefect to have rigged the accounting of small firms and taken money and usurped some land for friends. The evidence was incontrovertible and the sub-prefect proposed that he be replaced. The prefect overruled him and simply demanded of the mayor that he keep better accounts in the future. Contrast to this treatment the harsher punishment of suspension meted out to a mayor of Lorraine who had merely paid his son the old secretary's salary after it had been cut by 100 francs. In a strongly Catholic area, during the height of the laicity conflict, one cannot help but believe that political motives were behind such a measure. Such illustrations lend an undeniable atmosphere of hypocrisy to French political and administrative life in the nineteenth century. How curious to watch self-righteous prefects take an about-face with the change of a regime and mock their own rhetoric. Here, for example, is the moderately Leftist prefect of Moselle in 1844 damning Legitimist mayors; then in 1851 he weeds out those mayors of the "party that wants disorder", about thirty in all on the moderate Left.[40]

Political hatchet jobs increased markedly again under the Third Republic, mirroring enhanced politicization and polarization at the grassroots. I have found an excellent file for Lot in that period, and would estimate at least three-quarters of suspensions or revocations to have been politically inspired.

Here are some random examples I have taken from this unusually thick dossier. In 1886 a mayor was revoked for taking a fictitious secretary's salary. In the same year, another was dismissed for opposing the public vaccinator and another, for doctoring electoral lists (when even ripping a poster could lead to suspension). In 1888 one was revoked for insolence toward his sub-prefect, another for criticism of the President of the Republic. By the early 1900s issues such as the expulsion of religious orders and separation of Church and State provoked a good deal of dismissals. The Comte de Toulouse-Lautrec, indignant over the *inventaires*, was one of the most prestigious mayors to be axed.[41]

Besides *opposing* the state, mayors became objectionable too when they used the power of the state to their ends. As usual, Professor Weber's work is fundamental here. State sources of possible corruption obviously grew as the century advanced. The more state aid the more chance for graft. One sub-prefect noted this whole development, the taking of too much milk from the state cow, remarking, as he suspended a mayor: "I really hope that a vigorous example will prevent such practices from becoming normal in my district. . . ." This mayor had gotten resitution money for a farmer whose barn had "supposedly" burnt down. Even politically favorable mayors got themselves in trouble. A Radical on whom the government had gone easy for a while continued to appropriate state funds in different ways, especially by making up phony paychecks for functionaries. He was revoked in 1897. Tampering with electoral lists continued to be a major cause of suspensions (which always preceded revocations); but a fair amount of such cases *also* included this illegal use of state funds. Thus one mayor had placed a poor sharecropper on a list for medical assistance (illegally) and then used him on the electoral lists, and changed them around into the bargain. First suspended, he was then dismissed. (He had also fought the operations of the welfare bureau, as did several other mayors in this file.)[42] It is easy to exaggerate such sources of local discord and the importance of each of these cases. Ours is an age of dissensus, and this makes us sensitive to any historical conflict we can find, no matter how small. Most nineteenth century mayors, I imagine, enjoyed quite decent relations with their sub-prefect; most probably got along quite well with their municipal council, or the majority of its members.

Part of the reason for the latter was the personal nature of nineteenth century local politics. It was not yet the age of the committee, of the team of anonymous experts descending for an afternoon's consultation. The cultivation of mayoral personality and authority was essential to his position. He personified the unified commune to the outside world. In a recent political study Jack Hayward still sees the French mayor's role as far more important than the council's; for the council "consists mainly of leisured notables who regard their election as a recognition of social status and economic success." Confirmation comes from Bertrand Hervieu, who remarks that "the mayor exercises his power in a very autocratic manner, very personal. The municipal council participates only a little in decisions, and absenteeism at meetings seems high."[43] So the French mayor has more importance than the British, which is, of course, a contemporary estimate, but probably valid in the nineteenth century too. Even the fact that the vast majority of mayors were chosen from within the council does not invalidate our argument, for once differentiated officially, most knew to make use of their perquisites. Moreover, many who were not chosen were easily malleable illiterates, or incompetent men. Such was the case where my interviewee's father reigned. Elsewhere, a group of republicans were perhaps exaggerating when they referred to the municipality of Rocaix in 1881 as composed of "ten blind intellects, hardly knowing how to sign", with the mayor dominating these "municipal satellites"; but probably not by much. On ballots for another council a disgruntled voter scribbled "ass", "imbecile", "pig", and so on for the candidates.[44]

We have mentioned the above-average incidence of authoritarian mayors in the nineteenth century; as much as upon villagers that trait grated on council members, who might resent the mayor's domination and his capricious habits. Besides his position and literacy, one last reason the mayor could dominate council members is because he was usually older than the majority of them, which factor came into play along with his greater longevity in office. It was, after all, a patriarchal century, in which one deferred to experience.[45]

Mayoral patriarchs who changed the order of meetings or refused to discuss certain matters are legion. At a village of Puy-de-Dôme in the 1860s there were several petitions mounted by councillors about a mayor who overrode them on choice of secretary, water allocation, repairs, and the like. The prefecture, having substantiated the protest, did nothing about it, which was often the case. It was usually easier to replace councillors than mayors. Council protests sometimes reached the Ministry of the Interior, who nonetheless relied on his prefect, and really sub-prefect, for a final judgment. (The sub-prefect was of course closer to the mayor.) These protests convey a tone of despair, exasperation, even a feeling of impotence in the village. One such petition involved a mayor of Cher, almost illiterate himself, who kept arriving late to meetings and mocked the choices councillors proposed for posts like secretary.[46]

Councillors' resignations were a weapon to be used when all else failed. But my impression is that these were taken less seriously by the administration than the resignation of mayors, especially irreplaceable ones. Six councillors who gave up their posts at a village of Lot in 1893 cited a mayor who "believes himself to be above the laws of his country", noting that "he wants to govern by himself and treats his electors as slaves." The Ministry of the Interior simply dissolved the whole council and proceeded to new elections, for this was easier than tampering with a mayor who had been there a long time. Moreover, a dismissed mayor might foment opposition; re-elected as councillor, he might become a new source of trouble. At another village of the department, a mayor wanted to transfer his road surveyor out of the commune, against the wishes of the council. In this case the sub-prefect admitted that if the mayor hadn't twenty-five years tenure behind him, he would not accede to the demand; but reluctantly he ruled with the mayor. Another whole council of the area resigned because the mayor would not consult them on repairs; the sub-prefect simply accepted it.[47] Much easier, then, to get a more congenial council than a more congenial mayor.

Of course, it might work the other way too. Councillors might miss meetings or erect against the mayor's concrete proposals such a wall of inertia that he himself had to take action. A mayor in the Toulouse area was driven to resign in 1855 by a council that was prone to absences and constant bickering, to the point that no business could be completed. It was rather like the stone of evil (in the Bible) blocking the road to unity. The prefect, however, would simply not accept this mayor's resignation, waiting for new council elections that would change *its* composition. But another mayor near there was forced to resign by the prefecture for his weakness: almost illiterate and plainly feeble in health, he could not keep the council within proper bounds, and discussions simply rambled, or unravelled in discord.[48]

Disgruntled councillors, like priests, might use columns of the local press to ridicule the mayors with shafts of pettiness. The *Impartial de la Nièvre*, 14 October 1868, carried a very partial article by a councillor-*notaire*, who accused the mayor of Blet of living only two months a year in his commune, tampering with the health service, and generally being insensitive. Brought to court for libel, the councillor received a month in prison and a fine of 1,000 francs. At other villages such fights were sources of polarization and dissension. Again, notables spread politics rather as farmers sow. In 1910 one mayor of the Puy-de-Dôme got into a fight with a dissident councillor and finally knocked him down. The incident divided the commune in two and provoked anxious letters from a deputy of the area to the prefect.[49]

Some chronological distinctions are in order here. The last case I mentioned for 1910 involved "socialist" dissidents (though they were probably not true socialists at all). It is fair to say that divisions in the commune and others of that time were so acute because they were already political or party-oriented ones, or at least ideologically reinforced. Earlier in the century political standards were less important than the men themselves. People at the village level had mostly thought in terms of personalities, or men against men, clan against clan—a Namierite set of cliques trading amongst each other.[50] Jealousies in the earlier era were often unalloyed by ideology. Nietzschaen *ressentiments* naturally thrive in claustrophilic atmospheres, as they still do in small departments of large organizations. If villages were not airtight or complete "citadels", they were to some extent self-sufficient before 1880. One sub-prefect noted the kinds of jealous divisions that plagued his part of the Gironde in 1840: artisans fearful or resentful of bourgeois; one influential family trying to "repress" another; ambitious men who wished to dominate the mayor or supplant him. Another official generalized on a smaller area around a commune of the Puy, 1855, noting: "It is proverbial in the *pays* that inhabitants of this commune have always been divided among themselves: seven or eight want the *mairie*, each for his own advancement, and all are ready to unite against the one invested with this function". It is striking that only on the festival of the Emperor—a matter that was "*hors-village*"—could everyone get together there.[51] The isolated unity we hear about from Weber was in this case a figment. Paradoxically, the "figment" of national patriotism made it a fact!

Jealous letters, complaints addressed to authorities and taking mayors to task were perhaps less common than those denouncing priests or Third Republic teachers. For one thing mayors were often called on to validate such petitions or even to compose them. Still, we do have a goodly number, of which I cite but a few examples from some of the departments I have canvassed in detail. For instance, a mayor's assistant who wanted the *mairie* wrote a series of letters to the prefecture of Haute-Garonne in the 1850s, castigating the administration of the commune, and noting, among other things, that the mayor permitted, even encouraged, the theft of rabbits. It looked like he was scraping the barrel, and a justice of the peace, who made an investigation, found that the assistant was indeed envious of the mayor's popularity in the village and clearly wanted the post. At another village during the early 1900s a series of petitions poured into the prefecture, denouncing the mayor's handling of financial affairs, as well as other business. On investigation it was found that some signatures were fictitious and that others were gotten by deception—people not knowing (like Maugham's verger) what it was that they were signing. The key signatures were by reactionaries—frustrated candidates for the mayoralty.[52]

We can also study certain problem villages, like alcoholic Beaudéduit in Normandy, and note a persistence of internotable jealousies, though where to demarcate chicken from egg is hard. Who starts what, and why, in such conflicts is more completely analyzed in chapter four. Here the priest was a perpetual opponent of the mayor in the first half of the century and by his intensity attracted other notable opponents to his side. In the 1820s an ex-mayor, promoting his son for the post, made life miserable for the actual mayor, mounting petitions and finally provoking that mayor's resignation in 1826. Another man resigned in 1839, after eight years of personal, trivial problems, confessing that "I have become a very bad mayor." He had been strongly criticized by opponents for not repairing the priest's house; and though the prefect begged him to remain in ofice, his resignation was final. Yet another mayor there resigned in 1852, after troubles with neighboring communes and with his own council. Then he returned in 1855, instantly complaining about a bully of an assistant. In 1859, this mayor was found plastering the village with signs that ridiculed his assistant—shocking behavior, according to the justice of the peace. And so it went—at a poor village admittedly prone to such conflicts municipal life was anything but calm.[53] And once again, these petty placard wars testify to a higher degree of passions than we would perhaps impute to village politics. I have seen a typical placard in orange, composed by a frustrated mayoral candidate, that literally screams corruption in its large capitals, accusing the incumbent of racketeering.[54]

All along we have been alluding to the mayors as important agents of ideology in rural France. It is now necessary to be more precise about this ideological influence. Firstly, there was his *economic* influence which in turn changed the course of ideas. Judith Silver has shown adeptly how mayors, as well as other local notables, were stimulators of the economy under the Second Empire, acting as *traits d'union* between village and government. By installing a road or telegraph, as well as by more explicit means, they facilitated the transfer of civic ideals from the center to the periphery.

Mainly, this means patriotism. Weber's view that most villagers before 1880 were deficient in national patriotism must again be qualified. In fact mayors had long been attentive to the problem of stimulating patriotism at the grass roots, and they took their orders from the prefect, who in turn got his from Paris. When, for example, the Bourbon regime looked unstable in 1829, prefects had mayors try to prop it up in the provinces. In Haut Rhin, the prefect asked mayors to display busts of Charles X at all town halls and to survey ambulatory musicians and peddlers for songs or tracts that might be hostile to the government.[55]

Government festivals were also instrumental in inculcating patriotism, although we can never be ultimately sure how much they "took" in the popular consciousness. But the mayor, sometimes in competition with the priest, could be seen as a sort of local wizard or guardian of patriotism at festival time. Ministers of the Interior, especially by the Second Empire, wanted full reports on the degree of fervor and the effect of such festivals. At one festival in the Agenais, a mayor's assistant described proceedings to the prefect with becoming enthusiasm. Bread had been distributed to the poor, as in many localities, but better yet, "Our excellent Mayor took steps. . .to procure for us a display of illuminations rarely seen till now in our locality. . ." Dances were improvised, faces were "radiant with happiness", the emperor, as "pacifier of Italy", was on everyone's lips. At many other villages of the department we find the same kind of report: "illuminations rarely seen before" ("*inusités*"), flags, busts of Napoleon III or eagles, potato sack races, notabilities celebrating the festival "with all possible splendor" and "all the pomp that we could muster from local resources," to cite two mayors.[56]

These festivals may sound naïve, but they should not be underestimated. In our own world, as I note more fully in chapter five, we have grown old from amusements; but some of us may remember even the field days or July fourths of *our* youth and the joy of legitimized celebration. In wartime or revolution, mayors might, of course, go their own way. The principle of being *régimiste*, to which they held, was more uncertain at such times. Or they could use patriotism for their own ends. The mayor of a village in Gironde of 1870 had to get urgent repairs done on the church roof, but the Franco-Prussian War intervened and made money scarce. He asked the carpenter to "prove his patriotism" and do the work for free; perhaps after the war he would be paid. At another village of the department a year later, the mayor, as president of the welfare society, put on a lavish August festival, but was charged with using it as his own propaganda for Bonapartism.[57]

The problem of patriotism was part of the problem inherent in mayoral ambivalence itself. Mayors were obviously caught between government and locality, with one foot in each of two camps; but when it came to the crunch their centrifugal inclinations more often won out. As Hayward points out of the contemporary mayor, "The mayor, like the prefect, is both the agent of the central government and the representative of the local community, although he generally plays down the former role and often thinks of himself in opposition to the state rather than as its servant."[58] In nineteenth century France the tradition of peasant centrifugality was still strong, and mayors were often not much removed from peasantry, except by income. Moreover, government meant taxes and general interference, as Weber shows so well; before 1850 or so, it meant less as a source of aid or sustenance. Earlier in the century mayors took the side of poachers, of tax cheaters, of illegal woodcutters. In 1828, the "idée fixe" of an eighty-two year old mayor in the Cher was to fight the new forest code. This man wanted unlimited cutting rights for his charges and even in bed with fever still spoke incessantly about the problem. During disturbances in the Ariège and Pyrenees at this time, woodcutters could also get support from their mayors, sometimes torn between allegiances, but frequently siding with the "*pays*". From 1849 to 1851, when the central government hunted local Montagnards (or radical leftists), mayors frequently protected them; to turn them in was to lose the trust of the village. In Thabault's village, the coup d'etat of 1851 meant primarily the descent of capricious tax collectors and of military authority in activities of surveillance. Get them off our back, said Mayor Pouzet, in effect. The same feeling was seen in large parts of the South during the winegrowers' revolt of 1907. Despite Clemenceau's warnings, some 500 mayors resigned at that time.[59]

The mayor was interpreter of his village to those who could not readily understand its needs. He filled out his prefectoral questionnaires (revealing the state of mind of the commune), sometimes by rote, but sometimes also to instruct and to chide insensitive authority. If peasants marched around the cross for good draft numbers, he explained the custom to his town-bred superiors. He tried to get exemptions for peasant sons who were necessary to marginal farms; he supervised the signing of petitions, increasingly numerous throughout the century; and might even travel to a prefecture to explain why a teacher should be maintained in his village. According to Judith Silver, "political analysts have [mistakenly] portrayed mayors as yes-men of the prefecture", whereas "they were more interested in associating themselves with local rather than prefectural interests." The mayor *was* the *mairie*, he *was* the village: how not defend what you were?[60]

As the century progressed, he became more of an *economic* informant as well. He was a member of agricultural shows (*comices agricoles*), knowledgeable about the placing of roads and railways, sometimes a Homais in his encyclopedic grasp of the tiny details he provided the government. He told of the progress of farm schools, noted how crops were doing, and which farmers deserved prizes each year. Too often we forget the mayor as local enlightener, or spreader and incarnator of specialist knowledge, especially before the advent of the Third Republic's teacher. Mayors surveyed or gave advice on hygienic habits, one in 1850 preaching "pure air, healthy food, frequent baths and washing, clothes often cleaned, fresh linen and clean overalls." As seen, the mayor was sometimes *the* local newspaper reader, transmitting "affaires d'en haut" to his flock. He might fight for the establishment of adult classes. Later in the century he was a spur to cooperative farm movements and the setting up of organizations like brass bands. He also petitioned for new agricultural fairs, and organized measures against epidemics. Imagine him solemnly installing that new telegraphic office in his village, investing someone morally competent, like the schoolmaster and his wife, with this sacred, progressive new duty![61] It is the essence of nineteenth century enlightenment at the grass roots.

So mayors could be local *aristoi* by virtue of their many responsibilities. How then to measure their local "notability" or sources of status? Particularly given the fact that their prestige, more than that of, say, the Third Republic teacher, was usually intermingled with various other factors—financial situation, other political posts, farm, house, the number of men who worked their estate. Thus a report of 1829 on a mayor and *inspecteur-voyer* of Gironde notes succinctly: "These two men exercise a great influence; they are the biggest and richest landowners of the village." Certain mayors, even if not Tudesq's *grands notables*, had at the local level a preponderance so complete that the sheer fact of being mayor was comparatively unimportant (akin to Montesquieu's post in the *parlement* of Bordeaux). One man named M. Bézard was the largest proprietor of his village, president for over five years of its *comice agricole*, possessor of surpassing wealth for the area, and winner of forty-nine first prizes in agricultural shows! Another in the 1870s noted: "If I enjoy any influence in the canton of Castenet, it is solely due to my family position and to my landholdings, not to the modest and obscure function [of mayor] with which I have been entrusted."[62] Mayors like this one (and almost all others) also had honorary posts on the parish and welfare councils that conferred status. Their perquisites tumbled down like fruit from the original tree of wealth.

So to measure notability remains a precarious and somewhat artificial business. If, for example, we have elegaic tributes to mayors, as to curés, extolling their quotidian virtues, is not some of this evidence as suspect as the normal accolades you hear when an office worker retires? The eighty-two year old man who fought the forest code was "a respectable old man. . .charitable, obliging, excellent *père de famille*. . .extremely cherished in his canton." Since this is the prefect speaking to the Minister of the Interior we can perhaps take such a recommendation more literally than what we receive from newspapers or on tombstones. We note an example of the latter in Burgundy: "Man of heart, Good citizen, Administrator of integrity and justice." Another standard was "the best of fathers and of husbands." And perhaps more of a routine than a positive expression of devotion was the custom of presenting *brioches* to mayors, which began dying out in the 1880s. Mayors had squares or streets named for them; but it was not only as enlightened magistrate that one in Cher got such an honor (installer of mutual society, of roads, of more free schooling), but also as an important porcelain manufacturer in the region.[63]

These local notables, of course, had other rival notables with whom to deal or contend. Difficulties with the priests are reserved for a subsequent chapter; those with council or prefecture have already been noted. Certain mayors were already the noble squires of their village. Those who weren't must deal tactfully with that personage and with other *grands notables* of the region. The mayor was certainly taught to be flexible by the exigencies of his position. Given the nature of French regimes—the point is central throughout—he must learn to be a Barère, a Talleyrand, never a Saint Just. The changes came not only with each regime, but with each new prefect. In Vidalenc's Eure, the heir prefect of 1821 did a large investigation of all rural mayors, mercifully weeding out only the absolute incompetents. But by 1824 the replacement process was stepped up. Good votes must be delivered, or else.[64] So here we have some men who may be tyrants with the peasants, but who of necessity must slavishly kowtow to those above them. Perhaps that is simply social law everywhere.

Other mayors might be situated somewhat higher than the ordinary local notables, yet beneath those of vast regional influence. Their influence might encompass a canton or two, which was no mean achievement in the nineteenth century. Pierre Barral presents us, for example, the mayor of Saint Jean-de-Bournay, there from 1852 to 1867, a man who controlled the whole canton, who had links to the mayor of Vienne (himself linked to Paris), and who had privileges akin to Rogers Hornsby's, the baseball player who was sometimes allowed to call his own balls and strikes. This man, "convinced of his superiority", was untouchable by the sub-prefect. Links to the mayor of Vienne, a *grand notable*, might also read "dependency". A mayor of a village of Loir-et-Cher under the Second Empire derived almost his whole position there as retainer to the influential Count of Couvello. Mayors invariably would run into grand notables at political meetings held in the towns or at the local agricultural societies. They might procure favors for them, such as free drinks or advantages for a nephew. And if mayors were embroiled with prefects (Silver's thesis indicates a rise in such local challenges to authority under the Second Empire) it behooved them to get support from another higher notable, such as a deputy. Deputies, after all, were different than prefects or bishops; they came from the area and sometimes got their feet dirty.[65]

One of the chief problems we have so far avoided (by artificial means) is determining the importance of a mayoral position to someone who already had status and a number of other positions. For some who had local mayoralities might also have more wide-ranging offices above that one, and even a deputy position in parliament. Normally such a man must be mayor of a small town or at the least, a chief commune of the canton. Even after World War I, we have an excellent example of such a person in Jean Moulin, himself a sub-prefect, then prefect, who as De Gaulle's representative was tortured to death during the Resistance. When Moulin became sub-prefect at Chateaulin, a charming little river town of the Finistère, he naturally grew close with a doctor who was mayor of Carhaix (a *chef-lieu*), president of the *conseil general* of the Finistère, a senator, and the man who "is the leader of almost all republican politics in the department." M. Le Bail of Plozévet was both a mayor and deputy before and after World War I. Pierre-Jakez Hélias remembers how impressed local people were with this man. "He doesn't always stay in Plozévet. He goes to Paris to make speeches in the Chamber! He goes to defend people in the law court at Quimper." Just to be a *conseiller* of the department, *arrondissement*, or even canton gave one enhanced prestige and influence. Thus a report on another doctor, *conseiller* at the last two levels in the crucial transitional period of 1878-1882: "Good situation in the Commune. His influence is exercised over a large part of the canton."[66]

The problem is complicated when mayors were actual nobles. Incidence of mayoral nobility could probably be determined, but I will largely cite qualitative evidence and give some relevant chronology. According to Vidalenc's thesis on the Eure, 1830 was a great watershed (giving David Pinkney's conclusions some revision). In the 1820s the chateau had still been the political and social center of most villages, and these nobles were "often" mayors of the commune. Vidalenc enlarges for the whole nation, noting that "The Restoration. . .was then the great period of the nobility in the constitutional life of the country." After 1830 people at the local level were fed up with seigneurs — mayors who lived elsewhere — and now desired mayors and assistants "who were there when people needed them." A most important statement, indeed, contradicting once again Weber's idea of peasant atoms unconnected with the political cosmos, though for a relatively advanced department. The decline of noble mayors was henceforth precipitous. In the Eure, many were replaced by old functionaries of the Empire shut out during the Restoration. Thabault situates the change in Mazières slightly later. Before 1841, he says, nobles predominated as mayors, and then they were basically gone. The leftward shift in the South chronicled by Maurice Agulhon, which I discuss in a later chapter, would similarly doom noble mayors. It is perfectly predictable that they should hang on longest in regions like the West: in 1909 slightly under one-seventh of Breton mayors were still nobles. These nobles considered the *mairie* as much a part of their patrimony and human significance as the property they owned and are the strong crotchety types one encounters in Hervé Bazin's novels on the West.[67] I do not wish, however, to conclude a discussion of well-to-do or noble mayors on such a somber note: enlightened autocrats there obviously were, responding to local desiderata. One such was Albert-Auguste Flahaut, who as mayor of a village in Pas-de-Calais possessed 250 acres of land with many workers under him; to these men he loaned money and gave social services.[68] Again, it is far too easy to see such men through our liberal, bureaucratic, modern values system, though abuses (especially toward sharecroppers or other lease farmers) must have been fairly common. (I have seen many connected with the lay-*libre* school conflict of the Third Republic.)

We have discussed who mayors were. What were their day-to-day duties? How hard did these nineteenth century mayors work? This is hard to answer. Mayors in the sleepiest of villages might live a sleepy life, or deal with the most trivial, nonpressing of problems, as did Barthélémy Piéchut of Clochemerle; but my impression is that work loads were usually quite adequate. Aside from political duties, there was much additional paper-work, including reports, validation of certificates, electoral lists galore. There were marriages to perform, the supervision of military lotteries, verification of weights, measures, and quality of grain; welfare, garbage, and cemeteries to supervise, the maintenance of general order, surveillance of cabarets, the supervision of subnotables like *instituteur* and field guard, not to mention a sometimes debilitating, time-consuming relationship with the curé. But above all, mayors had to attend to the trinity of roads, church repair, and schools—an interrelated group of problems, given the competition for money.[69]

Roads were a key to much rural change in the nineteenth century. Eugen Weber, emphasizing the point in a well-wrought chapter, might also have underlined the local initiatives involved and particularly the role of mayors. For mayors, in general, pushed hard to get roads, and had to be cognizant of the various aspects of each project, particularly financial ones. Using road surveyors, they must prove the utility of a project— classify it, help determine its direction, and encourage or force certain property owners to divest themselves of terrain. They must ram budgets through the council and deal with the prefecture, oversee the search for gravel, coordinate plans with mayors of neighbouring communes. It was sometimes difficult to locate suitable highway workers. Sometimes the mayor might try to impress a field guard into part-time road work; one field guard from the Gironde resigned his post for this reason in 1878. When you look at council deliberations from typical villages, you find that the issue of roads frequently took the lion's share of meeting time.[69]

In church repair campaigns, priests took the major role, but mayors might rival their ardor. Mayors had to supervise accounts and pay each mason and carpenter; a budget report might run to over 100 pages. If matters went awry, if something failed to fit, mayors must accept responsibility. They must also choose among rival bidders and fight for government loans. These loans were given in installments, and the mayor, like a fellowship-holder, must send in his certificates to the prefect in order to show the progress of construction. In addition there were the "extraordinary impositions" in the commune—these could occasion much debate. And when a priest's house was to be bought or sold, there were lawyers and *notaires* to deal with; mortgages and therefore banks; and of course parish council and the bishop. Even to oppose church repair, as mayors often did, took time and energy, though some, to be sure, delighted in that sort of work—we will see it in the next chapter.

As for the schools, we must distinguish between reactionary mayors drawn to church schools (*écoles libres*) and progressives who from 1833 on wanted to pay for a lay schoolmaster and perhaps an upgraded school. Before 1880, even progressives chiselled on salaries, and this is in good measure why teachers remained dependent creatures. Mayors also had an enormous responsibility for the futures of the pupils themselves, in that they could supervise the admission and quotas of "gratuity" students, or hardship cases. Dr. Pouzet of Thabault's village set the limit at fifteen during the 1850s. There, roads and repairs to the presbytery, as well as a new registry office, superseded the school problem. Schools were often dilapidated and unhealthy places. To build one could take an awful lot of the mayor's time, and the great building campaigns of the late seventies and early eighties—the erection of *palais scolaires*, as opponents labelled them—drove out rival issues like church repair. At one village of Beauvaisie, the account book for school building alone from 1878 to 1880 runs to about 100 pages. Just for roof zincing (Coupeau's trade in Zola)—a matter of 775 francs—ten pages were allotted. Continually, there were the problems of supervision and verification, the many figurative headaches mayors must have contracted near the job. Problems of leases, government laws, suitable lodging for teachers (the cause of so many squabbles!) also weighed heavily. Mayors who supported school building or repair had necessarily to be propagandists. They were opposed by clericals, or just by penny-pinching citizens. At Loupiac in the 1800s the municipal council noted the real need for subvention of a girls' school, but also that "its inhabitants. . .are asking with great cries for the reduction of taxes, because of the deprivations into which the agricultural crisis has plunged them."[70]

It is not my purpose to discuss here the great school battles of that time. Suffice it to say that the school became an issue which demanded a good deal of paperwork and propaganda on the part of mayors; and that it was a central part of the struggle for local democracy, and seemed a key to the republican future at the grass roots. It involved quarrels between parish council and municipal council, Catholics and freer thinkers, the tightfisted versus the munificent citizens. Mayors supervised local ballots on how and where schools ought to be built.[71] So these schools, if a source of local pride, even an added feather in mayoral caps, were also a major source of worry.

There is evidence that the sheer growth of paperwork, especially after 1870, became too daunting for certain mayors to handle, mirroring the growth of what Albert Thibaudet once scornfully labelled "cette république paperassière." Despite more qualified secretaries — usually lay schoolmasters — certain mayors had a hard time keeping abreast. One in the Périgord tendered his resignation in 1911 "because of the incessant development of paperwork (*"travail d'écritures"*) in the *mairies*", and because of the necessity of training a novice secretary at that time. Agendas of council meetings were much more overloaded than earlier in the century. In just one session of February 1898 the council of a small town in Oise discussed distribution of clothes and food to the poor, pensions, free medical assistance, road lighting, road work, reimbursement for an architect, a railway, antiraisin tax demonstrations by grocers, rights of free grazing (*vaine pâture*), the appropriation of terrain for roads, and the building of a new well. Some of the issues were carried over to subsequent sessions. There were now more school problems, problems of hospitals, and of insane asylums, telephone installations, and the like — problems created by technology. Compare to the 1830s, when issues were more often "histoires de chiens enragés" — one of a few items actually cited by a local historian for a village of the Allier.[72] Work became more onerous, too, because of increased politicization at the local level. Here I do go along with Weber's estimate of a sea change, a growth in ideological life at the grass roots. This meant clericalism-anticlericalism, in the main; and, for certain mayors, pressures of choice and tact that were too much to bear. One in the Périgord reflected a situation not unlike a mayor caught between Resistance and *Milice* during World War II: "Old and broken. . .it's impossible for me to keep the administration of the commune of St. Clair any longer. Moreover, I can't hide the fact that being hardly interested in political [divisions], and having relatives and friends in every camp, I'm tired of these electoral battles that divide the most obscure of villages."[73]

In such developments the Third Republic seems to be the natural end point, as it is for all these chapters. After the categories are done with, one returns to the all-important fact of chronology; and for the history of French mayors, chronology is indispensable.

The coming of the Republic brought the "Revolution of the mayors" — the substitution, in 1877, of a council-appointed mayor for a prefectoral appointment in villages below *chef–lieux*. (The complete revolution for all communes occurred in 1883.) Weber believes this decisively introduced politics into most villages. So did the special aura of the Republic itself and its multiple promises: new festivals, cheap, more widespread dignities. And of course, the clerical issue, so nauseatingly central to so much of the country at that time also contributed to this politicization. One law relating to mayors could not have done it. No, it was a whole imagery associated with the Republic: its flag, its maps, its bands, its songs, "little things, one may say, but almost prehistoric vestiges [now] of a period when the word 'republican' had a meaning, and almost an explosive virtue. . .", in the affecting words of Marcel Laurent.[74] The Republic, despite all the bitterness it brought, brought its own symmetry, from which mayors benefited. And just as one sometimes gets a deep, necessarily ineffable feeling of how Catholic or noble France once was, so one sometimes gets a similar feeling about the iconography of this new Republic, taking France out of its long night (the metaphor is of the time) and into the light. Several years back I remember reading the signs on the town hall of a certain village, affixed there in 1889. One was for the centenary of the Bastille, "fortress of despotism where they locked up without trial the defenders of the people" (prostitutes included?). The other was for the centenary of the first meeting of the Estates General, "which delivered the people from the lords (*seigneurs*). . ." In other words, out of the night into day was the theme. (The analogy with Genesis is obvious.) That morning I had been following (in city archives) my rumpled mayors in affairs that took place in villages like this one. Then I left a traffic jam and wound through spiny forested hills to get there. The town hall was obviously built in the 1880s; at the summit, "R. F." sat upon a bed of sculpted green leaves. The building was most rudimentary, modest, almost toylike, with its dinky little balustrade above the door that looked down upon the gently descending slope of the square, where two children on vacation now played badminton among the cars; but where once our mayor made his speeches, raising the crowd to words like those on the building—"l'égalite des droits," "la fraternité humaine. . . ." Oh, what a squat, direct, foolish but admirable little building—so representative! So rational!

The 1870s were of course a bitter time at the local level, especially after 1875. As late as 1874 not so much needed changing. In that year the prefect of Gironde saw the need for a change of mayor in at most one-fifth of his communes. Recruitment from within the municipal councils was still working in a stable fashion; of 206 village mayors in three arrondissements, only twenty-four were not councillors. There, the prefect was still worried about forming a good solid Orleanist party under the *grands notables* of the area. The Republic was also up in the air at Mazières. Not until 1879 was a firmly republican mayor chosen there, and for a brief interlude it looked like the squires might return. In Oise, after consultation with his judges, *conseillors généraux*, and sub-prefects, the prefect believed that of 701 mayors in villages beneath the level of cantonal capital, only thirty to forty at most needed changing.[75]

Suddenly after 1875 came political changes. Where prefects had in the past considered various aspects of the mayoral personality, they henceforth considered his political orientation as the most important element. In their documents or lists they had always noted popularity, literacy, morality, and other criteria. More and more it was "reactionary but not militant", "a conservative without well-established opinions", "republican of long standing", "republican frankly rallied to our institutions", "Bonapartist devoted to M. Le Corberon" — these are from a typical document for Oise of 1881.[76] It should be remembered that even after the municipal election of mayors the prefecture still had some control over its mayors, and in cantonal capitals on up still had the nomination. Revocations were the prefect's province.

Everywhere, like the racket of gunfire or glassbreaking in Flaubert's Tuileries, one heard mayors chopped if they failed to adapt to the Republic. It was not the first time. In 1848, 50 percent of "February mayors" had fallen by July, some to emerge again later.[77] Now there was a similar prodding, an omnipresent use of pressure. Certain mayors who controlled whole cantons were particular targets. Thus the prefect moved against the mayor of Saint Martin d'Auxigny, a *chef-lieu*, in 1881. All the dirty words were trotted out: Catholic, conservative, clerical, reactionary. And on their side suspect mayors grew watchful. For example, a mayor of Cher writes in 1878: "I know very well that the administration is keeping its eye on me and is looking for opportunities to catch me in a faux pas, in order to get my dismissal." That very letter indeed did it — the prefect cited it in his own letter to the Interior asking for the man's revocation. A count at a nearby village got it in 1880 for failure to participate in the 14 July celebration — "a sanguinary day". A mayor in Oise, thanking the Comte de Cossé-Brissac for a new bell tower, a matter of a few spoken lines, was taken out of office in 1880. Nobles were finally decimated almost everywhere, except in the West. The Jules Ferry school also provided an issue for a rash of dismissals, such as of a Lorraine mayor, ex-Rightist deputy, and head of the crystal-making firm of Baccarat, who had vast departmental influence. Frankly noting that he was making an example, the prefect got rid of him, even while conceding the distinction of his man.[78] Rightist mayors felt that they were fighting for their religion, their locality, their independence. Who is to say that they were not?

In the West before 1877 the administrators had already been racking their brains looking for suitable alternatives, as a report of 1875 in the Morbihan makes clear: "There exists in the Morbihan, M. the Minister, a relatively important number of Communes lacking men endowed with sufficient education for the municipality."[79] It is not clear that the *révolution des maires* made matters any better there.

But almost everywhere, the transition was made. Between 1885 and 1914 the mayor, like the schoolmaster of the Republic, enjoyed an Indian summer of prosperity and of accruing prestige. The priest was rapidly being defeated. The Republic's prestige and symmetry was now at the local level the mayor's own. Mayors were more and more rural bourgeois.[80]

And if those officials generally benefitted from the victory of the Republic, the reverse was also true. The Republic at the local level was consolidated by the action and the gains of mayor and council. Ted Margadant, taking the long view past his own period, notes this well: "The subsequent evolution of the relationship between mayors and the state—obedient appointees during the authoritarian Empire, increasingly independent officials during the Liberal Empire, moderate supporters of the Republican regime during the 1870s, and elected leaders of Republican municipal councils after 1883—would make the gradual consolidation of Republican patronage through the institutions of local government."[81]

Of course, the dust never entirely clears, no victory is permanent, all contain elements of defeat; but this was perhaps the true heyday of both Republic *and* country mayor, except for those few reactionaries of the West who had problems during the religious troubles of the Waldeck-Rousseau era. The country was getting better and better; and the "Weberian triumph"—admittedly a two-edged sword—was also, in the main, a triumph for the rural mayors.

CHAPTER FOUR

Mayors versus Priests:
The Extension of Local Anticlericalism

We have now presented our priests and mayors and discussed them in a relatively airtight way. But conflicts or relations between the two, less publicized than those between curé and *instituteur*, seem to be a key to much of nineteenth century French history. Local history, of course this was; but more and more, historians recognize the local origins of great transformations, and realize the sagacity, even if exaggerated, of Lucien Febvre's statement: "For my part I've only known. . .one method, one alone, for really understanding and locating *la grande histoire*. And that is first to master in all its development the history of a region, or of a province. . . ."[1] In tune with this greater historiographical emphasis on local sources of disorders, and of new orders, it is fitting that the next two chapters deal with struggles between mayor and priest in nineteenth century France.

This quarrel has received little sustained attention, which is surprising, since it seems fundamental to many major developments: to the growth of anticlericalism and dechristianization, in particular, and to the coming of a "république au village," as well as the political anchoring of national regimes at the grass roots. Apart from works like Maurice Agulhon's, which only allude to it, we have very little of substance on the mechanics of the conflict, perhaps because the details were so often petty: disputes over benches, keys to church, last rites, flags, oaths, squabbles over building funds. In presenting some of this material here, I am obviously presenting the tip of an historical iceberg: for a single department one could find enough evidence on the conflict to form a book, especially in departments already favorable to anticlericalism. The notion of a "stalemate society" in nineteenth century France can now be revised.

Village France may have been backward, may have been relatively quiet, but rural consensus was much less strong in a nineteenth century of conflicting notables than it is today, when all stand equally on their feet, no longer needing guidance in the business of life and diversions.

Mayors and priests, each in their different hierarchy, each considering themselves as important or more important than the other, fought constantly against each other in the nineteenth century, and sometimes the incidents they provoked were magnified by village opinion or by the local press; but it would be wrong to dismiss all such imbroglios as mere "histoires de chiens enragés" or "affaires de clocher". Two competing wills were fighting for an important hegemony. Mayors, we have said, were frequently authoritarian creatures, as were curés; each liked to show superiority. All through the century we find mayors trying to have curés appointed that they could dominate (and vice versa). It was an attempt to gain the upper hand in the village, a naked bid for control. Few, however, arranged matters so cozily as a mayor who had his relative installed as priest, a man over eighty, almost blind, and completely deaf. (Unfortunately the vicar-general got wind of this man's inadequacy and had him replaced, while the prefect, who had been taken in by the mayor's report on the priest's health, severely reprimanded this official.[2])

To certain mayors I would impute a spirit of prankishness—of *taquinerie*; waddling, sanctimonious curés could obviously impel such people to play their tricks, as rigid authority did for Groucho Marx, or for his script-writers. In the 1850s a mayor gave the business to a young vicar by taking the torch from the Saint Jean fire and putting it elsewhere, placing unauthorized objects on monuments, and conveniently forgetting to consult the parish council in various matters. His sub-prefect saw this as mere dog-in-the-manger behavior, so usual as to merit no censure. At three villages of the Cher the sub-prefect simply threw up his hands, refusing to make cataracts out of trickles: between one mayor and curé, involved in a placard war at one of the department's most backward villages, this was just a "petite guerre;" at another these "misérables rivalités" were dividing the village; at the third he recognized the need for a new mayor, in order to end "all the intrigues. . .the little passions."[3] And prefects, too, were inclined to minimize the importance of such rifts. When a sub-prefect reported on an electoral battle between the two notables in Vaucluse, 1852, the prefect, in a letter to the Interior, simply imputed it to a normal tussle for "influence that Mayor and Curé struggle after [;] both, moreover, have quite irascible characters." Even directives from the Minister of the Interior inclined toward a quietly directed laissez faire policy, or at least toward moderation. Thus when a mayor buried a man at Le Thor who was declared (by the priest) unfit for Catholic burial (1839), the policy of the authorities was to keep these opponents from stirring up more discord in the village. The Minister of the Interior took care to emphasize that this should be a general policy in such cases. (By the Third Republic, as we shall see, the balance was completely tipped toward the mayor, and when, for example, the curé at Ille-sur-Sorgue in 1877 complained about the mayor's reservation of burial plots for freethinkers buried *sans curé*, the prefect fully supported the mayor. All he asked was that his subaltern change the formula to "someone not having belonged, or having ceased to belong, to one of the cults recognized by the state."[4]

Mayors also found occasions to squabble when the parish or welfare councils met. These rifts frequently mirrored a larger one between the municipal council, or some of its members, with parish councillors. In the *arrondissement* of Narbonne, 1867, says the sub-prefect, very few communes did *not* have such divisions.[5] Mayors, of course, had a say in all allocations — specifically, whether a priest or his church deserved finanical aid — and they could gain political leverage in that way.

Now nothing is more trivial than the recitation of marital quarrels, and each tiny bone of contention the self-righteous contestants see fit to invoke. Lawyers can teach social historians a certain exasperated patience in this regard. But trivial nicks do pile up, and sometimes they lead to a deep gash. My theme here is that taken together, no matter what their individual nonimportance was, these quarrels helped change ideological life at the grass roots, or at least to inflame it. When, for example, "Deplorables Divisions" arose between mayor and priest at Brosses (Yonne) in the 1830s, these were trumpeted loudly in an article of that title by the *Journal des villes et des campagnes* (14 September 1832), a journal appearing every two days and published in Paris. On that one village we have complaints and countercomplaints until 1839, filling a large dossier; these include several collective letters by the municipal council, opposed to an authoritarian mayor and siding with the priest. But in the same department during the 1830s a collective complaint *against* the priest was signed by over 100 inhabitants and the whole municipal council at Charmoy. The problem there was the refusal of burial, a familiar one in this period.[6]

Refusals of burials, indeed, led to many of the quarrels between mayors and priests that one finds in the archives. In some cases the priest, Catholic, probably felt sincerely that he had a legitimate reason for acting as he did. In other cases he was probably using refusal of burial as a political tool in his battle for village hegemony. We find plentiful refusals both in the West and in the more anticlerical departments of France. In Ille-et-Vilaine there are representative cases at Saint Médard sur Ille in 1835, where the dead man in question was the mayor's former assistant, and at Feins in 1832, where refusal bred scenes of violence. In almost all the cases I saw, the mayor complained to the prefect in behalf of the dying or dead person. Far south the mayor of Saint Léonard in 1841 denounced a priest for refusing religious burial to a boy with croup who had lost his voice and was unable to confess. At nearby Arnac-La-Poste in 1868 a refusal of burial led to serious riots, with the mayor, left-leaning, on one side, the priest and his cohorts on the other. Weber has clearly shown that quarrels over burials demonstrated a certain amount of popular resentment against overcharging priests. Mayors could then stir up latent hostilities that had already been there. The same was true of the countless times curés decided not to marry a supposedly immoral couple, or one tainted with Protestantism.[7] We have many examples of such divisions all over France.

Miserable quarrels? Of course, but they could drag out for months, even years at a time, to the exasperation of higher authorities who wished to maintain order in the countryside. One such scandal erupted at Les Cars (Haute-Vienne) in the 1830s, splitting the commune in two. From the sub-prefect we hear of a mayor who is "very simple but full of probity and rectitude. . . .", victimized by a priest who fights over state and church property, refuses to officiate at marriages, insults the mayor's wife by accusing her of adultery, and yells at him in church. One of their quarrels had come when the priest rang the church bells during a storm and the superstitious mayor told him to stop, fearing that this would bring *more* thunder. From the archbishop, in his correspondence with the prefect, we get the portrait of a mayor who withholds keys from the priest and who has allowed someone to open a cabaret in the stable, where the priest kept his horse: an intractable man, in short. At Lagnes (Vaucluse), during the late 1820s, mayor and preist fought over the amount of money designated for church candles, the time of mass services, and the ways of celebrating the festival of Charles X. This quarrel, complicated by anonymous letters sent to the prefect and, according to the mayor, by the collusion of his ex-assistant with the priest, grew into what constituted a major political power struggle there.[8]

If these problems appear silly to us, and probably somewhat silly to prefects, it also behooved the latter to survey them in order that rural tranquillity—that supreme ideal—should not be overly disturbed. Local order was an obvious necessity for any political regime getting established and legitimized at the grass roots; in the nineteenth century all regimes had to do that.

The sheer amount of correspondence that related to these problems means, depending on one's viewpoint, either that they were important, or else that they acted as smokescreens, impeding treatment of more significant issues. Anyone who has studied the growth and functions of modern bureaucracy must give some credence to the latter viewpoint. My own opinion is that both may be simultaneously correct.

Just to read through all the correspondence related to private bequests (*legs*), which I have not done, could take a long time. At Les Esseintes (Gironde) in 1862 the question of how to interpret one such bequest divided the whole commune, with mayor and priest predictably on opposite sides.[9] Church building and repair have also been noted as a major source of paper waste in the nineteenth century. Having tried systematically to go through some of the massive correspondence for Gironde alone, I have been utterly defeated by it. What I do find is that mayors, stimulating the penny-pinching sentiments of citizens, could again stimulate anti-clericalism by opposing priests on these matters, as they did with burials. One hears this note sounded in a deliberation of the municipal council at Queyrac, 1842, signed by the mayor and all councillors: "Ah! what has resulted, in effect, from all these useless and arbitrary expenses. . .troubles and divisions!" Here the sub-prefect supported the priest and parish council. Another curé of the area demanded a transfer (soon to be granted) because of a bad climate and poor health, all exacerbated by a stubborn mayor and retinue who had promised for years to proceed to repairs and had never done so, while also cutting off the priest's supplemental income. In this place the mayor won, but the archbishop put pressure on him to begin repairs before a new curé was named. Mayors who had done their promised repairs could then use that as a stick with which to flog uppity priests, as at Brécy (Cher) where a priest allegedly planted trees on the property of his *presbytère* and obstructed a new road there. What kind of behavior was this for such a well-treated priest? the mayor wished to know. We've given him 20,000 francs for his church, he declared to the prefect.[10] One does not know what action was taken.

Fights over the *presbytère* have already been noted — priests demanding repairs, trying to plant in the garden, cutting down trees, and thereby provoking conflicts with mayors who loved nothing better than to affirm their full rights. One problem that vexed authorities: did curés have the right to glean firewood from *presbytère* property? A letter from the Minister of Cults to an archbishop, 1845, averred on this subject that it was mostly a communal problem, to be decided at that level (by the mayor). The letter came in answer to clerical complaints over refusals of their privilege to take firewood (*affouage*) in Haute-Saône. What we find is that the mayor and local hounds were usually strong enough, especially in anti-clerical areas, to prevent priests from obtaining the wood.[11]

Also innumerable, or at least impossible to quantify, are affairs relating to church keys, bell ringing, and displacement or removal of benches. These heights of pettiness were frequently symptomatic of a wider split. Typical is a problem in a commune of Oise, 1845, where the "curé-desservant" had denied mayor and councillors entry into the bell tower, and changed the locks, so that their keys would not work.[12] Here were literal *affaires de clocher*, quite worthy of Clochemerle; or what Parisians like Balzac saw as "les mares stagnantes" — repulsive, bickering, trivial affairs of rurality at its very worst.

But pettiness is also found in Napoleon, in religious wars, and in many formally great events. Who *doesn't* wish to assert himself? Even the cream of egalitarians do. A propos, Richard Cobb has composed some excellent, apposite pages (in his serendipitous manner) on the superiority complex of urban *sans culottes*, who at a crucial point in the Revolution raised themselves above their station. Though he refuses to agree with sexual interpretations of men proudly holding their pikes, Cobb does see them using their imagistic regalia to advance themselves.[13]

Similarly with mayor and curé: two images, frequently two deluded "*grands*", locked in conflict. In the village of Vaucluse we have a protracted battle under the Second Empire between two such deluded grandeurs of this stripe. The antagonists, almost archetypal, were the bright but mercurial Abbé André and the equally authoritarian mayor. Abbé André, at Vaucluse from 1851 to 1866, was a maverick prone to running afoul of authorities. He had an exalted opinion of himself, and as supervisor of the archaeological digs of Roman ruins at Saint Véran reserved the right to refuse admission to the site. One visitor wishing to see the area was told: "The curé of Vaucluse only disturbs himself for crowned people." The man reportedly said that he was King of Bavaria and was admitted. For years the mayor tried to get rid of this curé, and André retaliated by writing a book on despotic mayors and bishops, the tyranny of transfers (*déplacements*) noted in Chapter II. The mayor attempted to tax the priest's dog, and other such quarrels continued elsewhere, after he was transferred, almost to the curé's death in 1881. (André was inappropriately interred near the fountain of Vaucluse, Petrarch's inspiration of love.) There were many other violent disputes much like this one. At Velleron (Vaucluse) in 1836 the curé got into a shouting match during mass with the mayor and his assistant, while members of the parish council tried to restrain him. The dispute occurred during a local festival, ostensibly over the amount of money the curé could collect in his *quête*. At the height of the quarrel the curé, known for his violence in other posts, hit the mayor and his assistant and was given fines totalling 100 francs and condemned to fifteen days in jail. For the Limousin, Alain Corbin has similar examples that need no repeating. Judith Silver quotes a priest of the Vendômois (under the Second Empire) whose language about a mayor is as exaggerated as André's and that of his opponent: "M. Bagan Pasquier [the

mayor] only serves the interests of hell-the apocalypse [is] his mythology. . .
he speaks of the Virgin Mary as about a female prostitute. He recognizes
the Eternal Father as everyman."[14]

We have seen what cards mayors played against curés; how did the
process operate in reverse? Refusal of Catholic burial was one often-used
strategem which could force a mayor to give way to the curé's will, the use
of anonymous letters another possibility. But mainly, those curés in conflict with mayors tried to pare away in small ways at the rival's position,
whenever possible. This could take the form of something so petty as
moving benches from church, (for example, at Châteauneuf du Pape,
1839)[15] or engaging in unauthorized building and repair. Such incidents
might, however, backfire and lead to transfers.

It should not be thought that mayors and priests *never* agreed on
matters; it is only that my emphasis in this chapter goes to sources of conflict, not consensus. In the West, of course, one can adduce many
examples of harmonious relations, some already given. Even in less clerical
regions you have effusive curés saluting, as one did, "the happy effect of
good harmony that reigns between us, the salutary push the [mayor] gave
to work on the church. . . ." This curé continues: "May God deign to
reward him and his family from now on." Moreover, nonenergetic mayors
could easily slip under the curé's influence, as they would do under the
literate *instituteur* of the Third Republic. Such, for instance, was the case
at Gradagne (Haute-Garonne) in 1852.[16]

To return to the mechanics of conflict, and ramify its components: in
these battles between mayors and priests, already underestimated, what
students of the problem (Roger Magraw, François Bellon, Agulhon) do not
see fit to notice is the rush to enlist "subnotables" on one side or the
other. Primarily, this meant the pre-1870 *instituteur*, who was normally
someone's underling. We already know of the pre-1870 schoolmaster as a
pawn of the priest—bell ringer, church sweeper, and general subaltern.
But this category is too confining, and quite aside from the "red"
schoolmasters of 1848[17], the archives suggest more importance and elas-
ticity to the ante-Ferry teacher than we have hitherto supposed.

On curés versus *instituteurs* one can find evidence even in Catholic
areas as far back as the 1820s. In one village of the Vendée such a rift went
on for at least five years during that decade. In a village of the Limousin in
1842 a priest pulled a teacher by the throat and insulted him. He had
already paid 150 francs damages for a previous insult. And in several areas
we find priests using pressure tactics on teachers which would become
much more common in the era of the Ferry school: refusals of absolution,
anti*instituteur* sermons, pressure on pupils at catechism, and so forth. A
petition from the councillors and major property owners of Billé to the

prefect of Ille-et-Vilaine in 1837 noted measures taken by the curé to discredit the schoolmaster and schoolmistress there. The sub-prefect of Fougères subsequently confirmed the charges and said the curé had been involved in similar matters in other villages. This curé said that all teachers who graduated from the normal school were impious, and that any mayor who supported them would be buried with his dogs. The priest had also hit a child who went to the teacher's school and refused last rites to a dying fifteen year old girl who had been a pupil of the *institutrice*. At Mornay (Saône-et-Loire) in 1846 a curé used sermons and opportunities at catechism to rob the teacher of pupils and give them to his sister, who taught at a rival Catholic school. The prefect, emphatically not a Third Republic prefect, said nothing could be done, unless the teacher wanted to prosecute, which of course he could not do. At Moulis (Gironde) a teacher ("with broken heart") found his mutual aid society attacked as a secret group in inflammatory clerical speeches.[18] In most villages, particularly under the Second Empire, priests reigned strongly over teachers. and the battle would remain unequal until the Third Republic. Teachers who were secretary to the mayor as well as the priest's domestic, cantor (*chantre*), and bell ringer obviously had little time or leverage for revolt. In the late 1840s one from the Vosges complained that he was "like a slave to the priest." In a canton of Oise, 1847, twenty-one teachers signed a petition asking for the abolition of humiliating duties like cantor, sacristan, and bell ringer. (In 1843-44, 94 percent of lay teachers in Côte-d'Or were cantors, 51 percent in Gers.) One surmises that only in "detached" departments like the Yonne could most pre-Ferry *instituteurs* have any significant autonomy or prestige.[19]

It is not my intention, however, to enlarge upon the early schoolmaster as a separate animal of importance; for that he was usually not. Rather, his importance before 1870 frequently derived from an alliance with the mayor against the priest, or by embroilment in the struggle of commune versus church. According to Theodore Zeldin, he often helped the mayor in Second Empire electoral battles, but Zeldin offers no evidence for this. We do find other subnotables like tavern keepers or innkeepers involved in electoral battles before 1870, usually on the left-wing side. This is the case, for example, at two villages of the Yonne in the early 1850s. And in an above mentioned quarrel in that department over refusal of burials (1836), the mayor had the schoolmaster give last rite prayers instead of the recalcitrant priest. One can surmise that these would be electoral friends in such a politically aware area, as would certain road surveyors, yet another "subnotable."[20]

In Catholic areas teacher and priest normally allied *against* the mayor, though we will never know the extent of struggles for the teacher's allegiance, nor whether plums were always dangled as payment. Teachers, especially earlier in the century, were probably happy to have church-related jobs and could be relied on to support the priest if the mayor was a threat. But mayoral alliances with schoolmasters can be found even in the Vendée and as early as the 1840s. In one village of that department we hear of these two figures ganging up on a priest, who was in turn fined for defaming the municipality. Here, as was customary, the bishop supported his priest against an "ignorant" mayor and "immoral" schoolmaster, while the sub-prefect and prefect backed the latter against a "turbulent priest." That priest ultimately left the commune. In 1854 a mayor and teacher at a village of Saône-et-Loire acted to remove a priest from the village, and even though opposed by the prefecture, kept fanning the flames, harping on words the curé had used in sermons. They were not successful in removing him. On the other hand there are places even outside strong Catholic areas where authoritarian mayor and priest held down independent schoolmaster, as at Montmort (Saône-et-Loire) in 1867.[21] Radical teachers were often as painful to mayors as to priests. And the prefectoral administration before 1870 was sometimes hostile to independent-minded teachers, too. An anonymous letter written in the Yonne of 1854 deplored the firing of teachers in his village and in others of the area by an administration protecting fanatic priests, even against the advice of local municipal councils:

If the schoolteacher irritates anyone they ask for his resignation, without a motive. . . .if he resists, if the muncipal council resists they suspend him without saying anything and name a commission that will do anything they ask. It's said that all this is done to make the government hated.[22]

This letter is important. It shows that local notables (municipal council or teacher) could be arrayed against more conservative superiors, the latter trying to stem the tide of educational laicity and republicanism in a department that welcomed it. In some cases one also sees the teacher dominating a weaker mayor and/or council, though this would be much more frequent when Ferry's black-coated town clerks dotted the country after 1880.[23] But of course many teachers were already town hall secretaries before Ferry; in 1833 they had 54 percent of posts in the Basse-Alpes, 33 percent in Gers (1843) and 69 percent there in 1865. Their literacy could be used against the other village literate par excellence, the priest. At Saint Hippolyte (Vaucluse) in 1862, a mayor's letter of complaint about a curé is written on school paper, in fine handwriting obviously the teacher's, and in language probably the teacher's as well. (The teacher, by the way, is highly praised in this letter.) Taking an interesting tack, this mayor tells the prefect that if the curé isn't replaced "religion will irresistibly lose out at St. Hippolyte," for everyone there detests the curé. The prefect, however, turned a deaf ear to this protest.[24]

What interests me most is how the pre-Ferry teacher frequently found himself caught between two authoritarian, opposed mentalities, unsure himself which way to go. It reminds one of two notables fighting over the dying Hippolyte in *Mme Bovary*, or of a typical Third Republic cartoon, where priest and *institutrice* each pull on the ear of a rural child, wishing to enlist him. In the evolution of anticlericalism before 1870, teachers were as much the pushed as the pushers. At Blauvac (Vaucluse) in 1864, an *instituteur* felt himself hopelessly divided in allegiance, and hoped only for reconciliation of the mutually antagonistic mayor and curé. Writing to the prefect, he asked: "While awaiting this reconciliation, I would be infinitely grateful, M. Prefect, to know if, when M. Mayor has me compose, as clerk, reports, letters, minutes against M. Curé, I should do it or not." At villages of Haute-Garonne and of Oise, curés attacked mayors by attacking *instituteurs*, who were seen to be too friendly to them. Teachers often had no one to turn to for advice, and must have been in many cases perplexed as to which side should be chosen. And *they* were the easiest to dismiss of the three figures. From roughly 1843 to 1863 there were fifteen *instituteurs* at a village of Gironde. In an example cited by Meyers, the teacher was too much of a lay cleric for his mayor and too immoral for the priest. An inspector's report of the 1830s reveals the schizoid type of teacher "imitating in his gestures and language the parish curé for whom he [is] sacristan or devoted servant, [yet] invested with the dignity of Monsieur the Mayor to whom he is a most humble aide. . . ." Peasants chimed in that teachers were too busy working for both mayor and curé even to stay in a classroom all day. We have a typical letter of protest on this from a man in Villeneuve-Minervois to the Ministry of Education in 1860. But the main point is how teachers might be an entering wedge propelled by the *mayor*, a key weapon used in anticlerical battles before 1870.[25]

Plain political differences were often the key to mayor-curé conflict, especially during or after changes of regime. I find the Revolution of 1830 an especially signal date in the growth of French anticlericalism, this despite the revisionist work of Professor Pinkney, for whom that Revolution brought little change at all. René Rémond, however, supports my chronological viewpoint, noting: "In the history of political anticlericalism the date of 1830 has a very precise significance: the revolution was accompanied by an explosion of popular anticlericalism. . . . Long contained within the bounds of measured expression, if not repressed by constraints and fear, it suddenly pours forth. . .and inspires every kind of excess." This historian continues in a more striking fashion: "Yesterday in the opposition, it [anticlericalism] is today in power or on good terms with its occupants." Here I believe Remond goes too far. Given the state of rural France, which most of France still was, no ideological movement could become widespread in the provinces without some gradual maturation. I am more willing, however, to accept another theory of his, that before 1830 romanticism was quite often theocratic and that after that date (he might have cited Stendhal's *The Red and the Black*) it is more usually allied with anticlericalism.[26]

The very *language* for such a conflict was lacking before 1830 as neither the words "anticlerical" or "anticlericalism" had yet been coined, though of course the phenomena were known. Even the word "clerical", used in a political sense, dates only from about 1815, according to recent dictionaries of etymology. The gradual "conceptualization" of the nineteenth century, facilitating the growth of ideology in the rural world, is a subject in itself.[27]

After 1830, mayors, chosen by prefects from within elected councils, became stronger, partly because of the new anticlerical wave everywhere; and priests in some ways became weaker. Adrien Dansette may be exaggerating when he says: "A piece of gossip from the mayor. . .was enough to have the priest sent to another parish." But he goes on to cite eloquent evidence that in "the single year, 1837, 3,500 priests were moved." F. Pomponi may similarly exaggerate when he calls mayors of the post-1830 period "césars de village" — men increasingly unwilling to suffer competition; but in some villages that was certainly the case.[28]

And so after 1830 one finds a significant transformation in relations between mayor and curé. The transition is noted in several local studies, less well-known than the work of Maruice Agulhon, but perhaps significant enough to change our thinking on these matters. (Agulhon of course situates the great sea change in the Midi during the 1840s and makes 1848 the point of "révélation.")

One study on a village of the Yonne is particularly instructive — the Yonne being one of those departments that was always evolving from one minoritarian viewpoint to the next: Jansenism, Protestant stirrings during the 1820s, anticlericalism as early as that period, and socialism and syndicalism by the turn of the century (the area forming men like Paul Bert and Gustave Hervé). For J. P. Rocher, who focussed on the conflict of a mayor and priest at Villeneuve-L'Archevêque (Yonne), the year 1830 was a particular turning point in the growth of anticlericalism. The struggle there began with the priest's failure to take the oath of allegiance to the new regime of Louis-Phillipe. The mayor himself had come into office with the regime and so took the oath seriously. Then the curé refused a religious burial to one of the inhabitants, and he and the mayor continued to fight over other petty affairs. But the political quarrel between an

Orleanist mayor and Legitimist curé was the fundamental one; and the mayor, by taking the public attitude. "The curé has wanted to teach us once and for all how to do without his ministry. . .May this lesson bear its fruits!" helped, thereby, to spread an *ideal* of anticlericalism in that village. Finally, it was the mayor's own campaign (the prefectoral administration much more circumspect), and the simultaneous stimulation of public opinion there, that made the priest resign his post in 1835. But this sort of thing happened in other villages. And from Henri Forestier's more general study of that department we see a contributing factor—a sharp rise in Protestant anticlericalism after 1830. Newspapers like *L'Union* (1848) celebrated victories over the "sacerdotal yoke", while Protestantism was often considered by the opposition as a cover for free thought.[29]

Moving to the Vaucluse, part of a whole region that was soon to move leftward in a significant way, we find more evidence of mayor–curé battles just after 1830 and which seem to be significant patches of the larger quilt. Orleanist mayors fought Legitimist priests all over the department, and the government would obviously support, or at least condone, such activity. Many priests, refusing to sing Louis Phillipe's *"Domine salvum"*, were brought to heel by mayors. One recalcitrant vicar of Ille-sur-Sorgue not only refused the oath, but also tried to prevent the "Marseillaise" from being played on the festival of Ste-Anne. Then this "ultra-Carlist," as the mayor called him, hit one of the musicians and broke his instrument. The mayor got the police to report on his actions. Formal complaints allowed one to gain legitimacy, the local upper hand. Just after the Revolution a petition signed by twelve men at Oppède reveals how a curé's antigovernment stand (anti-Louis-Phillipe) led to anticlericalism there. The petition is addressed to the prefect:

> We love religion, we love the ministers of this religion, if they restrict themselves to their duties. But we detest them if instead of setting a good example by their conduct, they irritate the inhabitants of their parish by their irreligious acts, to the point where the temple is deserted; if to attract an indulgent eye from their superiors they go with sword in hand to force the votes of peaceful electors.

It is significant that the blame also falls on the curé's superiors, that is, on the church in general. Another petition from people at Sarriens to the prefect in 1833 drew 150 signatures, about one-quarter X's, on the subject of the curé's antigovernment stand. Such petitions were often formulated, or at least validated, by the mayor.[30]

In Y. Déret's study of a cantonal capial near Moulins he attributes the same kind of weight to the 1830 upheaval (whereas in Roger Thabault's Western commune the documents are silent on 1830). Here (Dompierre-sur-Bèsbres), there had been mayor-priest conflict in the early twenties, and then a lull. After 1830 a new mayor, a prominent land owner and somewhat anticlerical justice of the peace, assumed office. Right away he fought the clergy, vocalizing his antipathy especially for callow seminarians: "But once the seminaries vomited out a stream of young priests for us, then the population suffered for it, not only from their ridiculous fanaticism, but even more their excessive ambition. . . . My relations with the ecclesiastical class of the canton of Dompierre are very poor (*"de toute nullité"*). . . ." Anticlericalism continued apace when a new mayor took office, and the curé there also adapted gladly accepting the Republic in 1848.[31]

It is not worth enumerating all the times that priests ripped or snatched away tricolor flags after 1830, but incidents of this sort also intensified conflict. A good dossier on Breteuil (Oise) reveals this and other kinds of discord there. At that commune the *instituteur*, who was the priest's cantor, became an insurgent, demanding over his superior's wishes that the whole song commemorating victims of the Revolution be sung. When a curé ripped a flag at Tremblay (Ille-et-Vilaine) in 1831 the mayor and council threatened to resign if the prefect didn't act; and the priest was taken to court. That problem arose at nearby Plesder in the same year, at Saint Marc, and at many other places in the department. Generalizing on his district, the sub-prefect of Saint Malo in 1831 said that only five or six of some sixty priests were submissive to the new regime. The sub-prefect of Fougères noted of the curé mentioned above that what he said "was false like everything that priests say." This, of course was the conservative West, where Legitimism would long remain a potent force among priests and among some mayors, too.[32]

Electoral battles between mayor and priest were also numerous after 1830, though again we must confine ourselves to a purely qualitative reckoning. We can only emphasize the kinds of conflicts involved, and for that only a few examples will suffice. To chronicle each egg that was thrown, every kind of pressure used, would end up as *petite histoire*. In 1834 the mayor of Robion wrote the prefect of Vaucluse, reminding him that he had already twice resigned because of the unpunished conduct of the priest there. The letter is very bitter, averring that the priest is politically seditious, has refused to sing the *"Domine salvum"* for Louis Philippe, and has worked for another mayoral candidate in the coming elections. Moreover, the priest gives big lunches for groups of farmers and neglects religious duties like first communions. Adding to the change, the mayor says that the curé bowls almost every day and even on Sunday (before *and* after vespers), in front of numerous spectators. At these games he hears all sorts of curses and generally unedifying language. This, of course, was a serious charge, for no moral notable was supposed to become overly familiar with the flock. In this case the archbishop supported his curé, and we have no evidence that the prefect tried to have him ousted, nor do we know whether the mayor could incite popular opinion against him. In 1843 the mayor at Saint Méloir-des-Ondes (Ille-et-Vilaine) complained to the prefect that the priest fought his reelection and that of three municipal councillors there by overt and less overt pressure. In a village of the Limousin during the same year the priest accused the mayor of retaliating against his political opposition by beating drums with others on the square outside the church during mass. This was also a village of interminable quarrels between parish council and municipal council.[33] How much political influence did the priest *actually* wield? This requires further study, but at least in the West his influence remained strong until the advent of World War I. Lynn Case's generalization on the Second Empire — that to a peasant "the priest in prayer was natural, the priest in politics. . . ridiculous" — is unprovable. In direct and in many indirect ways the priests could have influence at election time.[34]

Especially was this so in times of flux. It has always fascinated me, for example, that 83 percent of adult males voted in the April elections for the assembly of 1848. Where is the lack of patriotism that Weber finds in that world? But the election, held on Easter Sunday, was popular in good measure because of local notables and their actions, not just because of patriotism. Priests read out recommended candidates from the pulpit and composed electoral bulletins for parishioners. Excercised by laws the Republic contemplated making or had made, especially in primary education, the priests set to work guaranteeing correct votes, mainly for moderate or Rightist candidates. And behind them lay the more powerful voices of the bishops, trying to coerce them into correct action through diocesan circulars, as archbishop Saliège would do at the time of Jewish persecutions in World War II. Wrote one curé of the Vosges in 1848: "Where is the parish priest who cannot dispose of ten to twenty votes? There are some who can get hundreds. . .I have just learned this instant that secret committees have been organized in the whole diocese by Mgr. [the bishop]. . . ." Mayors obviously worked as hard as priests in this election, directly responsible to their new prefects (*commissaires*) for political information and aid at the local level.[35]

Under the Second Empire the mayor's role as local manager of elections for the government would become even more pronounced. As Zeldin has pointed out, "Through the mayors of France the government could speak to every man in the country."[36] The mayor could use that portion of the government pork barrel at his disposal against priests. If a man wanted a road to his farm or a postman's job for a nephew (government jobs increased throughout the century), he had better be on the mayor's side. The mayor supervised voters, sometimes with schoolmaster or postman at his side, and removed posters inimical to his candidates. Now the Second Empire for its first ten years was quite conservative and clerical, but increasingly after 1860 mayors found opposition on both clerical Right and radical Left; and in the former group priests employed the pulpit, confessional, and personal visits to fight for Legitimist, ultra-Catholic candidates.[37]

The mayor's political role as state appointee was balanced against the curé's religious prestige. If priest had his cassock, mayor from the time of the July Monarchy had his tricolor sash as well as other emblems. He was thus an authority invested almost numinously with local importance, and it is perhaps time that we add to D. G. Charlton's fine notion of "secular religion" in the nineteenth century by speaking of "political religiosity", particularity when political power carried with it an ideological orientation opposed to established religion. In many villages of France in the nineteenth century there is an established religion; therefore, politics must always be to some degree religious. Only when this established religion loses its importance do philosophies like anticlericalism ultimately lose theirs as well; just as a counter-culture evaporates when the established culture itself is done with.[38]

In more Catholic regions, and even in those that weren't, we sometimes find a trend opposed to what has been indicated. Priests lost prestige, and were opposed by mayors precisely because they failed to satisfy the religious desires of inhabitants. They ran into trouble for opposing superstitions, for shortening masses, or simply for not paying enough attention to people. In the West, particularly, we find mayors in conflict with curés because the latter *don't* suffice. There are numerous mayoral letters, or petitions with signatures validated by mayors, demanding a new, more serious priest, or a new church branch (*succursale*) in some hamlet. One typical letter was written by "the mayor and inhabitants" of Messaie (Vienne) to the archbishop of Poitiers in 1847; the writing seems to be that of a teacher or other educated person. Here the mayor and his signatories stressed their "undying attachment to the Catholic, Roman and apostolic religion," the difficulty they had in reaching the present church in bad weather, and the insufficiency of its present priest. When the curé of Mortemart (Haute-Vienne) tried to install a new saint to replace the old one in church (1843), he was opposed both by the mayor and by many inhabitants. This led to distrubances that were investigated by the police. At a village of Oise, 1841, the mayor protested when a curé forbade the ringing of bells at twelve midnight on Resurrection day: this had been done "for centuries; since the world began. . . ."³⁹ For all of this, I cannot substantiate Corbin's view that priests themselves were significant agents of anticlericalism. Only a minority must have frustrated true religio-superstitious desires in this manner.

Probably just as many were agents of anticlericalism by the espousal of a *leftist* viewpoint, though again we are talking about only a small minority and one that was largest at the time of the revolution of 1848, and in the South. I have seen various reports on leftist curés in Vaucluse. At Cadènes in 1850 police reported on a priest who held that it was "always with reason that a people rose up to make revolutions when this same oppressed people endured the yoke of kings who were only tyrants." In the same year police reported on a curé at Villars who led a demonstration and waved a red scarf. And then there was Curé André, mentioned above for his problems at Vaucluse, who also fan afoul of the mayor of Lagnes in 1864, because he had purportedly drunk toasts—"I drink to the health of the Reds"—with some leftwingers opposed to the mayor.⁴⁰

Even in the South, however, the action generally went the other way. A long letter written by a mayor and assistant in 1848 at Bedoin speaks of the need (à la Robespierre) to "purify" the *patrie* and stem the "impure torrent of corruption." In fact the mayor wants to settle a score with the priest there who, he says, has been an instrument of religious and political division for ten years and has had the pretension of governing the commune, imposing himself by will or by force upon preceding mayors. The letter clearly shows how mayors used political changes to legitimize their animus toward a rival authority. In the same year curés were physically attacked by an irate population at villages like Mormoiron and Vauganis, and a placard had to be tacked up by government authorities: "The Prosecutor of the Republic invites all the inhabitants of Vauganis to respect the person of M. Curé. Any attack, any word. . .can bring prosecution against its author."⁴¹ If 1848 is seen by Agulhon as the culmination of a growing village awareness of the outside world, of concomitant anticlericalism and republicanism (in the Var), of *sociabilité*, what he does not sufficiently outline is the role of mayors, and to a far lesser extent, of dissident curés as orchestrators of such sentiments in the Midi.

We have seen that a few local studies allude to the mayor-priest conflict after 1830 as a factor in the development of anticlericalism. Do any continue to watch this development after the inception of the Second Empire? There are only a few. Roger Magraw, in a study of popular anticlericalism in Isère under the Second Empire, imputes to the mayor-curé conflict a large role in this ideological development. He traces conflicts at representative villages, and finds, as I have found elsewhere, that the strains between notables, exacerbated by the prefectoral-episcopal gulf, profoundly affected local populations. One such imbroglio at Corbas near Lyon attracted attention in national newspapers like *L'Univers*. Here the mayor, supported by a majority of the population, opposed the curé on matters like costly church repairs. There are petitions signed by *pères de familles*. The mayor writes a letter to the emperor himself, asking for support against a rambunctious curé and episcopal administration. The mayor says that no bishop will ever consider his priest wrong (often the case in my own researches). A court orders demolition of the curé's repairs, and he and some pious women barricade themselves in church; a crowd of villagers smash windows and knock off the roof of the church. The curé refuses to baptize children of the mayor's adherents. The bishop finally transfers his priest but punishes the commune by putting in no replacement until 1869; then he restores the old curé. The conflict continues into the seventies, making anyone with anticlerical inclinations more anticlerical than previously. Again, the analogy of a counterculture or generation gap comes to mind; excesses of the parents bring out excesses of the children, and vice versa. Indeed, the clergy, like parents, offered injunctions that inhabitants of Isère, like Marcilhacy's Orléanais, found stifling. All this bred anticlericalism, with the mayors as catalysts.[42]

In a less known local study on this theme, François Bellon studies two nearby villages of Provence and tries to understand why one evolved to a firm republican position by the early 1870s, then to a radical republican position, while the other village remained conservative. Bellon focuses on the mayor's attitude to the church in each village. In the more conservative village the mayor cooperated with the priest; in the other one they tangled over the keys to the church, private schools, and church processions. The problem is, of course, partly chicken–and–egg; but Bellon concludes that the attitudes of mayor to priest, and vice versa (priest toward mayor) were a major factor influencing the political orientation (and hence, religious orientation) of these villages. But Gérard Cholvy, on another department of the South, plays down the influence of local notables in the evolution toward republicanism and anticlericalism.[43]

Before the Third Republic one can legitimately underline this theme of mayor-curé conflict, for it has too often been neglected or underplayed as part of a seedtime of the new ideological garden flowering toward the end of the century. With the reestablishment of the Republic itself, the theme simply becomes conjoined with others, or subsumed within them. Mayoral anticlericalism is now less autonomous or individual; well supported by government superiors, by the press, and by laic *académies*, mayors will now turn the tide against priests even in areas only moderately anticlerical. As for the clergy, even those who have never been political now begin taking conservative, clerical, or antilaic political stances.

If, as Weber suggests, the countryside as a whole became increasingly more political after 1870 so did the country curés. The year 1876, the year before the sixteenth of May, was for many a dividing line in that regard. The Republic was about to be taken over by Republicans, and priests often went from Catholic to Clerical. To illustrate how some were affected, a peaceful *desservant* at a village of Saône-et-Loire was to be transferred to another because he had quarreled with the mayor over the hot elections of 1876. Before that, says the sub-prefect, he had been "very well esteemed in the commune of Champagnant, to which he seems very attached personally." A sudden passion for politics, in the period of the Republic's triumph, changed all that. In the same department another priest had been politically moderate until the advent of laicity in the 1870s. Suddenly he began organizing religious demonstrations, which the mayor banned, and began attacking the Republic in sermons. The "douleur" he felt over the advent of the Republic and which he expressed in his letters seems perfectly sincere.[44]

Mayors were now supported by the revolution in imagery that accompanied the installation of the Republic, and this meant driving out ecclesiastical imagery such as processions, which came to be banned in many places from around 1878. One formula used by republicans was that they meant to "prevent inconveniences that could result from the passage of processions in the streets." By the early 1900s, in radical departments like the Yonne and in most others, few church processions such as the Fête Dieu were still permitted. Republicans were using such stock phrases as: "Considering that processions can be a cause of disorder in the commune and give rise to demonstrations and regrettable conflicts. . ."[45] Hesitant mayors—for example, one who would not put busts of the Republic in a school after the Ferry laws—were now dismissed. A mayor who allowed his commune to be consecrated to the Sacred Heart was severely reprimanded by his prefect in 1901, the latter under pressure from Paris; better was one who threw crucifixes into the latrine. Republican newspapers hammered at both priests and overly neutral mayors, and priests who verbally stepped out of line were subject to prosecution. Even to criticize the government for not repairing their churches could lead to a fine or transfer. Obviously those mayors who actively disliked priests were now sure of the Republic's support in local battles that might have been drawn or lost thirty years earlier. At Mazerolles (Vienne) a priest had been using an old chapel as a place to burn candles and celebrate miracles. When it fell into ruin he had a new one built and was drawing the population to it, but the mayor informed the prefect, and against local wishes it was promptly closed.[46]

In the intellectual history of the period there were new trends. In some ways the church tried to match the republican side at its own game, not only by competition between Catholic and lay schools, but also with a rival conception of patriotism, which has not been well studied by historians. Catholic newspapers in the years leading up to World War I celebrated their patriotism by opposing it to the inferior variety offered by the laic side. This patriotism, to be sure, was tinged with xenophobia, and references to Jules Steeg, "son of a Prussian," or to untrustworthy Jews are not uncommon.[47] The themes of nationalism, renascent Catholicism, and antilaicism all came together splendidly in these newspaper articles, as in one from *Le Courrier de Vitré* (November 20, 1910):

We are building Catholic schools because we want to make our children good Frenchmen, the best of Frenchmen, by teaching them the glories of the Past, the past that is so great, so generous, the past of the Fatherland, while simultaneously giving them lessons of the most pure patriotism.

Cardinals like Couillé of Lyon spoke in similar terms, and curés petitioning for transfers also found it wise to stress their patriotism.[48]

There were other forms of competition. If the laic school used slides, athletics, sewing clubs to make itself attractive, so could the church. Peace must be made with modern technology; in 1898 the prefect of Mende authorized the bishop of Mende to illuminate the towers of the cathedral at night. Fireworks were used in abundance, and at the end of one illuminated, almost Robespierrian ceremony "the last piece will represent a colossal crowned virgin, framed by two palm trees ten metres high, surrounded by glory."[49] Forms of tutelage were still being fought over, especially in Catholic areas.

And those mayors who were outsiders, in mortal danger of being purged, joined forces completely with the church. The nobles were especially fervent, supporting Catholic schools and marching side by side with priests during the Separation.[50] On the other side I have said that mayors could now be more brazen, more forthright. Indeed, some may have grown more authoritarian than ever before, bringing their latent tendencies out into this new, approved cultural daylight. A priest in Gironde complained that the mayor repeatedly held up payment of his salary, despite warnings from the municipal council, and allegedly said "that unwilling to be the servant of anyone he refused [precise hours] at the town hall. . . ." Strikes by curés thus became more frequent. Mayors were not only recalcitrant about repairs, but sometimes furthered the delicious beginnings of blasphemy—a global emancipation in this period. The mayor of Montgauzy (Gironde) supervised a civil burial in 1908 which drew a large crowd, then he had a café owner read an impassioned speech exalting free thought. The curé, who was scandalized, was allowed to go on a short retaliatory strike by his vicar-general.[51] At a village of Oise in

1901, the mayor decided to ring church bells for the arrival of republican dignitaries, overriding the curé. They fought over the ropes, the priest threw them up high and out of reach, and the mayor, trying to undo them, slipped and injured his chest bone. Mayors arbitrarily dismissed grave diggers or bell ringers, and were usually supported by the prefecture. They brought locksmiths to get church bells rung at times congenial to them. And they could now clearly dominate the priest on the welfare bureaus; by the law of 1879 it was no longer automatic for a priest to be elected by the often hostile municipal council. Chiselling on church repairs or outright denials in such matters became commonplace, too.[52]

Laicity was one of the key corrosive new forces involved, but it is again not my intention to enlarge here on the school problem that impinged on almost every church–municipality division, if it didn't indeed create a good many in this period. Laicity demarcated Right from Left, and contributed to the priest's growing isolation and to the decline in his prestige. If the Ferry Laws were attacked in the West, they were mostly accepted elsewhere. Universal literacy was becoming seductive to farmers, who envisaged filial emancipation. Laicity, then, was a prime component of anticlericalism and of mayoral victories over the priest. Claude Mesliand's model study of Pertuis (Vaucluse) nicely reveals this link of laicity with growing anticlericalism at the village level. The building of a laic girls' school in 1870 (rather early), the substitution of Marianne's bust for Christ at the townhall in the same year, and the full laicization of public school personnel by 1879 are all seen by him as dsecisive events there. More and more the isolated curé fights a one-man battle against a rising tide. In 1882 the mayor there forbids him the practice of certain rituals, like the carrying of the viaticum to sick people, and the curé in retaliation calls the mayor a sellor of cod's tails and onion heads, a buffoon. Civil burials rise radically, and so do successes of the radical party, with a general falling off of religious fervor even among the supposedly fervent. The curé sees the secular school and its ideology as a prime instigator both of anticlericalism and of dechristianization in this area.[53]

And the school's representative of course was the *instituteur de la République*. So the curé might now have two notables to fight. Again, to restrict ourselves to Vaucluse alone, we see the new alliance in a case at Saignon, 1889, where the mayor, complaining to the prefect about the priest's propaganda against the Republic, makes this a political affront not only to himself but to the teacher as well. At Sunday mass the curé had purportedly passed out to children a drawing representing a child caught between two policemen, with the inscription on it "the height of laic instruction." At Entrechaux in 1893 the curé blames the Panama Scandal on the laic school. At Mirabeau in 1900 a priest fights republicans generally and laic school specifically, and is dismissed. Examples could be greatly multiplied. And the strategems that one finds curés using in the West as retaliation are used, if with less frequency, here. The mayors of Malaucène and La Motte d'Aigues report as early as 1880 on curés refusing absolution to children who go to the secular school. At Cairanne in 1898 the curé writes articles against the "Godless school", places private school children ahead of *laïques* at a funeral, and, despite the archbishop's support of him, is finally replaced, with both the prefect and a deputy using their weight in the decision. The curé of Méthamis has been politically fighting the mayor and trying to use refusal of baptism to citizens as a tool in the struggle (1889). The curé at Lagarde-Paréole has been refusing places to an *institutrice's* schoolchildren in church. Here the mayor, a reactionary, backs the "polite, prudent" curé.[54] But one can see how the school issue became an issue of polarization in Vaucluse, as well as one that hurt the authority of the curé in a losing battle with teachers, who were frequently at one with mayors, enhancing the latter's strength.

All was not decline. Curés in areas like the West stayed on more equal footing with mayors than in the Orléanais or Provence, or had the mayor's support. At the national level Sacré Coeur, the Assumptionists and *La Croix* demonstrated a certain religious fervor presaging the post-1900 Catholic revival among elites and literary people. In the period before the war there would be a generalized clerical rebound at the local level against laicity, culminating with the Battle of the [text] Books in 1909 and the great campaigns for the building of *écoles libres* at that time.[55] Sermons grew more, not less, activist, and in Catholic areas priests were still formers of opinion.

In areas like Brittany it was nothing less than the last of religious wars. What to us is anachronistic stupidity was to certain Frenchmen the deepest thing life had to offer. What you ultimately believed. Who, in a nutshell, you were. Mind counted for that much. Elections were not simply elections. School was School. In the countryside political life took its hue from the fading rays on the village church. It was still an era that needed badly to believe.

Priests, of course, had more time for fervor than the average peasant. And fervent they were encouraged to be—in sermons and especially in catechisms. As the Bishop of Arras put it in 1882, "the curé, the chaplain, the vicar of today is the missionary for a new Propagation of the Faith."[56] If they became too vocal at elections, too openly propagandistic, bishops looked the other way or provided an alibi. This was the case at Courcelles-les-Gisors (Oise) in 1892, where mayor accused curé of handing out or having other people hand out antigovernment literature, as well as antilaic school brochures to children, and of provoking abstentions (only 96 of 180 electors voting at the municipal elections). At another village of the department the *desservant* gave a mass blessing to those who voted correctly and prayed for the fall of a government that had banished God from the schools. Prefectoral forms assessing character of priests now found more and more political black marks to put down by their name. "Electoral catechisms" were passed out by priests here, and even more so in areas like Brittany.[57]

Breton conflicts alone could fill several books, and I will not use them to do so here. Under that sad winter rain, however, these senseless, interminable battles over crosses and catechisms and *instituteurs* and meat-eating seem to us a kind of paroxysm or apogee, a summing-up. Even here, moorings were being loosened. One typical republican protest of 1904 against a cross replacement ceremony (*réparation*) is described in terms so finally redolent of the times that the historian cannot improve on them; for this is "The old land of Arvor, for so long enslaved by the tyranny of the priest, for so long overwhelmed and even annihilated by the black terror. . . ." Who will be at the procession? Why, "poor nobles (*hobereaux*), pseudo-descendants of the Crusades . . . pompous vergers, shouting cantors, bards . . . fanatic priests." [58]

How did it all occur? To neatly suggest anticlericalism as a city religion, or a country phenomenon, or as an obvious outgrowth of material progress, or indeed as a product of hard-hitting mayors whittling the authoritative timber of curés will sound inadequate. One plainly sees how syncretistic any answer must be. But the struggle of mayor versus priest is *one* cause of anticlericalism that certainly deserves a greater place in French historiography.

CHAPTER FIVE

Mayors versus Priests: The Lid of Repression

We have seen mayors and priests at odds in political and religious matters. This chapter will deal with issues which had to do with *outlets* in rural France—drinking, sports, sexuality, and popular entertainment, among others. Here I try to outline some of the ways this "lid" of repression, or at the least, of definition was applied by priests and mayors in rural France; and how they frequently competed over the same issue. The term "lid," applied to the actions of notables vis-à-vis ordinary men, may of course be a harsh one; yet in consonance with my general ambivalence throughout, I do not see it here as a totally pejorative thing. Let us proceed to examine the phenomenon.

The priestly lid was an immemorial matter. Church injunctions against dancing and various kinds of sports date from the early Middle Ages, though how these were applied varied tremendously according to time and place. In the nineteenth century the lid was a symptom of the larger priestly pique about loss of status. If the Pope banned bullfighting, priests near Nîmes did not worry much about carrying out the bulls; real bulls were no great competitors.[1] But the priest did fear competitors like the cabaret or the dance floor: these made important inroads on the church as the center of social activities (what it was in the boyhood of Thomas Hardy as well). Fear, according to Professor Marcilhacy, was one of the overriding psychological factors in the makeup of many nineteenth century clerics. But the curé as killjoy has been admirably discussed by Weber, as well as touched upon in chapter two, and one hesitates to dilate on this here. *Was* the nineteenth-century priest stiffer than his predecessor of the eighteenth or seventeenth century? Particularly those young seminarians bred and sent out from around 1820? More research is needed to determine this, but I think we can tentatively answer yes, especially given nineteenth-century perceptions of what constituted authoritarianism. Professor Silver underlines this theme of competition when she discusses clerical antipathy to dancing halls and particularly to cafés and cabarets in nineteenth century Loir-et-Cher. "Drinking places," she says bluntly, "challenged the church's position as the center of social activities."[2]

So we may begin with drink as a dangerous amusement. It was not only the activity itself (given meager purses) but the atmosphere that gave rise to injunctions. Cabarets and *auberges* permitted indiscriminate, unstructured, and unsupervised, therefore potentially subversive talk: they were "the parliament of the people", in Balzac's phrase. At taverns one sang, one cursed, and one stayed up late. One met a cross section of people—travellers, "foreigners" (often not foreign by our standards), and members of itinerant entertaining trades—that invited surveillance, especially when revolution or protest seemed imminent. Richard Cobb cites singers, jugglers, magicians, alchemists, readers in cards, patent medicine vendors, "and other similar, noisy, and ridiculous people" who were watched carefully by civil authorities. We might also mention itinerant book peddlers, who bore conventional, or nonconventional, wisdoms from centers of diffusion.[3] Newspaper readers were also found here.

It is not too much to say that the rhythms of ordinary rural life, almost classical, were altered by the romantic aura and opportunities for self-expansion afforded by such places, where they existed. The cabaret was a bit o. city out in the countryside, permitting extranormal communication; and it was in such places, sometimes run by radical *aubergistes*, or others thought to have a high degree of anticlericalism in their blood, that one could hear what the archbishop of Bordeaux called "the most detestable doctrines that up till now [1868] hardly dared manifest themselves in our most perverted cities. . . ." (The archbishop was warning one of his curés to watch out for this contagion.) It was not only that Restif's peasant might become a little more citified right here, and that the café was competition; but more, that it might harbor the worst anticlericals and potential destroyers of the church itself. If the church could offer no alternative, especially to youth, it was in dire trouble. Thus another curé of Gironde in 1859 implored his superiors to obtain 500 francs for repair money, so that he might have a foyer where young people could meet on Sundays: there they would be able to preserve their innocence and virtue, he said. In 1862 we find this same priest offering a letter of resignation from sheer fatigue after various battles of this sort. (Today, in this seaside village of Lacanau, he would contend with hundreds of bare-breasted women each summer—unclad mothers knitting on the beach, teenage daughters assaulting the waves, as if this mode had simply existed since the dawn of mankind, Perhaps it has!) La congrégation des enfants de Marie was another vehicle for absorbing the potential sap of youthful disorders, though as noted one member in *Clochemerle* would ignore percepts and get herself pregnant. A curé of Gironde in 1864 stressed the importance of this society in keeping young people from carnivals and balls, enrolling thirty-two of them at his village. Carnival, to him, was synonymous with drunkeness. It meant nocturnal outings to a neighboring village "in order to pass the night, without the least surveillance, to a very late hour at night. Judge the morality of their amusements," continued the priest, "and the danger of goings and comings in darkness [au milieu des ténèbres] and vast solitude! This disorder dates from time immemorial. It will be difficult to destroy it." How much these last lines substantiate Alain Corbin, who in some cases sees the priests themselves as unwitting agents of modernity.[4]

Growth of facilities, along with the expansion of the internal wine trade and increasing democratization of consumption, made alcoholism more not less of a problem as the nineteenth century wore one. Priests were not wrong to focus upon it. But as Professor Patricia Prestwich has noted, it was not wine drinking that was associated with a habit in France but spirits or cider. This made the problem particularly acute in areas like Normandy or Brittany, where—roads or no roads—local populations had some access to debilitating liquors such as Calvados. Drinking, says Thabault for his village, was also a function of leisure. Restricted to feast days for most people everywhere before 1850, it increased as the standard of living rose in the countryside. At first, however, there was a brief lag in the augmentation of drinking outlets. Napoleon III, fearing revolutionary opposition, authorized his prefects just after the coup d' état to close any suspect cabaret, café, or bar in their departments. They also had the right to fine café owners or reject applications for new licenses. By 1855 the number of cabarets and inns had been cut from 350, 424 to 291, 144. But by the 1860s the law was hardly being invoked, and by 1869 there were almost 366,000 in existence. Then came another slight drop after 1870, followed by a steady increase through the Third Republic to 1914. At Mazières the number of inns tripled between 1850 and 1880, and all became filled most Sundays. Drunkenness increased, as well as Sunday fights across from church. Rare was the Monday, says Thabault, which artisans didn't spend at the inn (this closer to 1880, probably). Moreover, with increasing specialization and government supervision, liquor was better and easier to drink toward the end of the century than it had been earlier.[5]

When bishops strutted around to the villages and handed curés detailed questionnaires to fill out, they put in a section on alcoholism and café attendance, as well as others on dancing, church attendance, and church repair. These questionnaires provide us with good evidence on church ideals of social control, though their students, such as Launay[6] for Nantes, perhaps use them uncritically. After all, village priests wished always to show their efficacy and good record, and would therefore falsify on the Panglossian side. But still it is worthwile to look at one such questionnaire for 1899. (Toward the end of the century, by the way, questionnaires were filled out annually: I saw some for each year of the 1890s.) This one is for Ille-et-Vilaine, and here I assess the problem of cabarets, and only with respect to women, for questions were now so detailed as to distinguish between sexes. By 1899, it seems, inn frequentation was normal for men, still abnormal for women, especially in this traditional region.

In my sample of villages, I have distinguished four categories of answers given by priests: the first shows a real concern about women going to cabarets, that too many were doing so; the second, some concern, that "some" were doing so; the third, only a little concern, that a few were going to cabarets; and the fourth, no concern or problem at all. Table 3 shows the results on forty sample villages:

Table 3. Priestly Concern: Women Frequenting Cabarets

Category 1	Category 2	Category 3	Category 4
9	17	10	4

Source: A. D. Ille-et-Valaine: 2V5-2V11.[7]

Clearly, curés of the West *were* worried about the problem of female drinking or café attendance, also seen in their accompanying remarks: "despite our reiterated observations" or, "the women go too frequently to the cabaret despite our reprimands," etc. If an occasional comment notes drunkenness as a general plague of the area, there seems to be no moral ire directed here against *men* who frequented the cabaret. The main point again is the fear of slippage in church authority. I reemphasize the fact that priests did not want to give a poor account of their performance, and that problems in these villages were most probably understated in questionnaire answers. In category three, for example, I placed the commune of Campel, where the priest said "few" ladies went to the cabaret; but in a questionnaire only two years earlier (1897), the answer was: "far too many, including younger women." Other examples of this sort make our chart too low an index of the female rejection of clerical teaching in the West, but do show the significance still attached to competitive outlets.

For indeed, what the café or cabaret did, providing a person had the money to imbibe enough, was to give him the very courage to jibe at authority. One also had to have the suppressed inclination to do so, of course. The prim *instituteur* of Clochemerle used a drunken fit to sound off against the primary inspector and inspector of the *académie*: hats off before *me*, Tafardel, he yelled on a spree. In a village of Oise, 1869 we see a perfect example of the café as "counter-church" (*contre-église*). Here the priest complained to his bishop about a group of young men whose masquerade party ended at a cabaret, where one rose on a stool and parodied the priest's sermons, inserting a number of off-color lines. In an area of poaching, theft, generally bad morality, and one where ideas derived from 1848 held some importance, "it's enough to make one burst into tears," declared the distraught cleric. The mayor, supporting the youths in this case, called anyone who criticized them a hater of pleasure.[8]

It was not by any means that mayors encouraged absolute freedom, only that some found it wise to be more lenient than priests. Mayors, after all, took drinks themselves. Certain council meetings were held at the tavern, as they are in some rural areas today. Too, this was that great intermediary era between traditional religion and in many places a slippage — to what? To modern scepticism, or an outright kind of hedonism? In most cases not, but rather to some intermediate standard of morality. To show further this difference in "lids": in 1855 a mayor of Haute-Garonne used police and field guard to survey a carnival and instructed them to allow singing and enthusiasm short of outright salaciousness or a charivari. When the priest said he heard a dirty song and wanted the mayor to bring testimony against its singers, he wouldn't do it, accusing the priest in turn of sowing potential seeds of discord in the village. The curé then wrote an hysterical letter to the mayor, underlining eight lines of it and threatening to go to the prefect if the mayor would not preserve public morality. The threat does not seem to have been carried out.[9]

Silver says that the political hierarchy also feared cabarets, but she does not really tell us how much. It is doubtful that many mayors would manifest such an obsessive edge to their worries as did curés. After all, when gendarmes came to investigate incidents, they usually ended up at table with a *coup* or two themselves.[10] Silver does quote a *procureur général* of 1861, who saw cabarets as places where country youth grew "corrupt, dissipating the fruit of their work" and lazy and debauched. Still, a fear of alcoholism or even of shiftlessness is different than a fear of mortal sin or of loss in status. It is true that both the local notables desired public order (one priest congratulating himself "for having done his best to make the love of cabarets and *of trials* [procès] disappear")[11]; but we should certainly distinguish between kinds of lids applied, and how these were perceived.

The point is best made by moving to the realm of dancing: were not priests applying undue censure to an activity that was generally quite harmless? Here we can distinguish between mayoral (or civil) censure, relatively tolerant, and that of the church, which was stick-in-the-mud and apt to produce fire where there was only smoke. If mayors accepted the status quo with certain variations, many curés didn't. It was rare to find the sort of religious toleration manifested by one curé of Lunel, and early on (1807), who defended dancing on the grounds that the Biblical David had done it. Particularly in the gay outdoors culture of the South, curés who did not adopt such an attitude could easily be seen as repressive, especially as southern regions moved Left and anticlerical after 1830. Instead, the fear of dancing was for certain clerics a monomania. "The torment of curés," says Cholvy of dancing in the diocese of Montpellier.[12] In the diocese of Aix it was no wonder that according to a curé himself (circa 1870) "the priest is regarded as a stranger, an adversary; he is observed, thwarted, denounced." In that southern department, much earlier in the century, a desservant had forbidden a lady to be a godmother unless she took an oath to stop dancing. Several years later at a village in Vaucluse the priest tried to exclude young women from the Fête-Dieu ceremony because they too had been caught dancing; but the arbitrary move elicited a letter of complaint from mayor to prefect.[13] More than Northerners, gregarious Southerners must have resented such injunctions or intrusions. This may help explain why the area went over so fully and early on to anticlericalism. Marcilhacy also emphasizes this clerical traditionalism on dancing in her study of growing anticlericalism in the Orléanais under the Second Empire. And Michael Phayer, an expert on the subject, sees dancing as contributing to the explosion of mayor-curé conflicts after 1830 (substantiating my own chronology), noting that town councils often petitioned priests for more liberality on the issue; and, even more generally (I wish Phayer's provocative views could be substantiated) that 1830 "may be seen as an important juncture in changing social values." Dancing, he maintains, had been more tolerated by priests before that date and especially before 1820 or so, when missionaries began to preach all over the country, lambasting in particular the modern, expressive dances like the Viennese waltz, reserved mostly for the bourgeoisie, but just beginning to percolate downwards.[14]

What I want to emphasize, then, is precisely this clerical creation of fire from smoke. There is a delightful Yiddish phrase curés might have heeded: "don't worry yourself into a pregnancy." (It can be applied to males or females.) For if peasant dancing had often been a utilitarian aid to courtship or a part of festivals, it generally remained unerotic even in the later nineteenth century. City dances in some cases would bear that element, but not usually country ones. Parents were about, partners changed fast, and as Michael Marrus notes "no meddling *curés* were necessary to enforce the strictures against self-indulgence."[15] But enforce they did. Animals losing their status bleat louder than those whose place in, or above, the herd is assured. And it may be that curés became more assiduous repressers in areas where they were already losing their hold. In religious Brittany, pardons went hand in hand with widespread dancing, despite the half-hearted clerical attempts to stop it, and dancing retained a healthier association with communal tradition. Elsewhere, curés expended a lot of energy trying to oppose Sunday dancing, thereby provoking cross burnings and other youthful disorders in retaliation. Phayer gives several good examples.[16]

Now mayors, too, set teeth against the more modern, entwining dances, of the type Emma Bovary practiced so scandalously at the Count's ball. However, such dances were infrequently seen among peasants before 1870. During the Second Empire a rural mayor tacked up a law restricting the amount of dancers on a floor and forbidding (upper-class) waltzes and galops unless authorized in writing. Couples who did dance together must maintain "strict decorum," says Marrus.[17] And few mayors would delight in the parodying of betters that accompanied certain dances, especially if those betters included themselves. They certainly strove to limit excessive enthusiasm that might lead to disorder or violence. But their modes of opposition were more measured, hence more palatable than those of the clerical side, and were not numinously dispensed. (Numinous blackmail might be the appropriate term.) Where mayors gave fines or oral censures, priests often refused communion, including the all-important Easter confession, to girls who danced, while their bishops and archbishops sent out the equivalent of papal bulls against the *bals*.[18]

More centrally, mayors were often in opposition to priests as a reflection of the wider tussle over just who should control the rites and rhythms of village life. Whether a conflict over dancing was pretext or substantive issue was not always easy to determine. It was sometimes the mayor's passive acceptance of dancing that galled curés; he didn't even have to be for it. At a village in Brittany in 1847 the priest criticized the mayor for permitting young people to dance, and then told him his own wife would be damned for it. (Sometimes it was more expedient to work on the presumably religious woman.)[19] It was another mayor's fault when a *bal* was held at the house of his servant in 1868. This dance captured many youths and married persons, an *institutrice*, and the son of the *instituteur*, and this in a less clerical region. Passive acceptance? No, the priest there saw this as part of a bread-and-circuses policy. It reflected, he said, the "tendencies of the civil administration, which does everything to amuse the masses who will soon end up wanting other amusements." Another priest, more liberal, was queried about this situation in the region and replied that little could be done about it. Yet another curé near there agonized over the possibility of trading dancing for religion in an area of indifference. All his people wanted, said the curé, was "just a bit of sermon (*"un tout petit bout de sermon"*) to *prove* to them that dances and balls are honest and innocent pleasures. It's a shame, they say, that our curé does not see the matter as we do!"[20]

The foregoing shows that not all curés were obdurate souls, for some obviously allowed dances, especially the older, church–sanctioned festive types, to go on; others evolved with their century, and were not paranoid about competition. Mundane normality, however, usually escapes the researcher and may prove nothing anyway. But when populations, and particularly mayors, noted their esteem for a village priest we may take it at face value that here was one who was "normal" (by our standards). For example, the priest who exercised at André Nègre's village of the Aude, during the latter half of the nineteenth century, was a "professional" — a landowner who did not hesitate to get his hands dirty, an energetic, intelligent, erudite man not at all interested in the subject of dancing.[21] The researcher, needing to make *his* subject interesting, may easily overestimate these sources of "conflict," which is perhaps one of our own numinous words today. An excellent account of a Pyrenean village around 1900 mentions how the priest in sermons routinely "spoke violently to young ladies to whom he forbade balls, threatening them with Hell fire." That warning, like the one against reading the *Dépêche de Toulouse*, seems to have been little regarded (there were no readers of the *Dépêche* there anyway); and "his role performed," concludes our author, "he was the best of men — good, simple, ready to serve, devoted." There the church was still a fundamental part of village life in 1900, and its ceremonies ardently attended. And the village inn, "foyer rural de l'époque", where dirty cards slapped away all Sunday, coexisted quite peacefully with it.[22]

Moving from dancing to other amusements and repressions, we see both priests and mayors as "civilizers," the latter notable often doing his civilizing in conjunction with someone else, like the schoolmaster. Mayors, of course, would have been loathe to initiate certain restrictions, being villagers themselves, if they hadn't also been connected to the prefecture and the consequent electricity of the central political order. (I exclude that minority who were completely self–sufficient and/or opposed to regimes.) In civilizing campaigns, it was frequently urban pressure groups, the prefect, and especially from 1880, the *instituteur* who impelled mayors to act. The signs on public drunkenness were printed in the city, not in Clochemerle. Mayors were also pressured to abolish violent games associated with festivals or *bals*, including *tir à l'oie* (hanging a goose up by the neck and beating it with sticks) or setting fire to dogs and shooting at them. In the work of John Merriman, we saw how mayors had defended local woodsmen from big-city laws until forced to do otherwise; and in the matter of poaching, prohibitions were probably forced downward, too.[23] With priests, some of the to-do about dancing was also a product of bishops' directives and their general policies.

We can see other sorts of percolations downward that reinforced repressions. Local elites firmed their ideas of stewardship in meetings of the little societies, exceedingly moralistic, that used to dot the provincial towns. They wrote essays on temperance, heard elevating discourses from Freemasons, disserted on catechisms. Their minutes and writings make touching reading today.

Then there was the repression of religious heterodoxy, specifically of Protestant sects, which was generally a problem in towns, but which set the tone of religious policy in villages too. To simplify rather brutally, Protestantism could not get a firm hold in France because local authorities saw it as a rival set of doctrines; and the evangelical societies promised just the sort of physical emancipation that entertainments like waltzes did.[24] Protestant evangelists, indeed, were travelling men, of the same suspect class as minstrels or itinerant organ-grinders, or even seasonal artisans. In departments like Yonne Protestantism was a patent stimulus to militant anticlericalism, and may have joined up with earlier subterranean forces like Jansenism to push that department toward socialism, as general secularism also spread. Songs in advanced areas of that sort, stimulated by religious bubbling, might be overtly political. A copy of one found on the road to Vermonton in 1854 went:

> . . .hunger arrives from the village, into the town, through the suburbs; Go therefore to bar its passage with the noise of your drums.

It continues as a perfect example of Weber's thesis on local politics:

> What do the ruined quarrels of cabinets matter to us? Is it still necessary because of these hates to arm our gigantic arms?[25]

The connection of Protestantism and its repression to our topic will be apparent when we descend to the village level and note its bases of support in a department like Yonne. In one report of 1846 on the subject, the mayor of Appoigny first mentions his tenure of sixteen years and what a hardworking, devoted magistrate he has been. Then he notes that those for the priest and against Protestantism are "well-married" couples, young ladies, and old women; whereas those for Protestantism make up a group that is active, troublesome, avid for the new: artisans, shopkeepers, inn-keepers, small bar-owners (*limonadiers*). In the middle is a noncommittal majority — "industrious and steady," mainly farmers. The mayor promises to keep a strict watch on Protestant preaching there. At another village of Yonne a petition of fifty-three names called for the right to hear Protes-tant preachers, and the justice of the peace distinguished two major cate-gories among the signatories: (1) "men of disorder" i.e., drunks, reds, bank-rupts, councillors from 1848; and (2) those who want to avoid paying for Catholic schooling in order to waste their money at places like the cabaret.[26] Protestantism was also a cover for fanatics (*exaltés*), said a sub-prefect, about another set of petitions. These were people who loved to create and read about scandal, and who wanted schools for two sexes.[27] If such Protes-tant longings did not constitute a general religious crisis after 1848, as one historian claims, they did have significance. Elsewhere I have called Pro-testantism one of the "dirty little secrets" of French history — the longing for a religious release from orthodoxy. Before the Third Republic, and especially in rural areas, Protestantism was perceived as another of those breaches against "public tranquillity," or even "food for anarchist hopes," as one Minister of the Interior put it in 1835.[28]

The repression of prostitution, more laudible, given the possibility of venereal disease, was another town issue, couched in similar terms and which may have influenced village notables' perceptions of sexual de-viance. A mayor who closed a house of prostitution at Joigny (Yonne) in 1858 significantly did so in the name of "honest" *pères de famille* and "public morality." Prefects left these delicate tasks to the judgment and discretion of local authorities, though prostitution seems to have been a significant problem only in larger towns and military garrisons. Period-ically the Minister of the Interior circulated questionnaires on prostitution, as on Protestantism or Judaism, to be filled out by mayors, for example in Yonne, 1869. We learn that in Auxerre there were twenty-five ladies registered, that roughly one-seventh were "sick," and that the probable number of unregistered women was closer to fifty. In the major five towns of the department we have fifty-four registered and about double estimated unregistered.[29]

Certain villages of other departments seem to have had problems in this area. I have, for example, checked files for Haute-Vienne. In Magnac-Laval of that department (1880) the mayor asked the prefecture for advice on how to deal with a woman he wanted banned, and again the prefect said it was his problem entirely. This prostitute had syphillis and spread it around, as had her latest lover and his motley predecessors. The mayor wanted to make an example for other prostitutes of the region, he said. At the large village of Condat the mayor also complained to the prefecture about working girls prostituting for soldiers there.[30] So some smaller places, usually related to industry or the military, seem to have been affected. It is well to remember that prostitutes, often on the run, were associated with vagrants and itinerants, a larger class of people feared by local authorities. Occasionally, a petition from the town indicated a certain groundswell of support for legalized prostitution, such as at Saint Junien in 1889, where about eighty people signed one, noting that over 1,000 men between twenty and thirty languished there and that a house of prostitution (*maison de tolérance*) was indispensable. The mayor validated the petition, but the sub-prefect rejected it, noting that the house, formerly open, had been rife with syphillis. (By 1900 it was estimated that as many as 100,000 people in France were infected, so the sub-prefect had grounds for his fears.)[31]

My main point is not to stress either Protestantism or prostitution here—neither were important in most French villages—only that their repression helped solidify the more general lid of repression used by local notables on all popular outlets and amusements.

Paradoxically, mayors and priests both derived notability from being custodians of entertainment themselves—curés in processions, until the Third Republic banned them; mayors at the *Fêtes patronales*. It was also ironic that these human embodiments of public order should stir up disorders by their own limitations, or by intrafrontal disagreements. Their quarrels could unravel the very social order they sought to uphold, for villagers (particularly before 1850) identified strongly with one village notable or another. A flurry of petitions often accompanied or were provoked as a by-product of such rifts. In 1836 the dismissal of the curé of La Bastide de Jourdans (Vaucluse), largely the mayor's doing, touched off a local civil war, with propriest forces ranged against promayor supporters. Troops had to be called in to quell disturbances. There was a similar popular uprising at Camaret in the same year when a priest was transferred out of the village.[32]

To further illustrate how notables themselves caused disturbances, we have two incidents in the Vendée of 1840 where a superstitious mayor complained that the priest was distrubing tranquillity by his dire predictions about the future. This is again the kind of paradoxical detail Corbin uses to prove the clerical background to the coming of modernity in Limousin. The mayor of the first village reported on the priest's New Year's speech of 1840, which said that violent changes would occur in France and which threw the inhabitants into a panic. In retaliation the priest wrote a long, disorganized letter profusely justifying himself, but police were sent to investigate and found inhabitants running around in fear of war. At nearby L'Aiguillon the mayor reported on a priest who spread the idea that revolution would come to France. People feared that the priest was blaspheming God and that the new harvest would consequently fail, and the mayor said he strove to reassure them. There the priest was sentenced to fifteen days in prison. At Louvigné in Brittany during the 1820s a mayor threatened resignation because the priest wanted to change the date of the local fair, and at Plélan the two notables quarrelled disastrously over the hour of a certain ceremony.[33]

Violence against priests is too well-known a theme to claim undue attention here, but should again be accented as the obverse side, the backfiring of a "lid policy." It was also a component in the development of anticlericalism and in growing consciousness of individual rights. A good example related to repression of amusement: at Saint Eulalie, about the mid-century, the curé found a father and some children playing marbles before mass and decided to confiscate them. The father then refused to pour wine at Mass, arguing back and forth with the priest on the altar steps (in *oc* dialect). Finally the priest slipped the marbles back into the man's pocket and made his peace with "fun." Weber has an example of youths throwing snowballs at a priest in Ardèche. The same thing occurred at a marriage procession in Caumont (Vaucluse) of 1855, where there was a general brawl before the café that night.[34]

Pent-up resentments were probably strongest in youth, who often had silent, uncommunicative families — a home lid — with which to contend as well. Composure was the ideal in many traditional homes. Moreover, offspring were economic tools, and not, as they would become among the middle-class, emotional ones. They were not well-schooled in enjoyment. George Bernard Shaw might later warn against mothers "exciting precocious sentimentality" in children, but the warning made sense only for the comparatively leisured. Of course children at least had nature games or grandmother's fairytales; whereas teenagers, already burdened by work, and by rudimentary knowledge, had no such imaginative outlets. But Jules Michelet exaggerates when he says there were no feasts in his younger period.[35] Of course there were; and this was the time to rag the curé, and have a little fun The curé of Saint Saturnin (Vaucluse) in 1838 complained to the archbishop that some youths had been leaping a wall to ring the cathedral bells and had been shouting at him. Twenty years later at the same place, a group of young women shoved and hooted at the curé and were then joined by a menacing crowd of both sexes, as he tried to push the girls to the back of the procession. (The mayor's assistant quietly watched and did nothing.) Processions of this sort could cause trouble because curés tried to establish an order contrary to what certain people desired. Again, this is the Corbin thesis amply on display. At Gadagne in 1849 people wished to return to an indiscriminate order for the procession of Filles de la Congrégation de la Sainte Vierge; whereas the curé, supported by the archbishop, wanted to give special honors (like carrying the Virgin's statue) to the most pious girls of the group. As evidence of a groundswell of opinion against the priest, we have a petition of at least 125 inhabitants of Gadagne asking for a return to impartiality.[36] Drunks often harassed priests as well, for instance at Bédarrides in 1851, where the police came to report on such a case. Violence against curés perhaps grew worse with the arrival of the Republic. A *desservant* of Puy-de-Dôme was assaulted in 1900 by stones and wounded in the head, sending him to hospital; but the authors of the incident were not located, perhaps because the Republic or local authorities had lost their investigative zeal.[37]

Carnival time was a natural for such violence. It was a period of relaxation and heightened liberty of language and action, a brief rupture of the social order, mirrored not only by the indiscriminacy of social intercourse between age groups, but also by role reversals, in which people acted like their superiors or inferiors. They were well made-up, of course, and they also donned masks. It was perhaps the same impulse that would be routinized in Proustian salons, where fin-de-siècle nobility slummed with Jews and homosexuals. But in folklore, there are quite a few tales on cheating or outwitting authority, or playing pranks on it.[38] Carnival briefly allowed one to do this. Moderate satire permitted people to blow off the steam of envy and channel it into humor. At the same time Carnival was one more of those seasonal, rhythmic festivals, like harvest rites or *fête patronale*, that was conservative in nature. It is only fair to note this ambivalence (ambivalence I myself saw at a pardon-cum-drunk in Brittany in 1970); and also, the magical utilitarian aspects of such festivals, in which one danced to have hemp or to make chickens lay eggs better. The main point is the speciality of festivals, including special foods, with local names, special songs, special dances. We could say that here was at once a controlled spontaneity within a controlled seasonal rhythm. For Jacques Humbert's Embrunais, an annual climb of Mont-Guillaume was a similar kind of seasonal release.[39]

Charivaris, which were mainly demonstrations during Carnival against social outcasts like adulterers or remarriers, also erupted against priests. Weber briefly discusses this, noting especially a revival of anticlerical charivaris against priests in the Allier during the 1870s; and I would speculate that areas more prone to anticlericalsim, like the post-1840 South, would find priests a more normal target than the traditional regions. For Vaucluse, however, I find only a few examples at the mid-century involving priests, such as thirty people at Lauris who made the priest the butt of their charivari (1852) and attacked him. There the police were called in to stop proceedings. We have reports of arrests after a charivari at Bordes (Yonne), 1853, directed against a priest leaving the commune. Its ringleaders were an ex*instituteur*, two municipal councillors and an innkeeper, probably radical. So there could be overt political overtones to the Carnival spirit; but along with Weber I doubt that this was usual.[40]

Both mayors and priests strove hard to prevent such occurrences, even though they afforded a nice opportunity to show disciplinary acumen. It is undeniable that certain charivaris were mentally and physically brutal. Mayors began to ban them from early in the century in different regions; what they were also banning was the culture of the Carnival—the various kinds of music and dances that accompanied these charivaris. Baby, in other words, was floating out with bath water. Local Basque poets, says Weber, had improvised charivari serenades. In many places there were local plays or farces performed during proceedings. Notables, and especially the civil administration, supported by schoolteachers, took the lead in repressing what a mayor had called in 1821 "disorders worthy of times of ignorance and barbarism." And mayors had to act according to directives *they* had from superiors. A file on revocations for Haute-Garonne shows one dismissed for failing to halt youthful disorders at church during a festival in 1854; another two years earlier was chopped both for drinking at the cemetery and for failing to repress a charivari that took place in front of the curé's residence at 1:00 A.M.[41]

Before 1870, mayor and priest were often together when it came to such disorders. Repression of unruly youth could be a common basis of agreement where few others existed. We know that mayors punished young people for outrages to "pères de famille" (a sacred category), that they sometimes reproached youths for speaking patois, and even (so we learn from a case of 1823) came down on them for speaking too loudly! (In the business of eradicating patois, we should add, mayors were perhaps no more or less zealous than priests: some clerics protected local tongues through catechism.)[42] But there were other forms of accord. For instance, Frédéric Mistral's mother had always wanted, she said, the name Nostradamus for her son, "first to thank the Mother of God, then in memory of the author of *Centuries*, the famous astrologer from Saint-Rémy." But both *mairie* and *presbytère* vetoed her choice.[43] Mayor and priest together quelled youthful battles between rival schools and villages in Gironde, 1834. The mayor (and the majority of inhabitants) at a village of Oise in the 1840s supported a priest who had been in the middle of a scuffle initiated by two women.[44] And if priests drew ire for changing ceremonies or acting arbitrarily, so did mayors. At a village of Cher in 1862 the whole municipal council protested against an "omnipotent" mayor, who had taken for his own profit the plot of fairground used immemorially for Saint Jean Day festivities.[45]

But it is certain common fears that I should like to underline here, taking care to reemphasize the difference in degree and in motivation. In certain areas the alliance might be cemented around that fear of Protestantism mentioned; this was the case for instance, at Rauzan (Gironde) as late as 1903. Both notables also feared parody or nose-thumbing behavior of any kind. Both watched for eruptions at cafés, though with different views of public order in mind. The needs of religion versus civil order might be summarized as follows: "don't go to café at *all*"; versus, "go only till ten and do not be unruly". In another village of Gironde, 1862, curé and conservative mayor together forbade the opening of a café-billiards spot, for the owners favored lay instruction and other "advanced" ideas.[46]

In addition, authorities had to prevent unauthorized card games, billiards, lotteries, and varied forms of gambling from taking place in villages. Sometimes these constituted urban infections passing into the countryside. At Ille-sur-Sorgue (Vaucluse) there was a floating game put on Sundays by big-city men from Avignon, upon which the mayor reported to the prefect in 1849. Two decades earlier at the same place a petition was sent to the prefect about such games, showing the strength of popular morality arrayed, sometimes in concert with authorities, against forces of immorality. (Earlier in the century this must have been stronger than later.) The petition ran as follows:

> As *peres de famille* having children susceptible of ruining Me, that's why I'm permitting myself, M. prefect, to write you a few words in order to teach you about the Conduct of the Cafes of Isle [sur Sorgue], without doubt M. Prefect does not know the manner in which it's played, well Sir. I dare to permit myself to tell you that in the Cafe . . . day and night they are playing games that have been prohibited for fifty years.[47]

The mayor of Mondragon complained in 1854 to higher authorities about young men squandering money on billiards, and wondered whether such immoral games could not be banned. In the same year the sub-prefect of Apt moved against a popular game called "La Bourre et la Bouline," a form of billiards allegedly ruining farmers in the area. Two years later there was a crackdown on a lottery for pieces of game (*gibier*) run at Camaret. (We will find crackdowns on lotteries in Yonne of the 1890s — for example, La Loterie des Enfants tuberculeux.) And at Lacoste, a village still tainted in its own eyes by the residence of the Marquis de Sade there, a medium made money in the 1860s by predicting people's life spans and talking to the dead. The man also preached polygamy and the abolition of marriage. Police feared the movement was gaining adherents in other villages and believed the man was ultimately trying to become mayor of Lacoste.[48] The most spectabular of all such "cons" in the region was a religious miracle at Saint-Saturnin-les-Apts in 1850. At a certain hour each day a girl named Rose Tamisier predicted that a picutre of Christ in the church would bleed. A few drops appeared and were convincing, until the hoax was uncovered. Many people were taken in overnight, including the mayor and sub-prefect, although the curé prudently reserved judgment. Such an affair was the sort of disturbance, the very kind of eruption of superstitious enthusiasm that both mayors and clergy saw as a threat to their tutelage and to the tranquillity of village life.[49]

If mayor and curé jockeyed for surveillance of moral behavior, rather like Homais and priest over the dying Hippolyte, some villagers for their part did not mind catching *their* putative superiors—curé and later, teacher—in moral disarray. I have dilated on this in Chapter II. Suffice it to say that neither priest nor Third Republic teacher should lose his decorum, such as happened in Bollène (Vaucluse), when a priest retaliated against six girls who were cursing him by slapping one, bringing a crowd to the scene. Neither notable should have a drink with the boys, much less get drunk; picture the scandal in 1897 when the inebriated curé of Saint Paul repeatedly fell on his face at the Apt train station, followed by some 200 jeering onlookers.[50] And the ultimate taboo for both curé and Third Republic *instituteur* was of course a sexual escapade.

For priests, a kind of vicarious substitute was the confessional; but it is not unfair to say the same of those on the other side of the barrier. For certain women, confession may have been a racy sort of rural amusement. Balzac has noted that the provinces in general frowned upon consummated love affairs; so again, confessional might be used to make vicarious fire from pale smoke. Also, as one nineteenth century writer declared, "Many women, and most girls are in love with their confessors." He was probably exaggerating from random evidence; but it is not impossible that the same sort of attachment arose in some cases as the one that exists between patients and psychiatrists today. Here was a case where the represser, the absorber, was also the amuser. But many curés used confessional as plain snooping, and were sometimes narrow-minded about sex even within marriage.[51]

A more common outlet for all sexes was village gossip—what Balzac calls in his irrepressible way "the small talk in which imbeciles take refuge." [52] No kind of document got me more into village France when I first set foot in archives than the many anonymous letters written or signed by ordinary men. I first saw how these plagued the *instituteur* of the Third Republic, especially the newly arrived; but all the village notables were prey to slanders, justified and not. At one village, in Gironde, 1871, all three—mayor, priest, and teacher—as well as the members of the parish council received them, or were denounced to higher authorities.[53] Priests and teachers were good targets precisely because they were in many cases "foreign"—coming from a different part of the department or region. And mayors often validated these letters, or gathered the simple crosses that indicated signatures, real or phony.

The point about priests, mayors, and schoolmasters was that they could never fully participate in village functions, although the mayor came closest to being one of the boys. What Van Gennep calls "secondary phenomena"—prefects or intendants, authority figures imposed from above—applies in part to village notables, but only in part.[54] As stressed in Chapter One these were in-betweeners, between what sociologists call the primary associations of family, neighborhood, local community and the less archaic, secondary associations associated with political and moral trusteeship. Before 1880, they read out the newspapers to people and connected them to the outer sphere. As far as games went, they would lose authority by giving themselves too fully to them. Also, they had begun cutting themselves off from the true reality and concreteness that used to keep popular symbolism alive. All popular games and rituals were connected to the earth or to real conditions. Notables were too stilted to let go; polymorphous perversity, in the catchphrase of Norman O. Brown, was not for them.

But my intention here—I said it in Chapter One—is not simply to lambast elites. As we know, none of the great ages of man have been eliteless. If notables provided a lid, they also provided the limits that gave coherence to rural life. Limits can be pleasant; so can a sense of hierarchy. Processions or festivals like *comices agricoles* looked silly to Flaubert, who neurotically contemplated the boring, booster speeches of nineteenth century Babbitts and chiselled out their dramatic pith in a memorable way. But Flaubert was far from the average rural person. We mustn't be so sophisticated as to bypass sensations of childish delight. The same goes for the medals or bits of ribbon awarded to faithful old sows. Catherine in *Mme Bovary* does not smile, but this does not mean her heart is dead, too. Flaubert simply could not penetrate that far. Cynicism is middle-class; you need leisure to be a cynic. We see such a gulf when even a wealthy cantonal mayor, finding himself in the company of prefect, bishop and *grands notables* at a Balzacian *soirée*, feels terribly out of place, cannot keep up with the nifty witticisms purveyed. He is still part peasant.[55]

Perhaps the traditional concepts of life and amusement can never be adequately understood by middle-class interpreters (which of course any interpreter is). I remember my grandmother, who was still in some ways a peasant, dancing at a wedding, dancing as unself-consciously as Brueghel's subjects probably did in their better years; whereas the middle-class people around her checked their steps, their clothes, who was there, what they should say, what image among several they should present.

One gulf is connected to the fear of boredom or death, which is essentially middle-class; peasant resignation precluded it. It is partly the fear of death that forces one to live self-consciously. It is also the absence of imposed rhythms. Peasants were not self-conscious. Their amusements were generally collective, not individual. They were not ravaged by the need to improve diversions. Pascal's theory of boredom was made for kings or aristocrats, not for people who rose at 5:00 A.M. Contemplating one's toe in a lonely room was Hell for Pascal, ludicrous hearsay to the man of the fields. For Sartre, Hell was mirrorless, but as Weber shows, few peasants possessed mirrors before 1880 anyway. They hadn't been educated to know that sort of Hell.

Of course they did have their fears — of nature, spirits, syphillis, war, taxes, and intrusions of all sorts. One would romanticize to say not. But they had no *concepts* of amusement as remedy or hygiene; perhaps it *was* that for them, but they needed no such perceptions.

In some remarkable pages Theodore Zeldin shows how difficult it was for middle-class men of sensitivity and refinement to enjoy themselves in the nineteenth century.[56] This leads me to reflect on the *mal du siècle* as a middle-class luxury, making literary capital out of pain, as Proust would also do. Masochism is middle-class. T. E. Lawrence gets himself beaten for a kick, and Woody Allen derives humor from self-abasement. If one couldn't get high on real fun, one could make fun out of suffering.

Nouveaumania is another besetting leisure tendency (and increasingly universal, as all in the West almost Lamarckianly acquire middle-class characteristics). For peasants, repetition was enough; the reassuring was O.K. It was a question simply of doing it once more with feeling. Here, then, is where the authorities applied the lid; not to new amusements, but to a rowdier interpretation of the *déjà vu*.

Rural notables were parent-figures, doing what parents have *always* felt compelled to do: tamping down with a flurry of adages and conventional wisdoms the springtime freshness each of us must originally feel inside. For popular amusements were a return to something primitive, original, spontaneous. They were a break from customary fetters, a rupture. Pulling rank was a delicious outlet of a different kind for notables. It was the power of returning things to dead center. Even today we all know which side of the desk we prefer to be on.

The difference today is that spectators and players, umpires and batters now melt together. Today we *all* wish badly, almost frantically to show someone, probably our parents, that we *are* diverting ourselves, and that life *is* bearable despite the amusements (pace Palmerston). We are now in fact an amusement culture; the lid has come off in spades. But there is also here what could not have been in a purely rural society: an element of vicariousness. Goethe said that too many immature minds make mature judgments. He might well have referred to historians like myself. But he might also point at the sheer saturation by which we now know many modes of fun *indirectly*. Amusements, to repeat, have made us old. In the nineteenth century the problem was not to choose between options, but simply to run the one play you had. To sing *your* songs, speak *your* patois, run *your* Saint Jean's bonfire, not those of the media.

To conclude less extravagantly, the lid applied by notables not only helped dictate what rural life was like, but also said something important about themselves and their relationships with each other. On the negative side, lidding meant much ado about little matters, inordinate repressions; on the positive, a sense of hierarchy and limits and of local bounds.

CHAPTER SIX

Classic In–Betweener:
The Village Schoolmaster
of The Third Republic, 1880–1914

In Chapter 4 I devoted space to the pre-Jules Ferry schoolmaster, portraying him (and her) in the main as "subnotable" — a tool of either mayor or priest. Doubtless, this grossly oversimplifies matters; the teachers did *not* simply take off in 1880 from out of nowhere. Some sources of their notability already existed in certain areas before that date.

Nonetheless, the Jules Ferry laws of the early 1880s brought them to the center, made them glamorous; and they now became the most perfect example we have of that ambivalence of station I note for all the village notables here. Their story conveniently closes ours.

"Black-hussars" of the Republic," in Charles Péguy's often cited words, the teachers figure prominently in most accounts treating the Third Republic. But what launched them to prominence? Historians usually emphasize the German schoolmaster's victory at Sedan in 1870, then the protracted struggle for the Republic that decade, as the motivating factors for Ferry's creation of a compulsory state school system in the 1880s. To give the shaky Republic a solid foundation, to develop loyalty to it in the thousands of communes of France, republicans turned to primary education as the best means of propaganda at hand. The profound educational transformation that ensued — making elementary school free, secular, and compulsory — made the village schoolmasters those who would henceforth make the republican system work.[1] In one fell swoop the teacher, representing his government, became "the great influence in the village," as Jacques Chastenet puts it.[2] This is standard fare on the subject, and quite innocuous so far as it goes.

What one needs to know, of course, is just *how* teachers established this putative influence in French villages. By what means could they attain notability? As notables what could they offer to the ordinary peasant of the Third Republic? Though we have excellent works on the *instituteurs*,[3] no one has yet given satisfactory answers to these questions, which seem so central to our comprehension of French rural life in its last period of vitality.

When I first worked on this problem, I restricted myself to a deep probe of five departments comprising the province of Brittany, anything but representative. But what I postulated was that if teachers could become notables even in this conservative-clerical area (and despite difficulties, they often did), then the process must have been similar throughout France.

My first point: in most country areas of France, *instituteurs* could be anything but the proverbial black hussars of Péguy. Their position in village life, as I detail it in the latter part of the chapter, was akin to that of a foreigner passing through a traditional milieu; teachers had to be ultradiscreet in private life, eschewing harsh verbal exchanges, drinks at the local café, compromising personal contacts, or romantic entanglements (which then included a misplaced glance!)—even unexpected attire.[4] The teacher as paragon of virtue and moderation—not only in the West was this the golden desideratum, but all over France as well. The difference between provinces was only a difference of degree. Politically, too, the *instituteurs* were not the fanatical propagators of Opportunism or Radicalism we hear about, but contented themselves, in the main, with quietly grouping republican enclaves where possible or with steering voters toward acceptance of a suitable ticket or man.[5] The West, of course, was still divided on the old lines of White and Blue. Where other political strains and more fundamental sympathy for the Republic existed, especially after 1900, teachers could be less cautious. But there were always constraints, for inspectors of the academy everywhere tried to keep teachers away from "the passions of party conflicts and petty divisions;" and teachers themselves valued their independence.[6] The point is that the teachers did not just descend from the train, wave the Republic's banner, and spread its gospel far and wide. They were far less explicit proselytizers than we usually suppose.

In fact, teachers gained most of their notability by means other than political, and then *ex post facto*, helped impose a comity where government was concerned—that is, that the Republic should exist. Building a reputation was often an arduous process, but teachers had several sources of prestige—the major ones being their literacy, their savoir-faire, their ability to render concrete services to villagers in diverse areas, and their accomplishments at school. The times were propitious for such a notability.

Before the advent of radio and television the teacher was, when accepted, a one-man diffuser of information and of culture in the countryside — "the universal secretary, the disinterested arbiter, the economic expert, the 'obligatory, laic and free' counsellor . . . the walking repertory of all human knowledge," as one commentator noted in 1913.[7] The schoolhouse at the center of the village now began to challenge the church as the place to which peasants came with problems. If, moreover, the teacher occupied the contiguous *mairie* as secretary to the mayor, which was so often the case, then his importance was even greater. At the *mairie* the teacher performed the function of legal advisor, where *notaires* or lawyers did not exist, and had to unravel complicated mortgages and wills. He wrote letters for illiterate peasants, duplicating the public scribe's work in larger agglomerations. (Needless to say, compulsory education would make that occupation an anachronism within several decades.) He gave needed advice on taxes. He might be called upon to resolve disputes. He was at everyone's disposition, a rural ombudsman, and mayors grew to be dependent on his skills, even in Brittany, where reactionary mayors often ruled the roost. When a teacher-secretary in Le Tour du Parc (Morbihan) was chastised for leaving his class to an immature monitor, the mayor there rose to the teacher's defense, going so far as to write the prefect of the Morbihan. In his letter he related to the prefect how he had asked the teacher to step outside that day to sign a paper. The letter testified to his boundless confidence in the *instituteur* as follows: "It would be very unfortunate if you penalized this teacher for such a little thing. We have never had such a good one since I have known this commune. He is very devoted to his class, to his work at the *mairie*, and performs services for all the inhabitants. As I am the cause of M. B.'s exit that day, if he receives a punishment or a transfer, I resign." [8] The teacher continued in his post.

By the eve of the war, most male teachers (some 32,000) were secretaries, and moreover there was now a Fédération des Secrétaires aux maires, instituteurs (S. M. I.) with about 30,000 adherents. As André Balz noted smugly: "Decidedly the times are rough for the little tyrants of the village. Formerly, [the mayors] did not hesitate to brutally dismiss from the town hall teachers who had ceased to please them."[9]

Not every teacher, of course, was town clerk, but there were many other services to be furnished outside the *mairie*. One was land surveying (*arpentage*), which teachers engaged in when no land measurers could be found. Even when a licensed land surveyor was available, the mayor might still have recourse to the teacher, who saved the commune money by doing the work free of charge. This occurred at Lohéac (Ille-et-Vilaine) in 1913, but there the teacher's primary inspector subsequently intervened, forbidding the teacher to survey again if that meant unemployment for a bona fide measurer. Many teachers must have been surveyors, though we have no figures on their precise incidence. The Duke of Rohan thought to devote a great portion of the Morbihan's conseil général meeting in 1903 to "Instituteurs géomètres." He maintained that so many teachers were surveying in that department that licensed measurers could not compete, and here he blamed the prefect, who stood up for the teachers.[10] Another function, that of tobacco store tax collector (*receveur-buraliste*), was also a controversial one for different reasons. Authorities of the academies did not want teachers to become sullied in business affairs. Only when virtually a whole village requested a teacher for the post would the inspector accede to the request, as happened at Saint-Sulpice La Forêt (Ille-et-Vilaine) in 1912. No one else was capable of collecting these special taxes, and the mayor assured the inspector that the teacher would spend no more than a half hour per day for this purpose.[11]

Teachers were also summoned for medical advice, since doctors generally practiced only in fairly large towns, and tiny villages were without them. With regard to medical care, a province like Brittany probably fared worse than most of France at that time. In 1893 the Department of the Côtes-du-Nord had sixteen doctors and eight midwives per 100,000 inhabitants while the national average was thirty-nine and thirty-eight respectively. The South was the area of the country with the greatest number of doctors per capita. Nuns were traditionally called upon to fill the gaps but, after the Ferry laws, so were teachers, particularly by the turn of the century. One ex-schoolmaster interviewed at Saint-Brieuc recalled numerous teachers of the seaside Côtes-du-Nord area ministering to common ailments and giving vaccinations in the prewar years. Both *instituteurs* and *institutrices* provided care. One female teacher of Lot-et-Garonne was honored by the Minister of the Interior in 1901 for her efforts at vaccination.[12] More generally teachers were called upon for first aid, especially by farmers who sustained bruises, scrapes, cuts. One would like to say also that teachers helped change the Frenchman's deplorable hygienic habits of the nineteenth century, but there is little evidence that the school campaign, especially before 1900, had much success in that area nor that it contributed to the teacher's standing. A teacher in G. Bruno's *Les Enfants de Marcel* (1887) notes: "Three-quarters of parents have an unbelievable fear of cold water."[13]

The major daily concern of French peasants was evidently agriculture, and so it behooved the teacher to become acquainted with that domain as well. Before outlining his agricultural endeavors, I want first to emphasize what neither Jacques Ozouf nor Georges Duveau has seen fit to notice: that rural teachers of the pre-1914 Third Republic had an extreme devotion both to the land in general and to the particular region where they taught. In Brittany the majority taught in one small area, which they grew to know very well in the course of their lives. A random sample of fifty *institutrices* of the Finistère reveals that forty-three were natives of the department, and that of the remaining seven, three hailed from Breton departments, leaving only 8 per cent of the total from other sections of France. All nine Breton teachers I interviewed were born, taught, and retired in the same department, except for Madame C. L., who taught briefly in the Finistère before reentering Ille-et-Vilaine. In Puy-de-Dôme, a random sample of forty male and female teachers of around 1900 indicates that 87 percent were born in the department; the remainder were from ones nearby. In a more accessible department, the Allier, the native teachers (in a sample of forty) dropped to 70 percent.[14]

There are other reasons for this concentration besides choice: inspectors of *académies*, particularly after 1900 and the beginnings of a glut, began discouraging "foreign" candidatures in favor of homegrown products.[15] Does this indicate the glimmerings of a regional consciousness we would never have imputed to the centralizing Republic? Perhaps. More important, normal schools generally recruited locally. The main point is not only that teachers often came from the region but that they cared a great deal for their environs. In many villages teachers composed definitive monographs on their communes,[16] and one of the author's interviewees, Louis Ogès, wrote a *Géographie du Finistère* that sold over one hundred thousand copies and went through several editions. Love of the land is a theme shot through Marcel Pagnol's portrait of his father, a teacher of the Midi. We should not leave the subject without also mentioning the famous *instituteur* Louis Pergaud, a giant idolized by his peers and celebrated throughout France for his exciting novels about animals, one of which received a Goncourt prize in 1910. Pergaud's knowledge of the creatures and topography of Franche-Comté was nothing short of encyclopedic. A peaceful lover of the soil, and the very antithesis of an ivory-tower academic, he died in the war, April 18, 1915, and was widely mourned.[17]

From my interviewees, too, I discerned a local patriotism not taken into account by historians, a trait quite different from mystical allegiance to one's country (à la Barrès). When in 1915 L. L. was trapped in the no man's land between the German and French trenches — his entire company already dead — he was obsessed by the idea of getting back to "ma Bretagne," meaning for him the seaside country around Saint-Brieuc. After playing possum for a whole day he regained his lines and subsequently returned to his native region. The Ogès (husband and wife were teachers) remember how they treasured the immediate area around Gouesnac'h (Finistère) where they began teaching in 1911. They took boat rides on the Odet river, fished for shrimp, walked in the woods; and though they could have obtained a better post, they faithfully remained there twelve years. When they transferred it was to a nearby village, then to Quimper — all in the same part of the Cornouaille region. In certain curricula, too, localism was stressed. Thus a teacher of the Allier in 1905 started one level in October with the geography of the village and its terrain, in November worked up to the topography of the department, and only in December got to the geography of France. A warm passage by Edouard Blanguernon also makes the point of local affinities, replying sharply to Maurice Barrès' criticisms of the teachers:

> Our teachers verify the history of France by that of region, of *petit pays*, with its crafts, its arts, and all that has characterized the life of ancestors on their little corner of earth, which has slowly formed the physiognomy of the race. They leave their schools, and where old houses persist, an old chateau, remains of ramparts, and old church, they lead their pupils. . . .[18]

The teacher, in short, shared with the peasant an intense feeling, a real respect for his *petit pays*, and this was important to his local standing. Not by nebulous republican formulae made in Paris could he conquer peasants fearful of "le hors-groupe" (Marcel Faure); nor by ethical dialectic win over "village opinion, like ours, which is clearly distrustful of the foreign and a little turned in upon itself" (Marc Bloch).[19]

Hence agriculture was a bridge between peasant and teacher. Once timidity wore off, farmers would ask teachers what methods to employ on their lands. They would inspect the teacher's garden to see which vegetables were taking the best that year. And the teacher was no passive observer himself; Alfred Gernoux, another interviewee, outlined the propagandistic efforts of his father in the Department of the Loire-Atlantique between 1887 and 1908: "He fought against fallow land, forced the use of liquid manure and other fertilizers, had nurseries and orchards created, had transplants brought from different regions and distributed them."[20] Such a man reminds us of an English country gentleman of the eighteenth century, a Turnip Townshend. L. L. recalls that just after the First World War he personally brought wagon loads of Tunisian phosphates to farmers of the Plouha-Paimpol region; and, despite their initial misgivings, got the peasants to buy them at a favorable price. Older teachers had similarly propagated the use of fertilizers in that region before 1914. And in the section of the *Manuel général* entitled "Questions diverses," teachers often forwarded difficult agricultural questions for answers. One in the Aisne (early 1914) demanded answers to various problems of potato planting.[21]

By the turn of the century *instituteurs* also helped spearhead the growing cooperative movement in agriculture, encouraging farmers to form common herds, for example, so that an individual farmer's emergency could be absorbed by the group. A fine teacher at Piriac (Loire-Atlantique) from 1898-1910 founded there the *Mutuelle de bétail* and became secretary of the society by virtue of his literacy. He also passed out pamphlets instructing farmers on the care of tuberculous animals. A teacher at Poligné (Ille-et-Vilaine) founded, like many others, an insurance society among farmers to recompense monetarily those whose farm animals died prematurely. Such practicality very likely made a great impression upon villagers, though for the latter teacher's inspector, who wrote a glowing report on him, the praise was due mainly because the teacher had translated an important principle into deed. It is probable, too, that teachers acted as they did at least partly because of their sanguine faith in the perfectibility of their fellow man. Certain *instituteurs*, it is true, got themselves into trouble for such activities. In 1906 a large "syndicat de négociants" at Rennes complained strongly to the *académie* about teachers representing the "syndicat Méret," a farmers' cooperative. *Instituteurs* were instructing farmers on how to join the union and how, thereby, to procure machines and fertilizers at lower prices, to the dismay of *négociants*. The teachers were permitted to continue such unionizing activity, and in coastal areas, too, schoolmasters played a part in the embryonic movement of fishermen's syndicalism as well. A. B., who taught at the new fishing school of Concarneau from 1901 until his death in 1907, was secretary of the local *Syndicat des marins pecheurs*. At a large gathering in his honor after his death, a deputy, a senator, the prefect, and a host of *instituteurs* paid homage to the late notable of that region.[22]

In addition to agricultural organizations, teachers founded many other local societies and cooperatives, again, more after 1900 than before. The year 1900 is a rough sort of dividing line, for by that time most expulsions of nonsecular teachers in public schools were completed and almost all lay teachers were now being equipped by primary normal schools with appropriate degrees. The comparative durability of the laic school allowed more time for extracurricular activities. Teachers also derived a new theory of mutual aid from Léon Bourgeois's influential doctrine of solidarism,[23] and it is partly thanks to the implementation of this doctrine in concrete form that peasants began to modify their individualistic outlook and return to the more collectivistic bias of the pre-Revolutionary era. A teacher from Saône-et-Loire noted that efforts like common wine cellars and mutual fire insurance companies would more and more "replace narrow individualism by the principle of unity and the spirit of cooperation."[24] Cooperative credit societies, initiated by *instituteurs*, proliferated in the countryside before 1914; also, cooperative societies for the old (*caisses de retraite pour la vieillesse*) as well as for specific occupational groups like rural firemen (*société de secours mutuels des sapeurs–pompiers*) or suppliers of flour to bakers (*société de panification*). Other kinds of groupings spawned under the teacher's aegis were shooting societies, temperance societies, antituberculosis societies, bicycle societies (just before the war), associations for former students, and orchestras of all sorts. Indeed, teachers at certain posts were required to know music. The mayor of Uzel (Côtes-du-Nord) requested a new teacher in 1904 who could lead the ensemble started by the former teacher there. Another mayor of Ille-et-Vilaine demanded a schoolmaster knowing violin. At Mornas (Vaucluse), however, a teacher who founded a musical society was accused of profiting from the sale of instruments to children.[25] It should be noted that rival Catholic shooting societies, orchestras, and other groupings existed in some villages, and that especially for teachers in the West attainment of recognition might be synonymous with bitter struggle or plain hard work.

It is easy to get starry-eyed about all these extracurricular activities and to forget that teachers also engaged in them for personal advancement, especially for the coveted medals of distinction that brought pay raises. Thus the teacher at Donjon (Allier), a year before his death, petitioned for a bronze medal, buttressing his case with a *vita* that included orphan administration, work in an antituberculosis society, and other such efforts.[26]

Teachers also taught peasants in a more formal environment, giving classes on agriculture, fishing, and a multitude of other matters by means of night adult courses, which burgeoned during this era. T. Chalmel, a fine teacher of the Saint-Malo area, who left a diary, had his thirty adults of the class of 1897 prepare reports on various kinds of agricultural problems. Teachers in the Department of Morbihan around the turn of the century taught about vicissitudes in weather, boats to be used for different kinds of fishing, the preparation and conservation of cider (always a significant topic in Brittany), and industry.[26] In such courses concreteness was, again, the teacher's selling point, and woe betide the *instituteur* who tried to foist theoretical notions like morals and civics upon adults. The barrier of anti-intellectualism was insuperable in the rural world. A letter from the mayor of Saint-Ouen la Rouerie (Ille-et-Vilaine) to the prefect in 1896 indicated that "our rural inhabitants. . .cannot comprehend the utility and importance of general education, nor the advantages of night courses, being only very vaguely conscious of intellectual and moral culture that has no immediate or tangible relation to pecuniary profit." The mayor and council of another village specifically demanded in 1895 that adult instruction relate almost exclusively to subjects like business letters, land measuring, and transplanting. And when teachers delivered periodic lectures (*conférences populaires*) to villagers, they were forced again to cloak any sort of propaganda under the guise of useful, tangible knowledge. Another *instituteur* who gave a lucid treatment of rural depopulation made certain to stock his exposé with numerous concrete references to regions as diverse as the Beauce and Poitou, to the different kinds of land-holding and farming procedures, and other influencing factors.[27] Teachers also held forth on the desirability of inoculation against disease, as well as on the evils of alcoholism, then almost a plague in regions like Brittany and definitely a controversial topic.

The teacher literally spread light when, in conjunction with adult courses, he brought a case of lantern slides (*projections lumineuses*) to illustrate his talk. The use of such projections was very beneficial to a schoolmaster's reputation, making of him, one supposes, almost a shaman in a period still lacking cinema or radio. For peasants who never left their department, save for military service, slides of far-off lands, or even of parts of France like Burgundy, must have been a marvel to behold. Only after the First World War, with increased mobility, diffusion of new media, a higher level of rural sophistication, would teachers lose this substantial monopoly on rural entertainment and thereby, a large ingredient in their notability.[28] But one should imagine the impact of these antebellum slide shows. At the village of Lhuître (Aube) talks on Tonkin and Victor Hugo were enhanced by slides. Five hundred people crowded into the school at Mäel-Carhaix (Côtes-du-Nord) in 1905 to see the "tableaux vivants" of Korea, complete with background music played on a phonograph belonging to the justice of the peace. By such means a teacher could win over a formerly hostile and reactionary area, buttressing his own position and hence that of the Republic. This is what occurred at Guégon (Morbihan) in the 1890s, where the lectures of M. Le G. attracted as many as four hundred people at a time, some from villages six kilometers distant. The sub-prefect of Plöermel exulted over the fact that even the hitherto antilaic mayor there had been proselytized. He lauded M. Le G. for having "obtained an unexpected success. . . which has had a considerable effect in the region." A teacher at Noyat (Puy-de-Dôme) was praised for similar efforts by his inspector, after garnering more mediocre reports earlier in his career. The political effect was, however, usually more implicit than explicit. And to balance the picture one comes across mayors like the one on Ile d'Arz, who burst into an *instituteur's* slide lecture on La Fontaine's fables in order to protest a coeducational gathering in such obscurity![29] But the adult course grew in importance during the Third Republic, and, like the banquet, became one of its most typical institutions. Under the auspices of *instituteur* and benevolent Republic, these night sessions permitted peasants to escape their isolation and meet one another for an evening of instruction.

Again, teachers did not simply give these courses out of the goodness of their heart. Academic honors in the form of medals, gifts of books, and consequent pay raises were partly based on the success of these adult courses, among the many other aspects of a teacher's performance. Two teachers of the Isère petitioned their inspector in 1899 for such honors, giving a detailed report on their adult courses and how well they were functioning. One used a quaint third person technique in his letter: "But if he [the teacher] enjoys some esteem in his little village, if he is the object of much benevolence on the part of inhabitants, he will not forget that he owes it in great measure to the adult courses he directs." This teacher had already received an honorary diploma and a gift of books; the second one was applying for his first "récompense".[30]

Motives aside, it is clear from all of the foregoing that the teacher who before 1914 might run the gamut from legal advisor to medicine man to entertainer, was clearly something more than the name "schoolteacher" implies. Multicompetence was nothing new for *instituteurs*. Before the Ferry laws they had, of course, worked for the curés as beadle, bell ringer, cantor, or church sweeper, and sometimes were reduced by indigence to full-scale farming, even to giving haircuts. In this way the emancipated teacher *qua* notable of the Ferry-Combes generation actually seems closer to his church-ridden predecessor than to the person who today in France essentially teaches and does nothing else. The operative fact here is obviously the spread of industrialization and concomitant growth of communications and prosperity in the twentieth century.[31] As in the cases of doctor, *notaire*, and village blacksmith, the teacher's competence to fill a variety of roles eroded after 1918. Before, he was a jack of at least some trades.

Further, in charting the range of the pre-1914 teacher's extracurricular activities, one is struck over and over by the fact that teachers were extremely specific in their concerns. Theirs was an Aristotelian world. Never could they have attained notability by being merely bookish types isolated from the daily problems of peasant life. Yet, through literature at least, the stereotype of overly idealistic ideologues has persisted in clouding our understanding of their rural role. In *Clochemerle*, the *instituteur* Tafardel is a priestly fanatic spouting bad Latin aphorisms and other pedantic items. Emile Zola paints the teacher Simon, in *Vérité*, as an analogue of Dreyfus and the incarnation of truth and justice. The teacher in Ernest Psichari's pre-war novel *L'Appel des armes* is portrayed, in a worse light, as militant Dreyfusard—a spiritual, almost abstract figure. And Jules Romains's Clanricard is similarly a mere symbol in *Men of Good*

Will, this time a symbol of prescience before the First World War. Even from Georges Duveau we get an anguished picture of "saints without hope" based too heavily on literary sources.[32] All this is not to deny the *instituteur's* idelaism, nor to deprecate a person "sans espérance" when ill-paid; yet it must be firmly stated that the village schoolmaster before 1914 was *also* concrete-minded and down to earth, and that this was the main ingredient in his notability. One must lay to rest the pervasive "type" he became at the hands of Parisian novelists.

Quite aside from the out-of-school activities mentioned, the rural teacher probably derived prestige as well from his daily in-school performance. Parents did not of course inspect teachers, but they had other means of evaluating their effectiveness. If their children appeared to be learning well or began to behave in an improved fashion, they applauded the teachers. They were interested as well in the schoolmasters' extracurricular efforts *within* the school, most universal of which was the school savings bank (*caisse d'épargne scolaire*). Teachers put aside the pennies of pupils and issued them passbooks, and children presumably thus learned thrift.[33] Parents were probably impressed by the knowledge of nature children derived from Thursday walks ("promenades scolaires") in the country led by the teacher, who explained plants or rocks or whatever subject was examined that week. To qualify this a little, it is true that the knowledge imparted was somewhat bookish and perhaps tampered with the peasant child's own naive appreciation of nature. Claude Duneton in *Parler Croquant* remembers having to say "étang" for pond, instead of the local word "gode," which meant much more to him.[34] Other "enlightening" activities like the campaign for school libraries meant less to peasant parents. The content of rural school libraries, however, is worth noting. The village boys' school of La Fontenelle in 1902 contained sixty-eight books, according to the teacher there. Of those roughly half were by well-known authors such as Balzac, Hugo, and Michelet. The others were mostly practical: *Les Insectes, Médecine vétérinaire, Géographie d'Ille-et-Vilaine*, and so on. A library in a modest village of the Allier (1910) had 510 volumes, as well as 95 for adults. In that year there were 1404 loans, and the teacher was praised by his inspector for having one of the best libraries of that district.[35]

More practical were the canteens that some teachers instituted in their schools and which gratified busy peasant parents. A teacher at Lizio (Morbihan), at first denounced by the local priest as a "firm Freemason," gained the admiration of a hostile village and mayor partly because of something so (seemingly) paltry as a canteen. This was made clear in an inspector's report of 1904. "The pupils like M. P. a lot. For a long time he has organized a *soupe scolaire* which I have seen function with great interest. M. P. provides free the vegetables from his garden and can thus give the children a hot meal at noon. That is one of the causes for the high number of pupils and good attendance. He is very esteemed by the population. On my visit to Lizio, I did not meet one peasant who failed to greet him and exchange with him a friendly word."[36] In poorer areas teachers would distribute schoolbooks free of charge, and sometimes other things, too. At Saint-Léger, a poor commune of the Loire-Atlantique, the *institutrice* in the first decade of the twentieth century gave out, besides textbooks, skirts and wool to girls, shirts and socks that she made herself to boys, and even *sabots*. The primary inspector of Nantes saluted her efforts, since such endeavors rendered school more congenial to children and parents and gave the teacher a good name.[37]

Peasants were "concrete," it must be reiterated; and the most tangible index of a teacher's performance was the number of successful candidates he could produce at the annual examination for the certificate of primary studies (*certificat d'études primaires*). Not only did the certificate bring status to pupils and parents but it also opened the way to bureaucratic careers and even to teaching itself. The certificate had been established in 1834 but remained haphazardly organized until Victor Duruy's time. By 1878, forty thousand were awarded in France, though these were of varying value. Finally in 1882 procedures were standardized. The selected candidates, who had to be at least twelve years old, traveled to the cantonal capital to undergo the oral and written test in the company of pupils from other communes. The examination and subsequent prize ceremonies became major events in village life, and as in Laurence Wylie's Vaucluse of 1950, children knew much was expected of them. The atmosphere of local drama was intense; teachers held the power of life and death over candidates. The certificate bore all the prestige of the great Republic itself. No wonder rural parents wanted one so badly for their children. Jean Orieux, in his memoir of peasant life, quotes the wife of a sharecropper: "Ernest has to pass. He is weak in arithmetic, but that doesn't matter. I will send a chicken to the schoolmaster, a ham to the inspector, and Ernest will pass."[38]

Nonetheless, children taking the test were often nervous. A composition written for the *certificat* examination of 1889 by a girl from Tréméheuc (Ille-et-Vilaine) indicated her precise impressions en route to the scene of the ordeal (this being the required subject of the exposition): "je fait un voyage ce matin pour venir a l'examen qui ma fait beaucoup plaisir mais un peu triste quand je pensait a cette examen La description du pays que jai traversé, jai passé par un chemin, jai apercu pleusieurs choses asses belles? Les impressions que j'ai eut sont que javait peur et je me demendait en moi même si jallais ettre admise et je matristé en pensant a cela car être ademise s'est une honneur davoir son certificat d'etude."[39] Needless to say the girl did not pass; but the success of other candidates redounded to the teacher's credit. A couple teaching at Saint-Frégant (Finistère) had done consistently well in this regard and were always praised by the municipal council, as in 1898 when seven boys and two girls (out of a total of eleven candidates) passed the examination. This pedagogical success buttressed the schoolmasters' high standing there, and when the couple left in 1908 after twelve years at the post, the noble mayor, M. du Plessix-Quinquis, made the following declaration: "The President [of the municipal council] reminds you of the unfavorable circumstances in which M. et Mme B. . .arrived twelve years ago in the commune: the school was completely disorganized. The population, having had for many years only teachers sent in disgrace to Saint-Frégant, was quite mistrustful of the new schoolmasters. . . . Although they hadn't the same political and religious opinions as the villagers, they avoided ruffling anybody, by their perfect tact, and have attracted the sympathy of all. It is with the greatest regret that all the inhabitants saw them depart the commune."[40]

It should be noted again that motives were not always of the highest in the race for certificates. Teachers at poor schools knew they were handicapped in the competition for advancement. And the pressure by villagers to produce certificates could be intense. For example, a man with influence over tobacco planters at Camaret (Vaucluse) canvassed signatures for a petition against the teacher there (1889), because his child had not received a first place in the class and had failed the examination for the certificate.[41]

Another obvious ingredient in attainment of notability was longevity at a post. Teachers who remained in one village for a long period had a better chance of earning great respect than those who remained only a short time before transferring elsewhere. I have surveyed a sample of fifty males teaching in the Department of Ille-et-Vilaine according to length of time spent at one village or town. From the sample I removed three teachers who died before age forty, two of them during the war. Given the high degree of displacement in early career (mainly, adjunct teachers moving to directorships), the overall findings for the other forty-seven show a remarkable stability among *instituteurs*. Fifteen per cent remained at one post for at least thirty years, 23 per cent for at least twenty years, 23 per cent for at least fifteen years, 28 per cent for at least ten years, and 11 per cent for less than ten years.[42] Moreover, when one considers that this was clerical Brittany, where harassment was sometimes fierce, the data suggest that all over France such residential stability was the case. And indeed, directives to teachers emphasized the desirability of long residence in one place. In an article of 1913, one teacher noted that "to remain for long years in one post has capital importance. . .[bringing] an incontestable authority."[43]

A few teachers taught throughout their entire careers in one commune, becoming more and more esteemed with the passage of the years. One such was the schoolmistress of Villesonges (Puy-de-Dôme), who spent her whole life there and had "the confidence of families." Another was J. D. at Bolazec (Finistère), who began in 1888 and retired in 1924. From thirty pupils at his debut he raised the enrollment to 127 (and three classes) by 1913, mostly at the expense of rival Catholic schools. Yet another first-rate schoolmaster taught at Saint-Etienne de Corcoué (Loire-Atlantique) from 1881 to 1921, spanning our period of the laic Republic. In 1893 his students had marched to a fire and formed a chain to pass water to the firefighters. Events of this sort — and of course the growing number of primary certificates turned out — placed the teacher and the public school on a solid footing there.[44]

Now the historian, once having listed these palpable reasons for notability, is tempted to satisfy himself with some conveniently syncretistic conclusion. Notability, however, implies status; and status certainly issues from fuzzier and more irrational attributes than mere actions on the notable's part (as, for example, those already detailed). There is as well a sort of imagery connected with any position, and this imagery is very important in any social hierarchy. Certain authors note this well; for example, Gustave Ichheiser: "An individual. . .is powerful, thanks to certain personality characteristics which have been lent to him by particular social arrangements and which can be taken away from him at any time by other arrangements. I call these characteristics pseudo and not real because they are only correlates of certain definite social situations. Yet, for the time being, they function as if they were real." Or, in the words of the rural sociologist, Henri Mendras: "All one's life is passed in conforming to the image others make of you, according to the position you occupy in the [French] village." [45] The teacher's image as notable was carefully cultivated; he usually dressed all in black, save perhaps for a white turned-down collar. His polished shoes and buttoned frock coat and crisp bow tie bespoke self-discipline. In the street he normally wore a hat of a bowler variety and sometimes a pince-nez. The great majority of male teachers had moustaches, less frequently beards, and their hair was close cropped. Moral rectitude, then, and acute differentiation from the ordinary peasant were apparent in the schoolmaster's outward appearance. H. L., an interviewee, recalls perfectly today the countenance of his first teacher at La Grigonnais (Loire-Atlantique): "He was impressive and dignified — just like a curé." Women teachers were similarly dignified in the long dresses of conservative color they invariably wore. Their hair was usually done in a neat bun (inspectors referred several times to the lascivious effect of hair "falling on the shoulders"), and they had to be impeccably groomed. Not to belabor the point, it should be emphasized how much a teacher's prestige depended, as did that of such traditional notables as curé and chastellan, on vestments, carriage, speech, and other imagistic concomitants of status. As Roland Barthès puts it, "Costume is, in the fullest sense, a 'social model,' a more or less standardized image of expected collective conducts, and it is essentially at this level that it is significant." [46]

Turning from ways one *might* become a teacher-notable, one is left with the problem of actually determining notability. At what point did a teacher get accepted as a "monsieur"? Certainly a teacher succeeded in the fullest sense when a reactionary mayor and population were forced to concede his ability. It was thus a personal triumph for the *instituteur* when over one thousand people in a clerical region of Brittany attended a fête of the laic school, as happened at Chéméré (Loire-Atlantique) in 1909.[47] Additionally, certain gestures of villagers manifested their respect for teachers. Monsieur and Madame Ogès remembered that the peasants of Gouesnac'h near Quimper always brought a pile of crêpes to them when a marriage was celebrated and that even girls who had not gone to the laic school honored the teachers in that manner. Schoolmistresses gave advice to couples about to be married or were the object of an honorary visit after the ceremony. We hear of teachers receiving special favors outside Brittany too, such as the only hunting permit in a village above Grenoble. Some rural teachers of the *Belle Epoque* undoubtedly became mayors on terminating distinguished careers, but the closure of most documents after 1914 impedes research on this subject. We know that the revered teacher of Mazières-en-Gâtine, portrayed in Thabault's *Mon Village*, did attain the office of mayor after the First World War.[48] Finally, one perceives the status of some teachers by the numbers of people attending their funerals. Madame T. Chalmel, who taught in the area of Saint-Malo from 1901 to 1924, died in 1936. A list of those who came to her funeral, appended to her diary, ran to almost 400 names! Little wonder that from about the turn of the century, the teacher was widely assailed as a king, as a Jupiter, as the omnipotent controller of *mairie* and village.[49] Such exaggerated depictions of the teacher by the right-wing press testify nevertheless to his having arrived. With curé and noble, even the Breton teacher was, at least in some villages, a figure of distinction.

The foregoing description of the teacher as notable begs the question: just how much influence did he wield? This is a thorny problem, and here I shall attempt to discuss only the obvious facets of the *instituteur's* influence, reserving the more questionable hypotheses for later.

What was the teacher's political influence? Jacques Chastenet, as I have said, entertained no doubts on the subject: "It is in great part to the *instituteur* that radicalism owes its triumph in the countryside, it is thanks to him that socialism begins to have certain successes."[50] This thesis has certain weaknesses. It neglects the importance of economic, social, geographic, and a host of other determinants for political behavior. An example that might disturb an intellectual historian is cited from André Siegfried by François Goguel: in the Vendée of the Third Republic cantons of granite were conservative while those of limestone were republican.[51]

Limiting my focus here only to Brittany, I would not go so far as to say, with Paul Bois,[52] that the *instituteurs* had no political effect whatever in the West. His study is based on the Sarthe alone; in Brittany two significant rural pockets were detached from conservatism just after the war, the Cornouaille (South Finistère) and the Trégor (roughly the western half of the Côtes-du-Nord). In the Trégor, a group of Radical notables were in part responsible for the shift, beginning around the turn of the century, and according to Gabriel Le Bras, the notables "found support in the families of *instituteurs*, the Trécor [alternate spelling] being a breeding ground for the Normal School (and thus for secretaryships to the mayors) . . . ." But again, reservations are in order. The Cornouaille was free of nobles, and the Trégor was bounded on one flank by a natural frontier, the Morlaix river, demonstrating the effect of the terrain upon political manifestations in the area. Both the Cornouaille and the Trégor contained numerous fishing ports, usually more left-leaning than the Breton interior.[53] In other words, other factors besides education came into play in such regions. To conclude: teachers could obviously aid in organizing republicanism in areas already susceptible to their influence. But even where favorite sons of the Right were inevitably elected in Brittany, teachers, it seems to me, helped impose that comity about the Republic's very desirability that I have mentioned. We cannot forget that certain nobles respected their efforts and implicitly accorded the Republic and its school recognition. Thus, even in conservative Brittany, the *instituteur* was of political importance by toning down the hitherto counterrevolutionary quality of the Right. And the teacher's action in politicizing the countryside in provinces already favorable to the Republic was usually greater.

The school and its teachers were instrumental in the eradication of illiteracy in France. Even in the West the conflict between *école libre* and laic school did not retard this development, for almost all children now learned the rudimentary skills of reading and writing in either school. By 1913 illiteracy in the entirely French-speaking departments of Brittany was almost a thing of the past: the draftees of the Loire-Atlantique were 1.4 per cent illiterate; those of Ille-et-Vilaine, 2.5 per cent. In the other departments of the province, illiteracy was still a minor problem: the figure for the draftees of the Côtes-du-Nord for 1913 was 7.9 per cent; of the Finistère, 8.9 per cent; of the Morbihan, 10 per cent. In 1899 the illiterate draftees of the latter two departments mentioned constituted, respectively, 12.9 per cent and 19.7 per cent of the total. This indicates that even in truly "Bretonnant" areas illiteracy was rapidly declining, due in great part to the school.[54]

The decline of regional and Breton tongues must be attributed not only to urbanization and the regiment but also to the influence of the school. Weber's work on all this makes any repetition unnecessary. We know that in a recent polemical bestseller Morvan Lebesque accused the *instituteurs* of the Third Republic of cultural genocide in Brittany, exonerating them only insofar as they were taking orders from more criminal superiors; and the charge is perhaps valid. Breton and other local French variations were condemned as early as the eighteenth century by the universalist philosophes of the Enlightenment, and the French Revolution likewise espoused the idea of levelling France into a homogeneous entity without regional tongues or traditions. France never really experienced such a folk-soil reaction to the abstract eighteenth century as occurred in Germany after the Napoleonic wars. Certainly in the thinking of a Michelet, for one, the cult of local specificity did emerge but not as an all-embracing system. The Third Republic, then, instituted an antipatois, antiregional policy that had long been in the air, and circulars sent to teachers in Brittany stressed the need for literally extirpating Breton. The primary inspector of the district of Vannes, in a report for 1903–1904, noted unhappily that children were still occasionally employing the "élocution vicieuse." It is difficult, despite Weber's assertions, to know how often teachers resorted to the proverbial punishment of tying a wooden shoe (*sabot*) around the neck of a child guilty of speaking Breton. My own opinion based on documents I have seen is that such punishments were quite rare. Pierre-Jakez Hélias remembers numerous oral admonitions against speaking Breton in class or in the schoolyard. But then after class the teachers' "greatest pleasure was to speak that very same Breton with their families and the townspeople. . . . Once they had finished being hussars of the Republic, they became men again." But at least during school hours the campaign was undertaken with vigor and seriousness, if not with the severity we sometimes associate with it. (For the children, as Hélias makes clear, it was less difficult to repress their Breton than to learn precise French, especially words for familiar things around the countryside.)[55]

To be fair one should reiterate the traditional importance of good French as an index of social status. The teachers saw themselves as democratizers; good language could only further the process. Breton or Provençal were considered retrograde. Teachers might proudly serve crêpes but they had little regard for an authentic regional tongue as something worth crowing about. That was past, in the worst sense, and they were future-oriented. It was an age of progress.

All of which points to a real paradox: while *instituteurs* respected regional distinctiveness, they also helped set in motion a process that would destroy such distinctiveness. There are other ironies. Teachers, I have said, were more earthy than has met the eye, yet by imposing the French language upon peasants they were bringing an alien and corrosive abstraction to the countryside—so says Claude Duneton. Duneton even avers—and this is more open to debate—that the good anticlerical teachers of the Repulic were propagating "a language of archbishops" belonging to a very unrepublican seventeenth century elite![56] There is no doubt, at least, that the teachers were the agents of a linguistic conversion that has helped bring the fierce reaction of French regionalism today. Like Jews who once despised Yiddish when it was a living tongue, Frenchmen now want to recover their once-scorned linguistic roots.

A last irony was that while inspectors denounced languages like Breton, prefects and sub-prefects did not scruple from using Bretonnant teachers as political instruments. Local Republicans, too, might ask authorities specifically for a Breton-speaking teacher to help with "republican propaganda," as was the case at Langoëlan (Morbihan) in 1908. One even comes across adult lectures given in Breton; one as late as 1902 at Le Saint (Morbihan) drew over 160 people. But there is no doubt that the school and its teacher, mainly antipatois, greatly diminished the use of regional tongues in France.[57]

Finally, one comes to the teachers as national influence, a welter of village notables creating through teaching and example a widespread mood in pre-1914 France. One definite ingredient of that mood was patriotism; and the patriotic *instituteur*, working from *Le Tour de la France par deux enfants* or the Lavisse and Aulard national histories, helped set a tone in antebellum France. It is fashionable, of course, to chart strong pacifist-socialist leanings in *instituteurs* from prewar times,[58] but the overwhelming majority were not of this configuration at all. At its height before 1914 the syndicalist movement counted only 4 per cent of the nation's 120,000 odd *instituteurs*, and almost all were urban. The typical village schoolmaster was perhaps no clamoring nationalist, but a professor of patriotism, in Jules Ferry's well-known phrase. One Breton teacher wrote the following poem in 1907 and dedicated it to his inspector of the Finistère:

Schoolchildren, joyous workers
Hope of France,
Let us write verse, our brothers and sisters,
Of these childhood friends;
But let us not forget the Fatherland,
That good and cherished Mother,
Soldiers of Revenge![59]

Another teacher, distinctly less nationalistic, wrote that "war is a horrible crime. . .however, there are legitimate wars from which no people can withdraw: these are defensive wars." Suspected as a pacifist, he would later fight and die in battle in 1916. Of thirty-five thousand teachers enlisted in the war, 8,000 died, and one can perhaps say that in words and deeds the *instituteurs* were the prototypes of a patriotic generation.[60]

They were also teachers of morality. The substitution of a morals and civics course for religious instruction in 1882 amounted almost to a revolution. Could morals, as Bayle had heretically wondered in the seventeenth century, be dissociated from religion and work? Ferry, Paul Bert, Ferdinand Buisson, all the great laic–positivist reformers thought it could, and they relied on their new village black coats to accomplish the trick. With the right sort of teaching given by an upright schoolmaster, Ferry believed that a generation of good, altruistic children and, thence, ethical adult Frenchmen could be fashioned. This teaching, he wrote, "seeks. . .to produce a moral act, to cause it to recur, to make it habitual so that it shall dominate life." But since Freud, most believe that many acts have an irrational, instinctual, or subconscious basis, diametrically opposed to what had been persistently inculcated as desirable conduct, and unsusceptible to preachment.[61] Usually when the dust clears one finds truth on both sides.

Was the village schoolmaster-notable a weighty moral pillar in the France of the Belle Epoque? At least certain people thought he was; a primary inspector noted the following about a highly rated teacher of the Finistère: "M. C., who has taught at Invillac for almost twenty-five years, has been able to exercise an excellent influence upon the population which is immediately recognized by the politeness and good spirit of the villagers." And an "instituteur d'élite" of Lot-et-Garonne was congratulated in 1909 for "a very great moral influence which has its source in the high character qualities of the schoolmaster."[62] Villagers, even some who opposed the secular school, certainly considered some teachers a second father or mother. One concludes that when you assume the teacher to be a moral influence, then *mutatis mutandis* he actually becomes one.

All of the foregoing treats the more enviable side of a village schoolmaster's existence. Outside the scope of this study, though also of great importance, is the enthusiasm so many had for classroom work. But now we must treat the drawbacks, or at least ambivalencies, of the schoolteacher's rural position. What follows may seem to contradict what has gone before, but only if one considers history and its figures consistent, all of a piece. It is my feeling, in short, that notability and insecurity could often coexist.

What were the sources of an *instituteur's* insecurity? In essence, the problem was this: better-off financially than most peasants, he was yet too il-paid to meet bourgeois standards. He was supposed to be a bridge to commoners (and usually of common origin himself); yet the teacher had to subscribe to an uncommon moral standard that separated him from the people. He was supposed to be a pillar of the coming order—"go forth, little spirit of modern ideas," said Ferdinand Buisson—but he never entirely abandoned his ties with the *pays* of his birth.

Fundamental to this ambivalent status was money, or the lack of it. Jules Ferry had said that his school laws would not only make primary education free, secular, and compulsory but would also emancipate the teacher by making him materially comfortable, a bourgeois at last. Needless to say this did not occur; and Antonin Lavergne's novel *Jean Coste* (1901) only capped a wave of protest initiated by disgruntled teachers themselves. Objectively we now know how correct Ferry's critics were. The basic salary scale, which, with a slight increase in 1905 and additions for outside work, obtained before 1914, is given in Table 4.[63] (Notice the inequality of salaries between sexes.)

Table 4. Basic Salary Scale for Pre-1914 Teachers (given in francs)

	Instituteurs	*Institutrices*
Fifth Class	1000 francs	1000 francs
Fourth Class	1200 francs	1200 francs
Third Class	1500 francs	1400 francs
Second Class	1800 francs	1500 francs
First Class	2000 francs	1600 francs

In theory communes of a certain size had to provide the teacher either lodging or an indemnity for lodging. Despite that, the salary scale was woefully inadequate and unjust, not only because of its low stipends but because of its system of promotions. The system was based upon percentages: 35 percent of teaching effectives had to be in the fifth class; 25 percent in the fourth; 15 percent in the third; 5 percent in the second and in the first together. To accede to the top salaries, the liveable salaries, could take a lifetime, and indeed, many teachers never reached the upper two classes. The remaining 20 percent of teachers were *stagiaires*, or untenured novice teachers, whose salary was a pitiful 800 francs without any other benefits. Until they passed an examination conferring the Certificat d'aptitude pédagogique (C. A. P.) they were doomed to remain in this servile state, and *stagiaires* of five years experience were not uncommon. The system of advancement was modified in 1902, but on balance teachers' salaries remained a scandal. The experienced German schoolmaster, for instance, received almost twice as much as his French counterpart in 1913; and the average *instituteur's* salary, even after 1905, amounted to little more than the average French industrial worker's wages and was below that of all other functionaries.[64]

What did this do for the teacher's village position? It obviously placed his income well beneath that of the bourgeois, and denied him social equality with the notables of his commune. And if the bourgeois skimped for puritanical reasons the teacher skimped out of degrading necessity. "The purchase of a pair of shoes is a catastrophe," as one wit put it.[65] When a decent pair of shoes cost fifteen francs he wasn't joking. Beginning teachers were worst off. One whom I interviewed in Brittany earned sixty-five francs thirty centimes a month in 1912, of which an incredible sixty francs was allotted for *pension*. Extra income for luxuries like a bicycle, indispensable for a daily seven kilometer trip, was just unavailable, given the fact that a used bicycle cost ninety francs.[66]

As if financial embarrassment were not problem enough, there were limits as to what one could or should do with the money one had. Peasants, who called teachers "mangeurs de fricot"—roughly, earners of easy pay—did not want to see them surrounded with comforts. The bias against conspicuous consumption ran deep in France, in part due to a heritage of taxation upon visible signs of wealth, in part due to scorn of *dérogement*—status suicide. And yet, peasants expected the teacher's belongings to be in impeccable order. These included garden, house, tea service, and clothes.[67] Such expectations were particularly high for a married schoolmaster who was a permanent fixture in the commune. But yet another paradox: teachers must absolutely not incur debts. According to both academy and villagers indebtedness, which was always a stigma in France, was doubly unacceptable for this important public servant. Files I have seen are filled with angry and often petty letters taking indebted *instituteurs* and *institutrices* to task. Butchers, bakers, grocerystore owners would not hesitate to write the teacher's superiors when he owed a few francs at the store—you almost sense the pleasure they got from doing so. Relaxed village camaraderie did not extend in such matters to the teachers. In 1893 the manager of the Paris department store, *Aux Classes Laborieuses*, informed the inspector of the academy of the Côtes-du-Nord that one of his *institutrices* owed twelve francs there. More representative of village vernacular is the following letter:

bain, 12 juin 1892

Messiu, je vous déclare qu'y a noblanche un instituteur qui est si endeté que il doit à tout le monde. Ca fais jolimant murmerer. . . .Si vous le nomié aieur, ca feré plaisi à tous les republicain.

And a teacher from the Agenais was criticized in even more extreme terms by a bookstore owner of Montluçon, who called his indebtedness "a premeditated robbery": the teacher ought to forego the café and pay him soon, he wrote the *académie*, or else his furniture would be seized.[68] Letters of this sort were conducive neither to a teacher's advancement nor to his village position. And when a teacher was in debt everyone knew it. The nature of the debt—whether it was medical expenses for children, books from Paris, or clothes—mattered little to the peasant.

Now the very fact that teachers owed money not only in villages but also in Paris stores indicates how far the communications revolution had come in France. Zola in his *Au Bonheur des dames* had first seen the implications of democratic buying under the Second Empire. Mail order catalogues, advertisements in the newspapers, and other enticements were then dangled before teachers who, more than most rural people, valued fine things and looked outward for their values. Yet teachers were confined in a rural world and prevented from adequately connecting with the urban world they knew outside. A teacher's daughter in Savoie recalls her young life as "one of strict necessities, never any treats". When her uncle sent chocolates from Chambéry it was a great occasion.[69] So that even when the teacher had an extra stipend as secretary to the mayor, even if his wife taught and added her income to the household, the strict rules emanating from villagers and more, from those great Protestant masters of the normal schools, Pécaut, Buisson, and Steeg, dictated monetary sobriety.

Teachers, however, were then criticized for the aloofness which their financial circumstances imposed on them. Why would they never relax, go on a spree? Aloofness indeed was connoted by the very clothes the teachers wore—crisp frock coat and bourgeois hat, pinned hair in the case of ladies. As Stendhal had called women's clothes "the artillery of love", so he might have seen teachers' vestments as moral artillery, even class artillery. And clothes were differentiators, as will be elaborated further on; classes were perhaps more reliably indicated by clothing during the early Third Republic than in the era when Père Grandet's bourgeois advisors all wore greasy, sloppy clothes. Add to this the fact that teachers were bookish, and that books, too, meant snobbery. Of course, teachers in self-defense might have asked: how else may I spend my discretionary income [when it existed]? With the café closed to them on moral grounds, with its homely diversions (smoking, cards, bowling, dancing) forbidden, what recreation was left, besides gardening and reading? But books were definitely abnormal. They lent the teacher an air of subversion.[70]

So the teacher was neither bourgeois nor proletarian nor peasant. Mona Ozouf and Jacques Ozouf both devote space to the problem and reduce it to this: lack of money kept the teacher out of the bourgeoisie; too much learning put him above the peasantry. My view, as has been seen, follows that of the Ozoufs, but their analysis needs to be given nuances. First, other village figures were similarly caught between these poles, for example, the *pharmacien*.[71] And what of the various functionaries—in what slot should we place them? Was not the teacher's outsider status in part due to his government post? Not only was he being paid for non-manual labor, but the pay came from Paris, which made him in village eyes a sort of *demi–rentier*. And everyone knew that the strings were pulled from elsewhere, that the teacher could not be his own person. The petitions and anonymous letters that inundated the files of prefectures and *académies* before 1914 were obviously sent in the conviction that the authorities would punish teachers who offended local opinion.

If teachers were neither bourgeois nor proletarians, what the Ozoufs fail to emphasize is that the education ministry wanted it that way. The myriad articles in education journals not only gave counsel on appearance, such as keeping hair trimmed or not slouching; they also recommended insistently that teachers keep apart.[72] *Instituteurs* must not become too friendly with anyone in the village, for they must preserve their special, unsullied status as guardians of future French citizens. Affiliation with any subgroup was suspect. An adjunct at La Rouexière (Loire-Atlantique) was chastized by the inspector of Ancenis for being too close to a group of young workers, thereby losing "the dignity and the consideration which an *instituteur* needs in order to succeed. . .in his task." Similarly, the teaching father of one of my interviewees, though very well-liked at Plounévez-Lochrist (Finistère), would have been, in the estimation of his inspector, "better respected if he showed himself to be less familiar with everybody."[73] This last statement gives a good indication of how teachers were forced by superiors to walk the tightrope between overcultivation and undercultivation of villagers' friendship.

Perhaps it is only by your acquaintances that you can ultimately be classed. But the teacher had no stable group of associates. He flitted from subgroup to subgroup, or perhaps over them, and in turn was viewed differently by each. When Theodore Zeldin noticed that the bourgeois was what you made of him, he could have transferred that theme to the teacher, who himself was a Pirandellian animal.[74] He was of course "neither bourgeois nor proletarian"; but to a sharecropper he *might* be a *monsieur*, while to a *fermier* merely "the schoolmaster". Even to a city colleague he would be of a different taint than to a country colleague. When all is said and done, the Ozoufs are correct: the teacher was an inbetweener. More research, however, will be needed to elucidate the varying nature of his rural marginality, the different points of view that made of him different people at different times.

When one talks of teachers caught between peasantry and bourgeoisie a corollary problem is the important question of *déclassement*. This theme, with variations, has received much attention in our own time—witness George Orwell on deproletarianized worker politicians or Vance Packard on rootless America—but in nineteenth century France *déclassement* was a hot political issue with its own peculiar flavor. The problem needs its separate historian. *Déclassement* was a central rallying point for Legitimists and the Right generally, and also part of the nationalist propaganda of a Barrès, whose favored word was "deracination." Education was considered the prime instrument of *déclassement* and on it a number of articles were written, one of the best by Emmanuel Labat in the *Revue des deux mondes* for 1913.[75] Labat painted a touching picture of Gascon peasant children, forced to go to school, told about foreign lands like Korea or America, given rationalist ideals made in Paris, and thus inoculated with scorn for their own tiny corner of earth To this sort of criticism the laic side felt compelled to reply. Félix Pécaut, grand master of the Higher Normal School at Fontenay-aux-Roses, acknowledged the problem but believed the school could blunt its impact by more attention to agricultural and rural matters; and anyway, other forces in society were drawing young people to towns, school or no school.[76]

In this debate few people stopped to consider the teacher himself as *déclassé*, except those writers who used the term in its more pejorative and partisan sense. But the schoolmaster, often *fraîchement issu de la classe paysanne*, was detached from his heritage much like an immigrant to America. The process was rigorous. Even before normal school, that "laic seminary" as some called it (notice the element of religious conversion), prospective teachers were marked out by their brilliance at the village school. Like privileged eighteenth-century Court Jews, teachers were offered a bargain: you, sir, may escape by virtue of your brains the burden of peasantry and become an *instituteur*. Take M. Auguste Bouet who became head teacher at Thabault's village of Mazières-en-Gâtine in 1881. Bouet's teacher had entered him for the lycée scholarship examination at age twelve. He failed because his peasant French made the word *vipère* masculine, not feminine, in an era when country people still said "un gros (grou) vipère." This error, says Thabault, really cost Bouet a university career. Instead, he took the primary route, ending up in Mazières, fifteen kilometers from home, and taught there from 1881 to 1925. The attachment to one area indicates at least some residual peasant identification, and undoubtedly that was a major part of his notability. Bouet wrote the local monograph, gave courses in agriculture, was secretary to the mayor, and ultimately became mayor of the village itself.[77] But only by divesting himself of a good deal of his heritage.

France is rethinking its peasant past, its lurching into modernity, and remarkable books like Duneton's *Parler Croquant* frankly treat the linguistic and spiritual impoverishment wrought by the nationalizing, antilocal Third Republic. The reader comes off very badly; in this book on Corrèze as in Lebesque's *Comment peut-on être Breton?* he is an agent of cultural genocide. Duneton remembers:

> As for the teacher Bordas, the "Monsieur", he was something different. Very simply he represented France, culture, power, in a word civilization, and he put his conduct on a footing with his very high functions. Although of modest origins and unavoidably a maternal speaker of Occitane, he refused with hauteur and a certain scorn to use that plebeian language.[78]

Again, few really look at the teacher himself as victim. Why should they? This person had won social promotion—what more could there be? And look at the letters of the inspectors, the optimism, the faith in the coming eradication of illiteracy and error, the bright forward-looking faith of mental and spiritual pioneers. To paraphrase Auden, had there been a problem we should have known.

Well, we *do* know there was another reality beneath this Ferryite one, perhaps not the ultimate reality, but nonetheless another level. Teachers in their polished and urbane French did try to grope back to what they had lost. A village teacher of the Vosges in 1914 hoped he could still retain some peasantness, as both his teacher father and grandfather had done ("They were peasants, they remained peasants all their lives"). Even in the 1960s Huguette Bastide, in her best-selling account of an *institutrice's* life in Lozère, writes plaintively: "I do not know how to warm up [to them], I answer, my stilted sentences irritate me. I'd like to speak patois to them, sit down with them and eat a piece of bacon or cheese. . . ."[79]

Language is obviously the key differentiator here between teacher and peasant. The gulf of language can easily cause trepidation in those who find it hard to switch idioms. Schoolmasters, bearers of good grammar, could never descend into the abyss of slangy French for that would be *dérogement* of the worst sort. Yet for schoolmasters in an area like Alsace or Armorican Brittany the problem of speaking ireproachable French had as its mirror image a second obligation. A primary inspector discussing a successor to the esteemed teacher of Lannion in the Côtes-du-Nord recommended that the new teacher there have absolute command of Breton. Almost all the inhabitants could understand and speak French, but in 1901 Breton was still preferred among the lower orders. "The Breton, the *homme du peuple*, of course, if by his nature timid, not very expansive, purposely distrustful. How can his reserve be conquered. . . if one is, so to speak, a foreigner to him?"[80] Here is the crux of the matter: even in a rural area where only French was spoken, the teacher, by virtue of his urbane language, was still set off as a kind of foreigner. And yet he was a half-peasant, frequently devoted to his natal area, but linguistically isolated in his own *pays*.

Language is obviously the key differentiator here between teacher and peasant. The gulf of language can easily cause trepidation in those who find it hard to switch idioms. Schoolmasters, bearers of good grammar, could never descend into the abyss of slangy French, for that would be *dérogement* of the worst sort. Yet for schoolmasters in an area like Alsace or Armorican Brittany the problem of speaking irreproachable French had as its mirror image a second obligation. A primary inspector discussing a successor to the esteemed teacher of Lannion in the Côtes-du-Nord recommended that the new teacher there have absolute command of Breton. Almost all the inhabitants could understand and speak French, but in 1901 Breton was still preferred among the lower orders. "The Breton, the *homme du peuple*, of course, is by his nature timid, not very expansive, purposely distrustful. How can his reserve be conquered . . . if one is, so to speak, a foreigner to him?"[80] Here is the crux of the matter: even in a rural area where only French was spoken, the teacher, by virtue of his urbane language, was still set off as a kind of foreigner. And yet he was a half-peasant, frequently devoted to his natal area, but linguistically isolated in his own *pays*.

A final note on *déclassement:* teachers normally taught their entire careers in a *petit pays*, but their sons and daughters, I would speculate, often migrated elsewhere. This problem of social mobility requires more research, yet there are straws in the wind which suggest that the ultimate defeat of the teacher's peasanthood was in his progeny. Three village teachers I interviewed chanced to mention their children. One couple, both teachers, had an only son, now a high functionary in the finance administration in Paris—a bourgeois in income and life-style. The granddaughter, also a *fille unique*, is "finding herself." Another teacher had a child who became an engineer in a big town. A third's daughter emulated her mother by teaching in the Girls' Normal School at Saint-Brieuc. I would also imagine that a substantial number of teachers' male offspring rose into the ranks of *professeurs*. Under the Second Empire, samples tell us that some 10 percent of secondary school teachers were offspring of schoolmasters. More qualitatively, Jacques Ozouf referred to a recent colloquium at the Ecole Normale Supérieure (Paris) where one university professor affected to apologize to his confrères for *not* being the son of an *instituteur*, as most there were.[81] The generational upward osmosis is universal, of course, and democratized avenues of advancement have in any event changed the status of teachers during our century. It is hard to know whether a grandson teaching at Nanterre in the 1960s had any more status than his grandfather at Nanterre-sur-Chantepie. But the point is the loosening from the land: uprootedness.

To return to the major theme of teachers' difficulties: John Cuddihy, in his book *The Ordeal of Civility*, defines modernization as "refinement."[82] For village teachers, refinement in language and comportment was a daily must. Even the *instituteurs'* dwellings had to be *comme il faut*, a reflection of their self-discipline. The teacher, you feel, was almost a new curé and indeed one finds, in a report as early as Victor Duruy's time, concrete evidence to that effect: "The teacher's house, as with that of the curé, should be the model house of the village: well-developed construction of course; sobriety, elegance, windows; and everywhere that cleanliness which is the poor man's luxury. . . ." In fact, we easily forget that rural notables everywhere were all to some degree surrogate religious figures and, as in early nineteenth century New England, "acted not as individuals, but as though they were clergymen and each profession were a church."[83] Teachers were as well the representatives of a new secular morality on trial, agents of a civic culture getting established at the grass roots. No wonder they acted like the saints people now remember them to have been. Directives from the *académies* or politicians in Paris repeatedly drove the point home lest they forget. For example, this circular of the inspector of Bouches-du-Rhône for 1882 states: "Our teachers must not forget it: teaching of morals imposes upon them, in turn, a moral obligation, that of putting their conduct in accord with their teaching. . . . The master is the example."[84] The example could never swear, never exclaim (the hottest kind of exclamation my interviewees used was *ma foi*), never verbally let go. And of course if the teacher was forbidden from being one of the boys in talk and action, he was also blocked in his intellectual aspirations. Gore Vidal complains that writers like himself never have anyone to talk to, and I suppose that some degree of isolation is common to all thinkers. But for the teacher fresh out of normal school, debouched into a spanking new world of ideas, the problem was acute:

who was there in the village who could seriously discuss Victor Hugo or positivism or even French foreign policy? Certainly those who came nearest to his station in life, such as the rural postman, the road surveyor (*agent voyer*), the mayor, were at the same time usually inferior to him in intellectual attainments. The young *stagiaire* or unmarried woman teacher hadn't even a literate spouse with whom to mull over matters. An *institutrice* of the Sologne, the type who seems to have been susceptible to depression, scratched in her diary 4 January 1893: "Solitude, a black cold, the humid walls in my room—nothing to read." A woman teacher of the Allier in 1895 equally deplored her complete lack of communication with the outside world; stuck with sixty-five children in her class, as well as adult courses and other duties, she felt she would go under, but was maintained at the same post until retirement in 1928! Another, teaching at La Tour d'Auvergne, was invited to a meeting in Clermont-Ferrand, but had to turn it down; for "one has to travel at night and often in very bad conditions."[85]

In a fine passage, Jean Guéhenno, a lifetime laicist of distinction, discusses the intellectual isolation that at least some teachers of the pre-World War I era experienced:

> They leave them in a frightening state of intellectual isolation. I think of the young schoolteacher at the age of twenty, when he leaves the normal school, so avid for knowledge, so magnificently curious, awakened to all problems. He takes his post, the smallest and most remote hamlet. And suddenly there is silence about him. An ocean of earth! Nothing but the inertia of the earth! Even anxiety disappears with so much serenity. And not one book! The pay is too meager to allow him to buy one. No one to talk with. What will-power is necessary then to remain preoccupied with the life of the mind. For the intelligence, there is hardly a more tragic adventure.[86]

From all of the foregoing it should be clear that intellectual, social, and moral isolation were inextricably mixed. And yet, simultaneously, teachers could be invited to every village marriage and funeral, and be consulted in every touchy dispute, as was the case with a teaching couple in Saône-et-Loire, among so many others.[87] Notability and isolation were not mutually exclusive. The teacher who coined the phrase "bien avec tout le monde, très bien avec personne" was probably describing the outer limit of acceptance.[88]

But the boundaries for maneuver, the tolerance for error, were very slight, and particularly in the case of village *institutrices*. For one thing, women were sometimes replacements for nuns, and since mothers worried more about their little girls' morals than about those of boys, their expectations of schoolmistresses, who usually taught girls, were higher than for schoolmasters. Then there was the Church itself, whose press at its worst caricatured *institutrices* as billiard-playing, cigarette-smoking, atheistic modern women. And some male teachers, too, set impossible standards for their female colleagues to follow. A lady teacher of the Vosges in 1897 complained that the *instituteur* there (Rouvre-en-Xantois) could stomach neither her seriousness—"it's pretentious"—nor her relaxed moods—"they're laughable." She ended her memoir philosophically, with the consoling reflection that all social positions require a "thousand daily renunciations."[89]

Among those thousand daily renunciations was dress. I have already touched upon this matter, but I stress here the special sort of sumptuary repression that was applied to women. Like males they could not condescend to casual attire; nor, like all women, could they adopt anything provocative (witness the scandal of Emma Bovary in pants). But neither could they soar into the realm of elegance. When a woman teacher wore a feathered hat or a *lorgnon* she ran the risk of appearing a social climber, of trying to be bourgeoise. As an *instituteur* of the Centre direly warned: "Daughters of peasants or of workers, the *institutrices* too often forget their origins and want to ape women of the world in their clothes and bearing." Mothers, especially, examined their dress compulsively, avidly searching for signs of coquettishness or "lack of correctness."[90] Look at the old photographs: the women teachers seem nothing less than dignified. On the other hand, however, *institutrices* must avoid stiffness and nascent masculinity. The term "bluestocking" (*bas bleus*), conventionalized by Barbey d'Aurévilly's novel of that title (1878), was the term of reproach for unfemininity, too much learning, and intractability. Dress, like language, was at once a great differentiator and a critical part of image—a tight-fitting thing both literally and figuratively. A primary inspector of the Allier, praising a teacher's appearance, said it all: "Excellent, at the same time simple."[90]

Marriage, probably as important as dress, presented similar constraints. Finding a suitable spouse helped raise your legitimacy quotient in a village, for the French were then hard on celibacy; but how to find that spouse? Male teachers could rarely marry into the bourgeoisie and at best might envision a match with a functionary's daughter or the offspring of a small shopkeeper. Peasant wives were also of course a possibility. But for women teachers finding a partner was infinitely harder, in part because their opportunities for courtship were more restricted, in part because of their learning, in part because of economic reasons. Peasants in certain areas looked on the *institutrice* as a "little doll," afraid to get her hands wet; and *commerçants* required a dowry, *rentiers* a goodly sum to make a match worthwhile. On the other hand, the single *institutrice* was probably more common before the turn of the century than after. Jacques Ozouf's study of the Manche indicated that the percentage of married *institutrices* in that department more than tripled between 1897 and 1922. After 1900, too, the administration and teachers at normal schools began vigorously to preach the virtues of marriages within the teaching community. Madame F. L. remembered how her headmistress at the Rennes Normal School warned the girls to keep themselves attractive in order to marry someone worthwhile, preferably a male teacher, and above all not to succumb to the blandishments of shiftless *coqs de village* for whom a young *institutrice* was a prized marriage prospect. Pauline Kergomard invited young schoolmistresses to shed their "monastic habits."[92]

When it comes finally to sexual constraints we enter terra incognita only beginning to be mapped by the likes of Professors Zeldin or Shorter. First off, we may say that neither peasants nor rural bourgeois notables were as sexually free as the urban working class or the dying Paris aristocracy. Peasants were constrained mainly by village gossip or, in areas like the West, by Church doctrine. Bourgeois morality is harder to capsulize; but I would say that one ingredient was the puritanism that went along with making money and keeping it. Central was the maintenance of family, if guides like Henri Baudrillart's *La famille et l'éducation en France* (1874) are to be trusted. Immorality would strike at the tight control of father over son and daughter, and destroy that well-ordered devolution of property for which the bourgeoisie has always striven. As for teachers, they had enough injunctions to last a lifetime, going beyond both peasant and bourgeois in this respect. There was, for one thing, the *Académie* sitting over them, and we know from Zeldin that the laic establishment, perhaps due to Protestant evangelical influence, was at least as puritanical as the Catholic one.[93] Dancing and smoking were doubly taboo because they were immoral and also because they showed the pillar of the Republic with his guard down. Villagers reinforced these standards, for they concurred with inspectors: teachers who took children from the fields had better be upright. Peasants permitted the teacher little deviation from the moral norm. Moreover, scandal-hungry themselves, they were prone to spreading rumors about this vulnerable paragon of virtue just to liven up a mundane existence. So even a wayward glance was open to much interpretation. How many teachers must have dreamed, like Zola's bourgeois Hennebeau in *Germinal*, of being for one day as sexually autonomous as a worker? This we will never know.

Since none of the standard authorities touch this subject I will have to use mostly the Breton sources I checked for solid examples. The trouble is that this sort of history easily descends into *petite histoire*. One thing we can say for sure is that women teachers bore the brunt of morals charges more often than did males. Just as they had to be prudent in their relations with the Church so also did they have to be careful to lead exemplary private lives. A woman teacher of Ille-et-Vilaine, though excellent in the classroom, was considered anathema at the village of Lillemer because she had had a baby too soon after her marriage before coming there. For the first year she was snubbed by most people, and right up until she left the commune three years later she was slandered in numerous anonymous letters. Another woman teacher came to the reactionary village of Marsac (Loire-Atlantique) from the Department of Gers in 1907. When the people heard that she had married a defrocked curé, their venom was unbridled. One of the anonymous letters in her file is a castigation of her morals and gives an indication of village pettiness at its worst, partly a reaction to "foreigners":

> Since last year, we have as schoolmistress a real run-around, she was kicked out of her own *pays* because she lived with her curé — they left together, since she arrived here he himself was at St. Nazaire she went to sleep with him every Sunday and sometimes more often they are married at present but they have a little daughter who was three years old before they got married and everyone knows that, all the same it's not necessary to make fun of us our daughters no longer go to school we'd rather they don't know how to read than to go a woman of bad morals. . . .

An investigation by the inspector found this letter to be a complete pre-fabrication; but by the end of the year the highly-rated *institutrice* had to leave the commune, transferred to the city of Saint-Nazaire where she taught from 1907 to 1936.[94]

Compare such imbroglios with typical suspicions surrounding male teachers. For example, a teacher in the Agenais was long suspected of carrying on with his female *adjointe* (behind his wife's back); but nothing was done, even when a package bearing certain unmentionables arrived at the school.[95]

In some other cases, however, sex scandals did have an adverse effect upon teacher's careers. An *instituteur* had been doing well at Le Pellerin from 1886 until 1897, when his wife's love affair behind his back came to the attention of the villagers. The French traditionally have made the cuckold an object of their mirth — the rural classic *Clochemerle* revolves around that theme; and this teacher was hastily sent to Touvois, an inferior post. Another teacher, a young *stagiaire* at Saint-Ouen-La-Rouerie (Ille-et-Vilaine), was sent to the Department of the Nord after two people spied him in the house of a thirty-eight year old woman "who is weak minded." Their description of what they saw through a hole in the shutters, certified by *M. le maire* as honorable testimony, was sufficient evidence for the inspector. The most spectacular case of this sort that I came upon involved an *institutrice* who was caught embracing a man on a beach near Saint-Nazaire in 1887. The detailed police investigation for "Outrages publics à la pudeur" contains more than a dozen testimonies of people who watched them from behind the trees on a hill overlooking the beach. An old man with a pair of binoculars called some youths to the spot to take a look and then more observers came over. The *institutrice* was forced to resign soon after.[96] She was eighty-odd years too early for sainthood.

In the latter two instances it is certain that the *stagiaire* and the *institutrice* had actually engaged in activities providing grist for snoopers' mills. The *institutrice* made no attempt to recant when confronted with evidence against her. At other times, however, *institutrices* or *instituteurs* were involved in sex scandals based on more ambiguous evidence. A major affair of this sort took place in the Finistère in 1907. A fifty-four year old father of two had been teaching at Gouesnou since 1880. From about 1900 he had fallen out with the mayor, who fired him from his post as secretary and accused him successively of brutality to students, drunkenness, and exploitation of children in the classroom. These charges were investigated by the inspector and found to be unsupported by evidence. Meanwhile, the mayor had roused groups of *pères de famille* against the teacher, a prelude to the scandal that followed. On 13 August 1907, the teacher (this is his version) was reading a newspaper in his favorite field near the village. Three young girls, two of them sisters, aged eight, eleven and twelve years old, asked him if he could see their cow, and one had him lift her up in order to gaze over the field. They went away shortly afterward. Late in the day their mothers charged him with serious sexual offences. The full report of the inspector of Brest, relating the detailed investigations he undertook, reveals to us the gravity of the affair. The story he heard from the girls and their mothers was that the teacher had called them over, encouraged them to do somersaults, and began to commit certain perverse acts with them. The girls returned home crying. The primary inspector noted that the mother of the two sisters modified her story several times. She was also known as a drinker and, being very poor, was dependent on charity administered by the mayor and a noble landowner of the area. Furthermore, the inspector noticed that the field was very close to a main road, making such escapades difficult to conceal. Finally, all three girls were pupils at the rival Catholic school. On the other hand, the girls sounded sincere to him, and the mayor supported them although he was certainly not an impartial bystander. This report, a model of clarity and balance, ended:

"It is difficult to conclude; but I am rather disposed to conclude that the teacher is innocent." The dimensions of the affair quickly widened. On 31 August the influential daily, *La Dépêche de Brest*, carried a long article entitled "Gros scandale en perspective," which sided with the mayor and his whole municipal council against the teacher. Other newspapers took up the case soon after. On 10 September a petition with 100 signatures of *pères de famille*, validated by the mayor, was sent to the prefect asking that the teacher be sent out of the village for "immoral acts." The *instituteur* did not resume his duties in the new school year, and everybody waited for the outcome of his trial at the *Cour d'assises* of the Finistère at Quimper. The verdict came on 4 April 1908, after a long closed-door trial, that is, with no minutes available, as befitted an affair of this genre: the teacher was acquitted. He retired in August, at a plausible age for retirement, but blackened for life.[97]

One should not think that the academy blindly protected the teacher even in such ambiguous cases. Although less capricious than villagers, inspectors, as noted, enforced the same moral standards and continually warned teachers not to give occasion for gossip, even going so far, in several cases, as to censure women teachers for bicycling through villages. The most closely watched teachers were those who could get into the most trouble, youthful *stagiaires* and adjunct teachers. Inspectors used the directors to inform them of the whereabouts and particularly the nocturnal habits of their young subordinates.[98]

Besides sex, the other great moral pitfall for teachers was obviously alcohol. In France a necessary concomitant of social intercourse has always been a shot of wine (the *coup de rouge*), but for teachers it was forbidden fruit. Use of spirits was damaging to the reputation of *instituteurs* who, themselves, taught courses on the evils of alcoholism. Marcel Pagnol describes the central position of "Alcool" in his father's normal school in the Midi. On the walls you saw livers colored a sickening green or purple, herniated aortas, twisted pancreas. Teachers strode forth, he says, anxious to fight the *trinité atroce* of Church, Royalty, . . . and Alcohol.[99] Of course they had read *The Assommoir*, great antialcohol document of the century, if not Pierre Loti's *Mon Frère Yves* (1883) on the ravages of eau-de-vie in Brittany. Yet to eschew the friendly drink was once again to isolate oneself. The pressure was very strong, particularly when the teacher had become somewhat accepted, to have a drink with the boys. Nothing was more socially central to village life. When a teacher did succumb too often, the academy pounced. A schoolmaster at Leuhan (Finistère) was transferred out of the commune in 1912 after twenty-five successful years there just because he was too fond of going to the bar with mayor and municipal council after meetings where he was the secretary. And of course, liquour problems brought other problems to the fore; fights in public, gambling, and indebtedness, all of which sullied a teacher of the Agenais who occupied six posts in just over two years.[100] There were teachers who drank on the sly, usually out of anxiety; generally the younger teachers and *institutrices* were most prone to depression.

At an extreme there was suicide. Take the case of two young *instituteurs* of Ille-et-Vilaine: the first began his career in one of the worst posts of the department, Saint-Colombe, where he was liked but was admonished by his inspector for not doing as much as he could. One morning he was found dead by his wife. He was twenty-eight years old. The second teacher, a twenty-two year old *stagiaire*, was sent from the cantonal capital, Saint-Brice-en-Coglès, to Gosné because he had been frequenting a lady with a somewhat tarnished reputation. After two months in the new post he too was found dead one morning. In neither dossier was there mention of previous physical ailments. Suicide is a logical hypothesis.

In other cases it is explicit. An *institutrice-adjointe* of eighteen years of age, fresh out of normal school, died several months after she began her career at Nozay (Loire-Atlantique) in 1888. She had hung herself. The inspector of the academy conducted his own investigation and found that the head schoolmistress "had been cold and hard with her young novice adjunct teacher as with those who preceded her. She had made her sleep alone in the *rez-de-chaussée*. She had refused to give her *pension* . . . Mlle T . . . [adjunct] was sickly, impressionable." A male adjunct teacher from the Pas-de-Calais commenced teaching in the Finistère in 1882 and was similarly alienated from the beginning. Here, the reasons were his poor knowledge of Breton, the country food ("insufficient for my well-being"), and perhaps also the effect of the climate and of being away from his own "pays." He committed suicide at Pont L'Abbé in 1891 after a mental collapse.[101]

I am, however, loathe to put too much emphasis here on psychological interpretations, given that it is hard even to decipher present-day motives of behavior. It is almost too easy to rest with the intangibles.

For the tangible problems of the village had more than enough influence on teachers. Two central problems were of course unruly children and also one that has been studied or mentioned so many times, the competition of *M. le curé* and his schools. In the West maneuvers like insults in sermons, pressures at catechisms, refusals of absolution were routine; but in no area of the country was the clerical irritant ever absent before 1914.

First communions were a particularly ripe occasion for discrediting the laic school. As communion drew near, the curé's requirements in catechism became stiffer, and by threatening not to pass the child on communion he could bring effective pressure upon parents of laic school-children. One of the teachers I interviewed remembers that as a boy in Plouha, a small town by the sea in the Côtes-du-Nord, he had made the mistake one night of peeking in the door of the schoolhouse at a local republican rally. At the meeting one of the favorite cries was "à bas la calotte" [Down with the priests]. When the curé found out that the boy and two of his friends had heard such unedifying words, he promptly announced that they would be expelled from their first communions, scheduled very soon after that episode. It should be noted that neither the father nor the mother of the future teacher was a practicing Catholic. Yet for them communion was an important social function highlighted by a great meal for relatives from far and near. The father was furious and went straight to the church. He asked the priest whether the boy knew his catechism. When the curé replied in the affirmative, the father told him that unless he allowed his son to take communion he would—and this in all seriousness—push the curé's head into the holy water. Realizing that the man meant what he said, the curé ceded, and the boy took his first communion. Few parents could emulate this example, and when a curé failed their children on communions merely because they were "laïques", as was the case at Plouzané-La Trinité (Finistère) in 1904, they could do little about it.[102]

Unhealthy schools and general conditions promoting exhaustion also contributed to the early deaths of teachers—especially females. All sorts of evidence about dilapidated schools could be adduced, but a general statement, from an article by a teacher of Haute-Loire, sufficiently indicates the situation that often obtained in poor villages, or ones where mayors refused repairs:

> Too often, through windows that don't fit well, through the rotting roofs, through the door that won't close, there penetrates with far too much facility rain, snow, wind; they sometimes call these schools "school-cemeteries", and in effect it is certain that they are extremely dangerous to the health of our masters. . . ."[103]

And such classrooms, it should be noted, could be overcrowded with seventy or eighty children.

Thanks to such conditions, women teachers particularly were susceptible to chest, throat, and lung ailments, to bronchitis and laryngitis. The testimony given by a young girl teaching at La Gallonnière (Ille-et-Vilaine) in the 1880s is repeated by many others in the documents: "My throat has become more swollen and I spit out blood, I can't stop coughing, and my voice gives out on me at every moment."[104] The great scourge of the era was obviously tuberculosis, and what was often diagnosed as bronchitis or laryngitis was really that disease. It was the most feared nemesis of teachers confined in places fertile to the disease. On the subject of tuberculosis, the doctors' letters in the documents supporting leaves for teachers are frequently misleading. One young *institutrice* of Ille-et-Vilaine was chronically ill from 1909 on, and a typical diagnosis was that of the doctor at La Mézière in 1910 who designated her ailment as simply "bronchitis with anemia." Not until 1917 — the reader must carefully thumb through the doctors' letters — was tuberculosis mentioned. The girl died three years later at thirty. A schoolmistress of Puy-de-Dôme had a medical certificate that in 1912 mentioned "bronchitis complicated by cardiopathy". The next year, 1913, she had "cardio-pulmonary congestion," and in that year she died (at thirty-eight years of age).[105]

I do not wish to imply that teachers were the only group which then contracted tuberculosis; witness the ravages the disease made on urban workers. Nevertheless, I reemphasize the critical connection between teachers' conditions of work and the disease. At Campénéac (Morbihan) the *instituteur's* run-down lodging in the prewar decades was scandalous, as the primary inspector of Ploërmel pointed out. Two teachers in a row had died there of tuberculosis, and the new one in 1912 was justifiably fearful for his family and for himself.[106]

Blame for the severity of tuberculosis among teachers must also be directed toward the educational administration itself, for its policy on leaves, vital to teachers who needed to recuperate, was hardhearted. To be brief, the administration did not encourage them. A report of the Minister of Education (J. Chaumié) in 1903 almost implied that teachers demanded leaves for frivolous and unsubstantial reasons: "But during the year we have not ceased recommending to the inspectors and to the prefects that they redouble their surveillance and only accord the leaves in cases of illness that are clearly established." As with pensions, the administration used a panoply of complex laws and regulations to make leaves difficult to obtain or to hold for a long time. Those granted were generally of three kinds: leaves on no pay, on half-pay, and on full pay. Predictably one must show perfectly incontrovertible evidence of grave sickness in order to qualify for full pay. Sometimes teachers with severe pulmonary disorders would have their first leave on their regular salary; but if they fell sick again the next would be on half-pay. Faced with mounting bills, teachers sometimes found it too costly to remain away from work. Tuberculous teachers often taught in dank schoolhouses for years after contracting the disease.[107]

It is astounding how often one finds the administration awarding a leave only when it was too late. For instance, the primary inspector of

Saint-Malo recommended in 1899 that a leave be given to the *institutrice* of Bécherel. The note to the academy was written on 4 April, describing the teacher's ailments as congestive pneumonia and pulmonary emphysema. On 7 April, three days later, she was dead (at thirty-one), with no mention of illness or leaves found in the dossier before the eleventh hour. Inspectors moralized more than they took action; on a teacher of the Agenais: "The master seems very tired out, his voice is without force; yet it seems that his efforts are increased because of his very lack of power."[108] Obviously these efforts in the face of losing odds were partly due to the pressures of the administration itself.

But despite all the difficulties I have mentioned in this chapter, the teachers of the time possessed great self-discipline, indeed cultivated it. And that finally, is what I wish to stress. "One must know how to dominate oneself"; "The master is the example"—these aphorisms really meant something to schoolmasters holding forth before the partly-draped map, a *Tour de France* in their hands. It is easy of course to sentimentalize; but it seems to me that today's reverse Whiggery, making history's progression scarcely more than a vale of tears, can be silly as well. Bergson thought that the sense of religion was inherent: it prevented man from caving in at the sight of himself. With teachers, however, those positive doctrines were learned elements of faith that worked like the real thing. Their acquired capacity for internal resistance to village problems made teachers the *instituteurs de la République*. No problems to overcome, no sainthood.

How then was the teacher an in-betweener and a paradigm for the pre-1914 Republic? First, he symbolized the period in microcosm, poised, as he was, between local and national Frenchness. Instrument of the latter, in the period when according to Weber France really became French for the first time, the teacher yet remembered the soil from whence he had come. When I interviewed a now deceased teacher at Ste-Anne-La-Palud in Brittany I noticed this ambivalence. The man could converse eloquently about universal ideals dating from the Ferry era and to which he still subscribed; but when he brought out a map to make a particular point, I knew he was a Breton through and through. On that map the village of Quéménéven appeared in great bloc letters, and Quéménéven is a hole-in-the-wall! I won't forget that moment, when he hunched over those village names which actually meant something.

The period 1870-1914 was also the great intermediary time in intellectual history when positive morality, having replaced church morality, had yet to be deposed by twentieth century relativism. It was the last period of rural notabilities, of tutelage. The organs of mass diffusion had not yet triumphed; but, given the literacy teachers provided, it was only a matter of time. Then the choices of urban existence would beckon—the choice-agony, we might now say.

Perhaps we don't realize how unsure of itself the pre-World War I Republic actually was. In fact its strength came from rallying against remembered foreign invasion and particularly against contemporary clerical enemies. These enemies helped cement ideals, as the ancient Egyptians became united by expelling the Hyksos. The Republic illustrates my own historical law—you are what you oppose. Without demeaning its positive philosophies, such as positivism itself, we should realize that these were far less clear-cut than they seemed on paper. Even what looks like 100 percent patriotism was actually bought at the price of tension, by the union of opposites. This is what Duneton means when he says that peasants fought in 1914 for national ideals but as rural people. Once complete, the national revolution would make such local patriotism, and perhaps all patriotism, a thing of the past. In our own country it is no accident that sons of immigrants were the most fervent supporters of the American Way of Life.

The Republic, *like* its teachers, was an outsider trying to get inside. Already by 1910 Charles Péguy was taxing the regime for having arrived; its stability was boring. (Needless to say, that stability would appear as a Belle Epoque to a future generation.) But was Péguy's aphorism—"all the mysticism ends up in politics"—ill-considered? Certainly he was correct in assuming, as I think he did, that a solid franc was no guarantee of happiness or longevity. When being fought for, the myth was vital. But all myths degenerate into outworn dogma, and the republican myth began to show its age. As Joseph Schumpeter pointed out back in the 1930s, systems can choke on success.

But our *instituteur de village*, when accepted, did become a notable in every sense of the term, even in reactionary regions. How then was his authority as rural notable diminished after 1918? How did he (and she) eventually become just a teacher, no longer the omniscient counsellor? Besides the evaporation of a clerical menace, one should mention various technological transformations. But certainly a full answer would require a book tracing all the mini-revolutions wrought by machines—something along the lines of Daniel Boorstin's *The Americans: The Democratic Experience*. More succinct is the pertinent anecdote related by Henri Mendras, who understands as well as any scholar the dynamics of rural French history:

> Four or five years ago, on the great square of a little town in the South of France, there was a magnificent cafe which was naturally called the Cafe du Commerce, and this cafe was little by little deserted, particularly by young people. It closed its doors for a year. One wondered: what is going to take its place? And after one year, there opened in place of the Cafe du Commerce a book and stationery store, selling newspapers essentially, magazines and pocket

books. That symbolizes admirably the passage of traditional Midi
civilization, where conversation was the principal social distraction,
to industrial civilization where the individual finds in the press and
mass organs of diffusion, the stereotypes he needs for his inter-
personal relationships.[109]

And it signals the end, Mendras could have added, not only of the
teacher as notable; but ultimately in our time of all rural notables.

Notes

CHAPTER ONE. INTRODUCTION

1. See Joan W. Scott, *The Glassmakers of Carmaux* (Cambridge, Mass., 1974), ch. I; Paul Bois, *Les Paysans de l'Ouest* (Paris, 1971), p. 197; and James R. Lehning, *The Peasants of Marlhes: Economic Development and Family Organization in Nineteenth Century France* (Chapel Hill, N.C., 1980), ch. 1. The hierarchy of peasants, based on amount and mode of land holding, ran from *fermier* down to day laborer.

2. Nonspecialists may consult any reliable history of the French Revolution and Napoleonic eras for the genesis of these hierarchies. The Minister of the Interior in Paris reigned over prefects in their departments (83 in our period), who in turn reigned over sub-prefects in the four or five *arrondissements* (districts) of departments, who in turn were above village mayors. The Ministry of Cults in Paris was often allied with another ministry, such as Education. Subordinate to it were the archbishops and bishops in the regional dioceses, and under them the village priests. The *académie* was a Napoleonic division for education—a large provincial school district. Under the Minister of Education in Paris were the inspectors of the *académies*, then primary inspectors in the *arrondissements*, and then village schoolteachers.

3. *Mon Village* (Paris, 1944). I use the English translation in subsequent chapters.

4. See Chapter 1 of my *Modern France: Mind, Politics, Society* (Seattle, 1980).

5. I use the words *instituteur* and schoolmaster interchangeably here. The term was coined during the French Revolution; *instituteurs* were supposed to "institute" the nation. The female is *institutrice*, school-mistress. I also use the specifically French word "laic" as a rough synonym for "secular."

CHAPTER TWO. PORTRAIT OF THE NINETEENTH-CENTURY RURAL PRIEST

1. See, for example, Edward Gargan, "The Priestly Culture in Modern France," *Catholic Historical Review*, 57 (1971) pp. 1-20; Pierre Pierrard, *Le Prêtre français* (Paris, 1969); and Joseph Brugerette, *Le Prêtre français et la société contemporaine* 2 vols., (Paris, 1935). The revolutionary books to which I refer by Weber and Zeldin are cited below. The diocesan histories are also cited frequently here. A fundamental work by Gabriel Le Bras is *Études de sociologie réligieuse*, 2 vols (Paris, 1956). One of his disciples: Christiane Marcilhacy, *Le Diocèse d'Orléans au milieu du XIXe siècle* (Paris, 1964).

2. Le Bras, *Sociologie religieuse*, II, p. 554. A good review of these writers' attitudes toward priests is in W.H. Williams, "The Priest in History: A Study in Divided Loyalties in the French Lower Clergy from 1776 to 1789" (Ph.D. diss., Duke University, 1965), ch. I. On the period covered by Williams, an excellent monograph is Timothy Tackett, *Priest and Parish in Eighteenth Century France: A Social and Political Study of the Curés in a Diocese of Dauphiné, 1750-1791* (Princeton, 1977).

3. Roger Magraw, "The Conflict in the Villages: Popular Anticlericalism in the Isère (1852-1870)," in Theodore Zeldin, ed., *Conflicts in French Society: Anti-clericalism, Education, and Morals in the Nineteenth Century* (London, 1970), p. 169; Bernard Plongeron, *La Vie quotidienne du clergé français au XVIIIe siècle* (Paris, 1974), p. 133. John McManners also emphasizes the good position of eighteenth century curés, in fine prose: *The French Revolution and the Church* (New York, 1970), p. 12.

4. Eugen Weber, *Peasants into Frenchmen: The Modernization of Rural France, 1870-1914* (Stanford, 1976), ch. II and passim.

5. On the West a nice evocation in Marcel Launay, "Les Procès-verbaux de visites pastorales dans le diocèse de Nantes au milieu du XIXe siècle," *Annales de Bretagne*, 82 (1975), pp. 184-185; Zola cited in Jean Rémy Palanque, ed., *Le Diocèse d'Aix-en-Provence* (Paris, 1975), p. 176.

6. Georges Clemenceau, "La Messe au village," *Figures de Vendée* (Paris, 1930), p. 104.

7. Zeldin discusses these activities in *France, 1848-1945, II: Intellect, Taste, and Anxiety* (Oxford, 1977), 1001; examples cited in Archives diocésaines de Bordeaux, series arranged by parish [hereafter cited as Arch. dioc. Bord.]: Curé of Haux to archbishop of Bordeaux, Dec. 16, 1896; and Archives départementales [hereafter cited as A.D.] Gironde, 1V61: sub-prefect of Lesparre to prefect, Oct. 6, 1900, on priest at Hourtin.

8. A.D. Vendée, 6V3: Bishop of Luçon to Minister of Justice and Cults, April 23, 1846.

9. See Judith Silver, "French Peasant Demands for Popular Leadership in the Vendômois (Loir-et-Cher), 1852-1890," *Journal of Social History*, 14 (1980), p. 279.

10. Curé's answer to archbishop's questionnaire, in Arch. dioc. Bord., Dec. 13, 1865, and various letters in file.

11. Abbé Pierre Brun, *Les Églises de la Gironde* (Bordeaux, 1957) and *Les Églises de Bordeaux* (Bordeaux, 1953); quote, p. 142.

12. Abbé B. Vidal in *La Semaine religieuse de la Lorraine* (Nancy), Sept. 29, 1894. See further discussion in text on the distinctions between "vicar," "desservant," and "curé." One might call a vicar a beginning or "assistant" priest. A "desservant" was a priest fully in charge, but without tenure, and generally ministering to the smaller, less important parishes. But as I make clear in the text the word "curé" was often used for men technically "desservants."

13. A.D. Saône-et-Loire, V40: Mayor of Cartevoix to pref., May 21, 1873; Minister of Interior to pref., June 6, 1873, confirms bishop's transfer.

14. Archives nationales [hereafter cited as A.N.] F^{19}2994: Mayor's deposition on curé of Cénac, Jan. 10, 1869; A.N. F^{19}2652: Extract of deliberation of municipal council of St. Priest, May 10, 1863, sent to bishop.

15. A.D. Gironde, 1V61: Minister of Cults relaying prefectoral recommendation of a priest in Gironde, March 18, 1874. A.N. F^{19}1994: Pref. to Min. Cults, May 26, 1836, on priest at Celles (Dordogne).

16. Pierre Simoni, "Notices nécrologiques et élites locales: l'élite Aptésienne au XIXe siècle," *Annales du Midi*, 87 (1975), p. 88. The article is on *Le Mercure*.

17. Bernard Guillemin, *Le Diocèse de Bordeaux* (Paris, 1974), p. 89; Arsène Thévenot, *Monographie de la commune de Lhuître* (Arcis-sur-Aube, 1903), pp. 316-321.

18. Austin Gough, "The Conflict in Politics: Bishop Pie's Campaign against the Nineteenth Century," in Zeldin, *Conflicts in Morality*, p. 142.

19. On the literary evocation of priests, I have learned from Paul Franche, *Le Prêtre dans le roman français* (Paris, 1902) and Jean Prévost, *Le Prêtre, ce héros de roman* (Paris, 1952).

20. Typical expense accounts for churches are found in A.N. F^{19}1770.

21. A.N. F^{19}4106. Bishop of Belley to Min. Cults, Nov. 23, 1842, on Ain village, then more correspondence; and Pref. of Ardèche, to Min. Cults, May 21, 1872, on Laval d'Aurelle, where no meetings had been held since 1867. Now they will get a new council and chastize the priest; A.N. F^{19}2653: Pref. of Tarn to Min. Cults, Aug. 11, 1843; A.N. F^{19}4106: Pref. of Aveyron to Min. Cults, and Bishop to Min. Cults, Aug. 4, 1857, on Mélac (Aveyron); and many other examples in A.N. F^{19}4106, such as pref. of Aveyron to Min. Cults, Jan. 8, 1854, on a village where water flooded the church through broken windows and nothing was done. The *fumier* example in Arch. dioc. Bordeaux: Treasurer of *fabrique* to vicar general, July 4, 1862.

22. Claude Langlois, *Le Diocèse de Vannes au XIXe siècle, 1800-1830* (Paris, 1974), p. 294; Guy Devailly, *Le Diocèse de Bourges* (Paris, 1973), pp. 76-77, 192; Guillemin, *Diocèse de Bordeaux*, p. 226; Nadine-Josette Chaline, "Le Recrutement du clergé dans le diocèse de Rouen au XIXe siècle," *Revue d'histoire économique et sociale*, 49 (1971), figures on pp. 397, 400, 405. See also Dominique Julia, "La Crise des vocations, essai d'analyse historique," *Les Etudes*, 326 (1967), pp. 250-251, on growing rural character of nineteenth-century clergy compared to the eighteenth century. Also Tackett, *Priest and Parish*, pp. 43-71, on eighteenth-century clergy's origins and recruitment.

23. Devailly, *Diocèse de Bourges*, p. 203.

24. Alain Corbin, *Archaïsme et modernité en Limousin au XIXe siècle, 1845-1880*, II (Paris, 1975), p. 991. Other figures in Jean Delumeau et al., *Histoire*

de la Bretagne (Toulouse, 1969), p. 440; Zeldin, *France, 1848-1945*, II, p. 995. I find the same problem in studies on social origins of students, for example in the otherwise excellent articles of Patrick Harrigan. Langlois notes many "rural" priests from suburbs of big towns and concludes: "Urban parishes include a rural population." *Diocèse de Vannes*, p. 316.

25. Jules Simon, *Premières années* (Paris, 1870), pp. 91-93.

26. Letters and circular in A.N. F^{19}2652: All to Min. Cults: Poitiers, Jan. 15, 1838, Toulouse, Feb. 25, 1835, and Nîmes, March 20, 1835. L'Abbé ***, *La Question de l'inamovibilité canonique* (Paris, 1873), p. 21.

27. Gerard Cholvy, *Géographie religieuse de l'Hérault contemporain* (Paris, 1968), p. 267. For preceding paragraph, *ibid*, pp. 240-260.

28. René Legrand, *Historique de la paroisse de Neuves-Maisons* (Nancy, 1974); quote, p. 27.

29. Arch. dioc. Bord: Letter from inhabitants of Haux to archbishop, Dec. 26, 1862; at Pellegrue, the old priest advised superiors not to replace him with someone too young. In ibid.: Jan. 18, 1866, to vic. gen; and A.D. Ille-et-Vilaine, 1V44: Subpref. of Vitré to pref., Feb. 28, 1842; subpref. of Fougères to pref., Dec. 25, 1840, contains bishop's appraisal; Arch. dioc. Bord.: Curé of Hostens to vic. gen., Dec. 16, 1865, on St. Magne. Literary works on clerical isolation are Alphonse de Lamartine's *Jocelyn* and Hervé Bazin's *Le Blé qui lève*. In Arch. dioc. Bord., the curé of Mouliets, June 2, 1867, to archb. notes that his transfer after twenty-six years near his family will now make him lose "les liens si précieux dans la vie isolée du prêtre."

30. A.D. Cher, 23M103: Pref. to archb., June 29, 1869, and archb. to pref., July 13, 1869; the case was complicated by its involving teacher and mayor against priest; Arch. dioc. Bord.: Statement of vic. gen., June 20, 1864, and letters of protest, e.g., *mère de famille*, July 12, 1863, to mayor's office.

31. Arch. dioc. Bord.: Mayor to archb. Nov. 7, 1869, encloses copy of priest's letter.

32. A.N. F^{19}: Pref. of Dordogne to Min. Cults, April 6, 1844, and bishop's note on transfer. See Marcilhacy on the *esprit de domination*, which "peut apparaître comme la revanche des avanies et des échecs, de ce que nous appellerions aujourd'hui, un complèxe d'infériorité, entrainant les curés dans une sorte de cercle vicieux, car plus ils s'affirment dans ce sens, plus ils nourrissent l'hostilité de leurs ennemis." *Diocèse d'Orléans*, p. 83. Arch. dioc. Bord.: Mayor to archb., May 15, 1860, and many petitions. On one letter from the priest, Sept. 15, 1866, archb. scratches "à déchirer"; collective petition from some councillors of parish and municipality to archb. July 19, 1834, archb. promising the priest's retirement.

33. Arch. dioc. Bord.: New priest at Bleignac to archb: Dec. 19, 1863, and June 4, 1864, thanking him for new post; Clemenceau, "Lavabo," in *Figures de Vendée*, pp. 41-42; A.D. Côtes-du-Nord, T. [*Dossiers par communes*]: Teacher at Loc-Envel to inspector of *académie*, Sept. 28, 1902.

34. Corbin, *Archaïsme et modernité*, I; quote, p. 647; pp. 670-671. Yves-Marie Hilaire, *Une Chrétienté au XIXe siècle? La Vie religieuse des populations du diocèse d'Arras, 1840-1914* (Paris, 1977).

35. A.D. Saône-et-Loire, V42: Copy of Min. Int. report on this priest of St. Serrin, Nov. 18, 1894; A.D. Ille-et-Vilaine 1V45: Subpref. of Fougères to pref., Nov. 12, 1900, (on Baillé) and Archb. to pref., Nov. 30, 1900, on transfer; A.D.Saône-et-Loire, V38; subpref. of Châlons-sur-Saône to pref., Sept. 8, 1862; A.D. Vendée, 5V2: Mayor to pref., July 24, 1866, certified by subpref., and Min. Int. to *conseiller générale*, April 23, 1861.

36. On the problem generally, I have learned much from Yves Raguin, *Celibacy for Our Times* (tr. M.H. Kennedy, St. Meinrad, Ind., n.d.) and best from W. Bassett and P. Huizinga, eds., *Celibacy in the Church* (New York, 1972).

37. A.N. F^{19}2652, a good file on the matter: Ordonnance, Aug. 21, 1814, confirming view of bishop; Min. Cults to bish. of Bourges on a priest of Cher, Feb. 1852; A.N. F^{19}2994: Curé of Beaumont to bish., May 26, 1839; A.N. F^{19}2652: Bish. of Valence to Min. Cults, Feb. 13, 1854; Curé of Crest to same, Sept. 2, 1852; Pref. to same ("confidentielle"), June 30, 1853: Final verdict Min. Cults to bish., Feb. 28, 1854.

38. Plongeron, *Vie quotidienne du clergé français*, p. 139; A.D. Vaucluse, V132: Archb. to pref., Feb. 7, 1863, moves priest involved with servant; A.D. Haute-Vienne, V10: Subpref., Dec. 23, 1860, on painting scandal at Les Salles; A.D. Oise, 1V110: Notices to pref., of Oise, July 2, 1890.

39. A.D. Ille-et-Vilaine, 1V16: Police officer at Rennes, Oct. 24, 1847, report; A.D. Puy-d-Dôme, V0321: Subpref. of Clermont-Ferrand to pref., Nov. 26, 1895, on *vicaire* at Courpière; A.D. Oise, 1V24: *Arrondissement* of Clermont, canton de Breteuil, 1831-1902: Subpref. of Clermont to pref., Oct. 5, 1861, and *commissaire de police* at Breteuil to subpref., Sept. 30, 1861; and A.D. Oise, 1V15: Bish. of Beauvais to pref., Oct. 24, 1859, and various police reports.

40. Gough in Zeldin, *Conflicts in French Society*, p. 143.

41. A.D. Saône et Loire, V41: Report, quoting villagers, by police of railways at Chalons-sur-Saône, June 1, 1904, confirmed by pref.; V38: Police report at Macon, April 4, 1874, and pref. to Min. Int., April 9, 1874.

42. A.D. Vendée, 5V1: *Procureur du roi* at Napoléon to pref., Nov. 1, 1835 (bishop suspiciously silent); and subpref. of Les Sables d'Olonne to pref., May 23, 1836, and petition here; A.D. Vaucluse, V132: *Gendarmerie* of Apt to archb., July 24, 1849, on priest of Beaumettes; A.D. Puy-de-Dôme, V0321: Director, Penitentiary administration of Min. Int. to pref., June 19, 1896; copy of last letter, June 10, 1896; subpref. of Riom to pref., Riom, June 6, 1896, for additional details.

43. Arch. dioc. Bord: Curé of Pellegrue to vic. gen., Jan. 20 and Feb. 22, 1869, on abbé; Lyonnais, and curé of Margueron to archb., Dec. 18, 1863, and archb. to curé, Oct. 24, 1865, on transfer; A.D. Oise, 1V13: Insp. acad. at Paris to insp. acad. at Beauvais, Oct. 13, 1859, sums up evidence (village of Rainvilliers).

44. See "Fontana du village," in Clemenceau's *Figures de Vendée.* Edward Shorter in his articles and *The Making of the Modern Family* (New York, 1975) is, of course, a pioneer here.

45. Weber, *Peasants into Frenchmen*, pp. 26-27; Corbin, *Archaïsme et modernité* II, p. 621.

46. A.D. Vendée, 5V2: Priest of Montchamp to bish. of Luçon, 1842: and curé

of Napoléon to pref., May 2, 1866. I have seen a 150-page letter of complaint from a village *institutrice* to her "father," the inspector at Pontivy (March 1895) in A.D. Morbihan, T1261.

47. The three examples are from Arch. dioc. Bord.: Curé of Mouliets to Archb., Jan. 3, 1863; curé of Créon to archb., 1880's (n.d.); and curé of Montbadon to vic. gen., Aug. 22, 1876.

48. Zeldin *France, 1848-1945*, II, p. 1004.

49. A.N. F^{19}2652: Bish. of Rodez to Min. Cults, March 10, 1835. Bish. of Nantes, Feb. 2, 1835, and bish. of Soissons, April 9, 1835, to same express fears of town influence also.

50. Article on bishop at Machemont (and other villages) in *La Semaine religieuse de Beauvais, Noyon et Senlis*, April 15, 1883.

51. A.N. F^{19}2652: Circular of bishop of Arras, Dec. 10, 1849.

52. Arch. dioc. Bord.: Curé of Rions to archb. of Bordeaux, Feb. 9, 1835.

53. See Tackett, *Priest and Parish*, especially for this, passim.

54. An example, in A.D. Oise, 1V74: Bish. of Beauvais, attestation of July 28, 1849, on "curé-desservants"; A.N. F^{19}2653: Letter dated March 25, 1848, national poll of 1830 cited by Langlois, *Diocèse de Vannes*, pp. 301-302.

55. Xavier de Chalendar, *Les Prêtres* (Paris, 1963), p. 158; Gargan, "Priestly Culture," p. 6, based on Chanoine Boulard's work; Pierrard, *Prêtre français*, p. 116; E.T. Gargan and Robert A. Hanneman, "Recruitment to the Clergy in Nineteenth Century France: 'Modernization and Decline'?", *Journal of Interdisciplinary History*, 9 (Autumn 1978), p. 288. Dioceses like Rouen and Besançon reached peaks of recruitment by 1830; Vannes had done so slightly earlier. See Langlois, *Diocèse de Vannes*, pp. 299-300.

56. Some typical letters in F^{19}2652.

57. The Allignol book (Paris, 1839) is also discussed in Gargan, "Priestly Culture," pp. 5-6; quote from abbé Joseph Dupont in Pierrard, *Prêtre français*, p. 105.

58. Abbé * * * *Question de l'inamovibilté*, p. 14.

59. A good file on this: *Fonds d'évêché* in A.D. Oise, 2V89: Binage 1861-1866.

60. A.D. Oise (*fonds d'évêché*), 2V92: Various letters and press extracts.

61. Harry W. Paul, "In Quest of Kerygma," *American Historical Review*, 75 (1969), pp. 387-423; Gordon Wright, *France in Modern Times* (Chicago, 1974), p. 327.

62. Gargan, "Priestly Culture," p. 15, on this.

63. One such testimony, admittedly in the West: A.D. Vendée, 6V3: *Garde des sceaux* for Min. Justice and Cults, report June 20, 1839, on Vendean priest: "Physicien, Homme de génie . . . inventeur de plusieurs machines utiles."

64. Zeldin, *France, 1848-1945*, II, p. 995; see also vintage Robert Palmer: *Catholics and Unbelievers in Eighteenth Century France* (Princeton, 1939), arguing a kind of Catholic enlightenment. Priests did have the tithe and other means of becoming cultured "aristocrats." One near Sennely bought his fine wine in Orléans, had fine silver and crystal, and many books. Gérard Bouchard, *Le Village immobile* (Paris, 1972), p. 244.

66. E.g., pref. of Cher, 1830 in ibid., p. 179; Weber, *Peasants into Frenchmen*, p. 364.

67. Pierrard, *Prêtre français*, pp. 97-98, is good on this.

68. See Chesterton's religious collection, *The Well and The Shadows* (London, 1935).

69. Gargan ("The Priestly Culture") summarizes the important work of Gaspard Latty, *Le Clergé français* (Paris, 1890); also, Gargan, p. 18.

70. Thanks to the curé of Ars there is still no dancing in that parish. Weber, *Peasants into Frenchmen*, p. 369.

71. On Lémire, Jean-Marie Mayeur, *Un Prêtre démocrate: L'Abbé Lémire, 1853-1928* (Paris, 1968); for next man, born in the country (1867-1955), article in *La Nouvelle République*, Jan. 14, 1977.

72. A.N. F^{19}5956 (Ardennes): Archb. of Reims to Min. Cults, July 24, 1888; A.D. Saône-et-Loire, V15: Bish. to pref., Jan. 10, 1893; A.N. F^{19}2653 (Vaucluse): Pref. to Min. Int., citing archb.'s letter, May 7, 1879.

73. A.N. F^{19}5955 (Ardèche): Mayor of Fabras to Min. Int., April 25, 1895, on no curé.

74. In Pierrard, passim, and Weber, *Peasants into Frenchmen*, p. 37; Pierre Barral, *Le Département de l'Isère sous la IIIe République, 1870-1940* (Paris, 1962), pp. 245-46.

75. Zeldin, *France, 1848-1945*, II, p. 1002.

76. In the diocese of Montpellier, ordinations tumbled under the Empire, so that in 1806 28 percent of the clergy were over sixty years of age; in the diocese of Bourges, 1820, about half the clergy was over sixty. *Devailly, Diocèse de Bourges*, p. 93; Gérard Cholvy, *Le Diocèse de Montpellier* (Paris, 1976), p. 203; Launay, in *Annales de Bretagne*, pp. 189-190; Palanque, *Diocèse d'Aix*, p. 202, 205; Chalendar, *Les Prêtres*, pp. 147-148: In 1901, there were 1733 ordinations, in 1914, 704.

77. Weber, *Peasants into Frenchmen*, p. 357.

78. Arch. dioc. Bord.: Priest of Montgauzy, to archb.; July 2, 1865. Weber, *Peasants into Frenchmen*, pp. 358-359; Langlois, *Diocèse de Vannes*, p. 355.

79. A.D. Saône-et-Loire, V41: Subpref. of Autun to pref., June 14, 1872, on Abbé du Four.

80. Letters in Guy de Pierrefeu, *Le Clergé fin-de-siècle* (Paris, n.d.), pp. 173, 177.

81. A.N. F^{19}6002: President of council of Espère to pref., Dec. 20, 1893. Pref. to Min. Int. (Feb. 11, 1894) agrees, with bishop, to hold new elections. Second case in ibid.: subpref. of Figeac to pref., Sept. 30, 1895. Independence was also little condoned by the Republic's government, who set the tone. For uttering a few words against the Republic, a priest paid a sixteen franc fine: *Lyon Républicain*, Aug. 7, 1877; third series: Arch. dioc. Bord., examples: Head of *fabrique* of Mauriac complains to vic. gen., Jan. 27, 1883, on lack of money; new curé of Rauzan to vic. gen., Dec. 25, 1902, on fights with *fabrique* and inherited debts; Thévenot, *Lhuître*, pp. 239-240.

82. Jacques Ozouf, *Nous les maîtres d'école: Autobiographies d'instituteurs de la Belle Époque* (Paris, 1967), p. 7.

83. Examples in A.N. F^{19}6002; Bish. of Cahors to pref. alludes to the problem, April 13, 1887.

84. France Duclos, "L'Opinion publique en Vendée devant la Séparation des Églises et de l'État" (masters thesis, University of Nantes 1974-1975), p. 15.

85. A.D. Ille-et-Vilaine, 5M [unclassed]: Subpref. of St. Malo, to pref., June 12, 1888, and catechisms in bundle.

86. A.D. Ille-et-Vilaine, 1V45: Mayor of Bléruais to pref., May 20, 1895, and archb. of Rennes to pref., July 15, 1895; petition, March 1894, to archb.; and subpref. of Fougères to pref., Nov. 19, 1901, notes persistence of problem.

87. A.D. Ille-et-Vilaine, IV8: Inhabitant of Mézières to pref., July 14, 1890.

88. Françoise Pastureaud, "Alphabétisation, culture, moeurs et croyances populaires: Le Marais de Monts, Saint-Jean-de-Monts, 1796-1903" (masters thesis, Ecole Pratique des Hautes Etudes, 1975), pp. 44-60 especially.

89. Quoted in Tony Judt, *Socialism in Provence, 1871-1914: A Study in the Origins of The Modern French Left* (Cambridge, 1979), p. 179; Gérard Cholvy, "Religion et société au 19e siècle: Le Diocèse de Montpellier," *Information historique*, 35 (1973), p. 230; Evelyn B. Ackerman, "Alternative to Rural Exodus: The Development of the Commune of Bonnières-sur-Seine in the Nineteenth Century," *French Historical Studies*, 10 (1977), p. 142. See also her full-length monograph, *Village on the Seine: Tradition and Change in Bonnières, 1815-1914* (Ithaca, NY 1978).

90. See the essays in Michel Bée, et al., *Mentalités religieuses dans la France de l' ouest au XIXe et XXe siècles* (Caen, 1976), especially the last half of Gabriel Désert's chapter on the Beauvaisie.

91. Pierrard, *Le Prêtre français*, p. 127, and his *Juifs et catholiques français* (Paris, 1970).

92. Interview with Mme Adam, Victoria, various sessions, 1980.

CHAPTER THREE. PORTRAIT OF THE NINETEENTH-CENTURY RURAL MAYOR

1. Louis Girard, in *Histoire de l'administration française depuis 1800: Problèmes et méthodes* (Paris, 1975), p. 13.

2. For the parental sense of being responsible for the village see Charles Schmitt, *Le Maire de la commune rurale* (Paris, 1959), pp. 30-31; on nobles, André Siegfried, *Tableau politique de la France de l'ouest sous la IIIe République* (Paris, 1913), p. 136; on importance of *mairie*, Jean Fonteneau, *Le Conseil municipal; lemaire—les adjoints* (Paris, 1964), pp. 131-133.

3. André Nègre, *St. Eulalile aux Bois* (Caen, 1970), p. 292. At Dommérat, visited by Daniel Halévy, the mayor's place was one of the best: excerpt in David Thompson, *France: Empire and Republic, 1850-1944* (New York, 1968), p. 129. In Thabault's village, 1905, the mayor's house was "beyond compare." Roger Thabault, *Education and Change in a Village Community: Mazières-en-Gâtine, 1848-1914* (tr. Peter Treagear; New York, 1971), p. 166.

4. Weber, *Peasants into Frenchmen*, p. 539, on mayor of a village in Hautes-

Alpes; Village of Décines (Isère) in Barral, *Département de l'Isère*, p. 524; A.N.F
bII Oise: Pref. of Oise to Min. Int., July 8, 1873; A.D. Haute-Garonne, 1M45.
Justice of peace at Villemur to pref., June 30, 1853, on mayor of Mirepoix; and
Thabault, *Mazières-en-Gâtine*, p. 32.

    5. Clemenceau, "Six-Sous", *Figures de Vendée*, p. 117.

    6. On bread and circuses see A.D. Lot-et-Garonne, M300: E.g., mayor of
Sauvaganas to pref., Aug. 16, 1859, distributing 150 kgs. of bread; or mayor of
Béagan to pref., Aug. 17, 1856, giving a large banquet for notables.

    7. Weber, *Peasants into Frenchmen*, p. 473, for one good example of mayor
reading newspaper to villagers, and ch. 27 on paucity of newspapers; mayor
petitions for school gratuity in the case of a policeman's widow's son: A.D. Gironde
O Loupiac: insp. acad. to pref., Dec. 23, 1854, on mayor's petition; and see Weber
on pork barrel, p. 539.

    8. I have culled many examples of mayors being difficult with Breton teachers.
For example, the mayor of Taupont (Morbihan) repeatedly dodging the teacher's
plea for wood in the winter of 1908. The stove was out of order, filling the classroom
with smoke. See my doctoral dissertation, "Pillar of the Republic" (University of
Washington, 1971), p. 98. Documents on workers cheated or put off by mayors in
A.D. Haute-Garonne, 1M63.

    9. Marcel Laurent, *Deux Communes: Vinzelles et Charnat* (Clermont-Ferrand,
1976), p. 101; Thévenot, *Lhuitre*, p. 208.

    10. Laurent, *Deux Communes*, p. 87; Edgar Morin, *The Red and White:
Report from a French Village* (tr. A.M. Sheridan Smith; New York, 1970), p. 168,
and André Burguière, *Bretons de Plozévet* (Paris, 1975), p. 46; A.D. Oise 301
[Communal archives of Bouillancy, *régistres des affaires*, 1808-1848]. The Courtiers
were sole judges in a variety of violent and/or sexual affairs. In Lhuître, some five
families dominated the *mairie* for over a century. They not only intermarried with
each other, but with branches of their *own* family. Thévenot, *Lhuître*, pp. 51-52.

    11. Judt, *Socialism in Provence*, p. 206; A.N.F¹611 Gironde 1870-1884: Pref. to
Min. Int., Feb. 14, 1874; Evelyn Ackerman, "Development of Bonnières-sur-Seine
in the Nineteenth Century," quote on p. 134.

    12. Henri Marc, *Histoire de Chenôve* (Dijon, 1893), p. 257; A.D. Lot, 3M72:
Document of 1874.

    13. A.D. Gironde, 3M503: Report of Aug. 2, 1840, on Lesparre; André-Jean
Tudesq, "L'Administration municipale dans le Sud-Ouest sous la monarchie de
juillet," *Annales du Midi*, 84 (1972), p. 485; A.D. Puy-de-Dôme, M01553: Ambert
(report on communes under 3,000, 1852) and M01548, Clermont 1837.

    14. Jean Vidalenc, *La Société française de 1815 à 1848* (Paris, 1970), I, p. 115;
Irène Délupy, "Pouvoir municipal et notables à Gruissan, village du littoral languedocien", *Études rurales*, 65 (Jan.-March 1977), pp. 71-75.

    15. A.D. Puy-de-Dôme, M01548: Subpref. of Riom, proposals for mayor and
assistant mayors, form containing income figures.

    16. A.D. Puy-de-Dôme, M01555: 1837 document and 1878, subpref. of Riom,
propositions; A.D. Gironde, 3M503: Lesparre document, Aug. 2, 1840; A.N.F¹611
Moselle: État des mutations for mayors; A.N.F¹bII Oise, *arrondissement* of
Beauvais: 1833 and 1871 document (*revenus annuels*); A.D. Lot, 3M72 [États
renseignements maires et adjoints, prefect's document 1874].

17. A.D. Gironde, 3M503: Pref.'s recommendation form: justice of peace at Créon, Dec. 11, 1835, on mayor for Carignan; A.N.F^{1}bII Oise: Pref. to Min. Int., July 8, 1873.

18. Tudesq. "Administration municipale," p. 486.

19. A.D. Gironde, 3M503: Chart of subpref. of La Réole, Sept. 28, 1870; A.N.F^{1}bII, Oise: Arrondissement of Beauvais, 1871 document given above; A.D. Puy-de-Dôme M0154: Subpref., 1837; and M01555, 1878: documents given above (latter with confusing categories like "propriétaires-marchands de bestiaux").

20. A.N.F^{1}bII Oise[11]: Prefectoral document on municipal councillors and mayors, Nov. 8, 1831, Clermont; prefect. doc. Nov. 17, 1848. On this one we have a veterinarian, an artist, a miller, a butcher, and a grocer all representing the lower-middle class.

21. Bibliothèque Nationale, Fonds Maçonniques, with details on occupations, a fine source for study.

22. For example, A.N.F^{1}bII Morb: Pref.'s form, 1826, on captain of a frigate re-elected at Languidic, income of 12,000 francs, Min. Int. note, June 24, 1823, on a man important in flax supply trade, retained despite complaints at Locminé.

23. Tudesq, "Administration municipale," p. 485; A.D. Puy-de-Dôme, M01555: 1855, document; an example of poor literacy in A.D. Gironde, 3M503: Mayor, St. Savin to pref., 1840, "j'ai lonneur de vous ecrire confidenciellement consernant nost elections . . .", typical of many. In poor departments like Lozère, prefects complained steadily about semi-illiterate mayors. See Bernard le Clère and Vincent Wright, Les Préfets du Second Empire (Paris, 1973), pp. 143-144.

24. More incompetents were probably found earlier in the century, such as a bumpkin mayor at Tangais (Ille-et-Vilaine), "un homme sans conduite, et qui se montre souvent ivre en public. . . ." A.D. Ille-et-Vilaine, 1V13: Subpref. of Mont-fort to pref., July 23, 1816; the document on marriage is in A.N.F^{1}bII Oise. In same file a prefectoral document of May 11, 1871, says that the mayor for Clermont is "un de ces espirts tempérés comme on en rencontre dans tout ce pays. . . ."; and A.D. Oise, M [unclassed]: elections in cantons. Prefectoral form of 1860 for Fériquières. A description of one mayor in A.D. Puy-de-Dôme. M01555: "Vieux maire dévoué, honnête" (Riom, 1855). Another factor worth noting is that older mayors had a developed relationship with prefects. In some departments they came regularly to the prefecture. At Cahors, mayors could come any day, while the general public could only visit from 2 to 4 p.m. Wednesday and Saturday (market day). And to be received at the prefecture was "a kind of consecration." See Bernard Le Clère, "La Vie quotidienne des préfets au XIXe siècle (1815-1914)," in Jacques Aubert et al., Les Préfets en France (1800-1940) (Geneva, 1978), pp. 49, 93.

25. A.D. Puy-de-Dôme, M01555: arrondisement of Riom, proposed candidates; A.D. Haute-Garonne, 1M47: Subpref. of St. Gaudens to pref., March 23, 1854, on mayor at Montespan.

26. A.D. Cher, 23M89: Mayor of Fussy to pref., Nov. 23, 1860; mayor of Allogry to pref., Oct. 10, 1862; municipal concillors of St. Thorette, March 1, 1862, after mayor's death (unanimous in support of his choice); mayor of Genouilly to pref., March 1, 1863; mayor of Arçay to pref., June 11, 1863.

27. A good bundle of justice's early lists in A.D. Oise, M [unclassed]: cantonal lists for elections of mayors and asst. mayors; A.D. Cher, 23M89: Judge at Mehun-sur-Yèvre, to pref., March 20, 1864, on man up for St. Laurent, and *Commissaire de police cantonale* of Bourges to pref., April 28, 1861.

28. A.D. Cher, 23M103: Subpref. of St. Amand to pref., Aug. 18, 1865, on Chaumont; A.D. Haute-Garonne, 1M45: Subpref. of Toulouse to pref., Aug. 10, 1854, on Baux; justice peace at Grandvilliers to pref., Aug. 8, 1866, in A.D. Oise, M. [unclassed]: elections of mayors and asst. mayors; and justice of the peace at Grandvilliers to pref., Aug. 28, 1860, on Beaudéduit; A.D. Cher, 23M103: Subpref. of St. Amand to pref., Aug. 7, 1868; and A.N.F. bII Cher 13: Pref.'s report on St. Saturnin, April 17, 1875.

29. Judith Silver, "French Rural Response to Modernization: The Vendômois, 1852-1885" (Ph.D. diss., University of Michigan, 1973), pp. 134-136.

30. Laurent, *Deux communes*, p. 92; several examples in Theodore Zeldin, *The Political System of Napoleon III* (London, 1958); and see Alain Morel, "Pouvoirs et idéologies au sein du village Picard hier et aujourd'hui," *Annales: économies-sociétés-civilisations*, 30 (1975), p. 172, on mayors as "véhicule des informations."

31. Zeldin's *Political System of Napoleon III* is fundamental for the Second Empire; see also Sherman Kent's *French Electoral Procedure under the July Monarchy* (New Haven, 1937). Even in the 1820's the prefect of Lot sent out a weekly house organ to all his mayors, asking support of progovernment candidates in the national election: Sherman Kent, *The Election of 1827 in France* (Cambridge, Mass., 1975), pp. 138-139. Silver, "French Rural Response," p. 121 (on Morée) and p. 90, substantiating the views of Sanford Elwitt in his general study of the Third Republic.

32. A.D. Haute-Garonne, 1M47: Complaints to subpref. of St. Gaudens in Feb. of 1855; A.D. Puy-de-Dôme, M01513 (Clermont Ferrand) has a thick dossier on free drinks and other corruption in a mayoral election at Gergovie, June 1900 (letters from wine brokers, cafe owners, etc.); mayor threatens *cantonnier* and gets a pension for a blind man in return for votes at a village of Lot (illegible) in A.D. Lot, 5M36 (various anonymous letters); another puts his imprisoned brother on list and another pressures field guard: A.N.F¹bII Meurthe-et-Moselle: Min. Int. to pref., Jan. 2, 1880, on mayor of Clazeures, and *Indépendance de l'Est*, Nov. 29, 1873, on mayor of Foughas. These are a few of many possible examples; Kent's first book, *French Electoral Procedure*, is also full of them. See also Eugen Weber, "Comment la Politique vint aux Paysans: A Second Look at Peasant Politicization," *American Historical Review*, 87 (April, 1982), pp. 383-84. This is Weber's most recent rejoinder — and an excellent one — to the theses of Charles Tilly and Ted Margadant on peasant politicization (noted also in my treatment). The article came too late to have a great influence on my own research or ideas.

33. A.D. Puy-de-Dôme, M01546: Case 1: Subpref. of Issoire to pref., April 11, 1860, on reprimand, but cannot yet dismiss him; case 2 (thick file): subpref. of Issoire to pref., Aug. 1, 1860 (Anzat-le-Lugnet), and numerous petitions from notables, but prefecture protects him.

34. A.D. Puy-de-Dôme, series 0, 0171: Mayor of Arlane to pref., Sept. 19, 1829, and prefect's *arrêtés* Oct. 9, 1829 on sentence.

35. *Ibid.: Percepteur* to pref., June 31, 1852, on mayor at Latour, 1831-1848; and *percepteur* of Sauxillanges to pref., May 10, 1850, exhaustive report on mayor at Lamontigie; on roads and "selling favors," A.N.F^{1}b Oise 11: Pref. to Min. Int. Feb. 21, 1830, calls it "disorders," investigations; see also A.D. Puy-de-Dôme, Series O, 0171. E.g. *agent-voyer* of Sauxillanges to subpref. of Issoire, May 8, 1851, on one mayor; *agent voyer* at Thiers to subpref. of Thiers, Dec. 21, 1850, on mayor of Pasliers.

36. A.D. Haute-Garonne, 1M47: Subpref. of St. Gaudens to pref., Sept. 14, 1854, proposes revocation; pref. to Min. Int. Sept. 25, 1854, executes it, on mayor of Poulat-Taillebourg.

37. For examples of the first type, A.D. Haute-Garonne, 1M47: Mayor of Mazières (pref.'s *arrêté*, Oct. 20, 1854) and Mayor of Montsaunes (pref.'s *arrêté*, Nov. 3, 1854) on violence; subpref. of St. Gaudens to pref., Feb. 14, 1855, on mayor and priest at Martres-de-Rivières; money troubles: See for example, subpref. of St. Gaudens to pref., June (?) 1854, on mayor of Signat and A.N.F^{1}bII Moselle: Pref. to Min. Int., April 28, 1855, getting rid of a mayor—"sa position ne lui laissait pas assez d'indépendance."

38. A.D. Gironde, 3M76: Justice of peace at St. André de Lubzac, on cantonal form, 1825 (no village given); A.N.F^{1}bII Oise: Min. Int. note, Sept. 4, 1825, on mayor of Canny (Oise); A.D. Puy-de-Dôme, M01546: *Commissaire de police* at Rochefort to *commissaire centrale*, Dec. 6, 1852, on mayor of Vernines; A.N.F^{1}bII Meurthe-et-Moselle (Communes A-F); Pref. to Min. Int., June 11, 1874 (asst. mayor of Auden-le-Roman.

39. See John M. Merriman, *The Agony of the Republic: The Repression of the Left in Revolutionary France, 1848-1885* (New Haven, 1978), pp. 107-113. The phrase "hecatomb of mayors" is cited by Eugen Weber in "The Second Republic, Politics, and the Peasant," *French Historical Studies*, 11 (Fall, 1980), p. 525.

40. Haute-Garonne, A.D. 1M47: subpref. of St. Gaudens to pref., June 22, 1855, and pref. to subpref., July 3, 1855, on St. Loup; A.N.F^{1}bII Meurthe-et-Moselle: pref. to Min. Int., Feb. 26, 1883, and councillors' petitions. A.N.F^{1}bII, Moselle: Pref. to Min. Int., Feb. 15, 1844, and Dec. 19, 1851.

41. A.D. Lot, 3M85: Min. Int. report, Feb. 4, 1886, on mayor of Meilhac; Min. Int. note, Sept. 8, on mayor, Peyrilles; Min. Int. note, Feb. 28, on Puy L'Evêque; electoral poster incident at Vaillac: Min. Int. note, Feb. 24, 1873; Min. Int., May 1, 1888, on mayor of Léobard and Dec. 2 on unspecified mayor; mayor of Aynac (Toulouse-Lautrec), April 5, 1906, Min. Int. note.

42. A.D. Lot, 3M85: On mayor of Terron (quote), subpref. of Figeac to pref., July 7, 1900 (prefect approves); on mayor of Cabrerets, Min. Int. reports Aug. 14 and 18, 1897; on mayor of Pruybrun, subpref. of Figeac to pref., Sept. 5, 1907, and Min. Int. to pref. April 4, 1908. I have gone into the Cahors file deeply, partly to avoid the charge of impressionism. In this file I saw *all* the cases of suspension and revocation and then took down typical examples and assigned weightings to them, rather than take a few examples from each part of the country. It was an unusually complete file. A national file on revocations earlier in the century is A.N. C977, well-analyzed by Merriman in *Agony of the Republic*.

43. Jack Hayward, *The One and Indivisible French Republic* (New York, 1973),

pp. 30-31; Bertrand Hervieu, "Le Pouvoir au village," *Études rurales*, 63-64 (1976), p. 40.

44. Claude Mesliand, "Gauche et droite dans les campagnes provençales sous la IIIe République," *Études rurales*, 63-64 (1976), p. 216; A.D. Cher, 23M189. Ballots from La Celle-Condé, May 1888.

45. In André Negre's Saint-Eulalie, the oldest councillor in 1843 was forty-three, whereas the mayor was already an old hand. (Negre, *St. Eulalie*, p. 270.) Another village historian notes, "les vieux restaient les maîtres jusqu'à leur mort. Les fils travaillaient docilement en domestiques." Pierre Manse, *Mérileu de mon enfance: La Vie quotidienne dans un village des Pyrénées au début du siècle* (Pau, 1971), p. 27.

46. A.D. Puy-de-Dôme, M01546. Petitions Sept. 30, 1861, and Feb. 21, 1863, by councillors of Gerzat to pref.; they added that the mayor spend a lot of time on a property far from the village. Case two: Ibid.: Min. of Int. to pref., April 3, 1862, on protests at Bromont-Lamothe; pref. sacks mayor. Case three: A.D. Cher, 23M89: Pref. to mayor of Cerbois, Nov. 20, 1861; light reprimand. A councillor, resigning, wrote the pref., Dec. 29, 1863: "M. le Prefet il est pas possible de vous relaté tant de choses qu'il se passe dans la commune, il arrive à toutes les Reunions le maire convoque à une heures, le maire vient deux heures a pres. . . ."

47. A.D. Lot, 3M84: Six Councillors of Caillac to pref., July 23, 1893, and Min. Int. note Oct. 31. (At Lumery in Cher, a mayor, according to the Minister of Interior "oppose une force d'inertie invincible" against councillors on all affairs; but he is not dismissed: A.D. Cher, 23M103, Min. Int. to pref., April 14, 1869.) Last cases: A.D. Lot, 3M84: subpref. of Figeac to pref., June 28, 1896; subpref. of Gourdon to pref., Sept. 15, 1892, on councillors of Meilhac. See also le Clère and Wright, *Les Préfets*, p. 144, for difficulty of getting rid of mayor.

48. A.D. Haute-Garonne, 1M45: Mayor of Laréole to pref., May 1855: pref. to mayor, June 4; subpref. of Toulouse to pref., Dec. 5, 1854, on dismissal of mayor at Puissegur.

49. Ministry of Interior police document, June 2, 1869, on sentence in A.D. Cher, 23M103; A.D. Puy-de-Dôme, series O [*versement inconnue*]. Deputy to pref., June 21, 1910, and *conseiller générale* investigation, June 19, 1910, on Mezel.

50. Excellently noted in Claude Karnoouh, "La Démocratie impossible: Parenté et politique dans un village lorrain," *Études rurales*, 52 (1973), pp. 24-56. See for comparison my "Oregon's Nineteenth Century Notables: Simeon Gannett Reed and Thomas Lamb Eliot," in Edwin Bingham and Glen Love ed., *Northwest Perspectives* (Seattle, 1978).

51. A.D. Gironde, 3M503: subpref. of Libourne to pref., Aug. 17, 1840. In the same file, a petition of 75 notables backing one man for mayor (to pref., Aug. 31, 1846). A.D. Puy-de-Dôme, M01515: subpref. of Ambert to pref., July 6, 1855, on Moersac and environs.

52. A.D. Haute-Garonne, 1M45 (among many examples there): asst. mayor of St. Cézert to pref., Jan. 5, 1853; second case (among many) in A.D., Haute-Garonne, 1M634: subpref. of Loudens to pref., March 1, 1909, with complaints on Cier-de-Luchon.

53. A.D. Oise, M. [communal file Beaudéduit]: salient letters among many:

mayor to pref., Feb. 28, 1821; petition for schoolmaster against mayor to pref., March 21, 1825; Dec. 5, 1839, another mayor's letter of resignation to pref. (with quote); other resignations to pref., March 17, 1852 and Jan. 22, 1855; justice of peace at Grandvilliers to pref., July 12, 1859.

54. Posters in large file on village of Sancoins, 1883, in A.N.F.[1] bII Cher 13 (St. L-San.). Pref. supports mayor. One also sees replies by mayors in local newspapers, e.g., mayor of St. Emilion in *L'Union républicaine* (Libourne) Oct. 21, 1880, on electoral conduct.

55. Paul Leuilliot, *L'Alsace au début du XIXe siècle*, I (Paris, 1959), p. 514.

56. A.D. Lot-et-Garonne, M300: Quotes: asst. mayor of Carmont to pref., Aug. 16, 1859; mayor of Larrigue to pref., Aug. 18, 1860; mayor of Labretonie to pref., Aug. 16.

57. A.D. Gironde, O-Loupiac: Mayor of Loupiac to pref., Oct. 11, 1870, extensive correspondence on repairs through 1880s; *La Tribune*, Aug. 27, 1871, attacks mayor; Budos on Bonapartism and file in A.N.F[1]b11 Gironde (1870-1884). This kind of detail may point to the 1850s as a period of peasant politicization. Charles Tilly, among others, points to the earlier rural upsurge of 1848. Tilly, "Did the Cake of Custom Break?" in J.M. Merriman ed., *Consciousness and Class Experience in Nineteenth Century Europe* (New York, 1979), p. 19. So does Philippe Vigier in *La Seconde République dans la région alpine*, 2 vols. (Paris, 1963).

58. Hayward, *One and Indivisible: The French Republic*, p. 30.

59. A.N.F[1]bII Cher 13: Pref. to Min. Int., Oct. 31, 1828, on Scincergues; John Merriman, "The Demoiselles of the Ariège, 1829-1831," in Merriman, ed., *1830 in France* (New York, 1975), pp. 98, 102, and Weber, *Peasants into Frenchmen*, on Pyrenees, pp. 59-60; Ted W. Margadant, *French Peasants in Revolt: The Insurrection of 1851* (Princeton, 1979), pp. 197-198; Thabault, *Mazières-en-Gatîne*, pp. 49-50; and Guy Bechtel, *1907: La Grande Révolte du Midi* (Paris, 1976), p. 147. (Mayors and councils resigned.)

60. For draft, Weber, *Peasants into Frenchmen*, pp. 57, 293; for protest at prefecture, Silver, "French Rural Response," pp. 141 and 170. Cf. Denis Brogan on village concreteness during Third Republic: "In most of the small towns and rural regions of France, you voted for or against the parish priest, for or against the local landlord." Brogan, *France under the Republic: The Development of Modern France, 1870-1939* (New York, 1940), p. 585.

61. Thabault, *Mazières-en-Gatîne*, pp. 75-80, 84, 97, 123, 166; Weber, *Peasants into Frenchmen*, quote p. 148 on mayor of 1850; Silver, "French Rural Response," on mayor of Aze, 1873, petitioning for wool and livestock fair, p. 102 (and passim); on epidemics: mayor of Civres-les-Mello to Min. Int., March 1830, complains of bankruptcy brought on partly by severe epidemic of 1821 when he had distributed funds: in A.N.F[1]bII Oise 11. (He received no money from the government.)

62. A.D. Gironde O-Lussac. *Inspecteur-voyer* of Lussac to pref., 1829 (n.d.); Silver, "French Rural Response," pp. 117-118, commune of Choué at the mid-century.

63. Examples in Maurice Agulhon, *La République au village* (Paris, 1972), pp. 248-249 (cemetery of Brignoles); Pierre Simoni, "Notices nécrologiques et élites locales: l'élite Aptésienne an XIXe Siecle," p. 92; Marc, *Histoire de Chenôve*, p.

257; Weber, *Peasants into Frenchmen*, p. 474; and François Escoube, *Mehun-sur-Yevres: des origines à 1914* (Bourges, 1973), p. 138 (on place name at market).

64. Jean Vidalenc, *Le Départment de l' Eure sous la monarchie constitutionelle* (Paris, 1968), pp. 213, 236.

65. Barral, *Le Département de l'Isère*, p. 518; André-Jean Tudesq, *Les Grands Notables en France (1840-1849)*, II, (Paris, 1964), p. 968; and Silver, "French Rural Response," p. 117-118, again noting earlier local politicization than does Weber (but for a fairly advanced department).

66. Laure Moulin, *Jean Moulin* (Paris, 1969), quote from a Moulin letter of 1930, p. 101; A.N.F¹bII Meurthe-et-Moselle: prefectoral charts 1878 and 1882 on mayor at De Gaulle's Colombey; Pierre-Jakez Hélias, *The Horse of Pride: Life in a Breton Village* (tr. June Guicharnaud; New Haven: Yale University Press, 1978), p. 135.

67. Vidalenc, *Département de l' Eure*, pp. 369, 284. He also cites great fears of the restoration of pre-1789 feudalism there. Thabault, *Mazières-en-Gâtine*, p. 34; Delumeau, *Histoire de la Bretagne*, p. 482.

68. R.H. Hubscher's article cited in Weber, *Peasants into Frenchmen*, p. 265.

69. Extremely thick correspondence on roads in A.D. Gironde, O-Lussac (4) and O-Queyrac (2). In latter: subpref. of Lesparre to pref. Jan. 13, 1872, on resignation of *garde-champêtre*, in office since 1853. To gauge time spent on road problems in councils, I have used communal archives: for example, registers in A.D. Oise ID17-3B1, *archives communales* of Bouillancy: from 1830s to end of century.

70. Last quote in A.D. Gironde, O-Loupiac (3), Mayor's declaration, July 31, 1884. A good communal file is A.D. Oise, 1M1, *archives communales* of Ivry-le-Temple; Construction of a boy's school and lodging for teacher, 1878-1880. My dissertation has much detail on school-building, lodgings, and the problems they entailed.

71. A good file is A.D. Gironde, O-Loussac, which has 700-odd slips of paper dealing with the problem of where one school should be built. Sharecroppers, vigorously opposed to any school, seem to have been pressured by nobles.

72. A.D. Lot, 3M86: Mayor of La Bastit to pref. of Lot, April 17, 1911. Subpref. of Gourdon to pref., April 26, 1911; A.D. Oise, 1D11 (Chaumont-en-Vexin). Deliberation of council, Feb. 11, 1898, and others; Y. Déret, *Dompierre-sur-Bèsbres* (Moulins, 1965), p. 257 on 1832.

73. A.D. Lot 3M86: Mayor of St. Clair to subpref. of Gourdon, Dec. 3, 1885; subpref. of Cahors accepts, Dec. 14, 1885.

74. Laurent, *Deux Communes*, p. 8.

75. A.N.F¹bII Gironde: Pref. to Min. Int., Jan. 22 and 29, 1874; Thabault, *Mazières-en-Gâtine*, p. 110; and A.N.F¹bII Oise: prefect's document of Jan. 28, 1874.

76. A.N.F¹bII, Oise (*arrondissement* of Beauvais): pref.'s form of 1881.

77. Tudesq, *Grands Notables*, II, p. 122.

78. A.N.F¹bII Cher, 13. Pref. to Min. Int., Jan. 31, 1881; mayor of St. Montaine cited in Min. Int. note, June 21, 1879, and next example, Min. Int. note, Aug. 26, 1885; A.N.F¹bII Oise II, Min. Int. note, July 5, 1880; and A.N.F¹bII Meurthe-et-Moselle (A-F). Pref. to Min. Int., Nov. 24, 1882.

79. A.N.F.¹bII Morbihan 11: Pref. to Min. Int., Oct. 30, 1875.

80. This is true even for councillors in *chefs-lieux*, it seems. For example, in A.D. Oise 107-1011 on Chaumont (a *chef-lieu*), of 12 councillors elected in 1908, the mayor is a *huissier*, the assistant a *rentier*, and of the rest, four call themselves *rentiers* and one is a teacher in retirement.

81. Margadant, *French Peasants in Revolt*, p. 34. To make the matter simpler, through mayors, the Republic could control municipal councils, and thereby the country. Of course, mayors had been elected by municipal councils in 1848, but the innovation had had no time to make the Republic secure at the local level.

CHAPTER FOUR. MAYORS VERSUS PRIESTS: THE EXTENSION OF LOCAL ANTI-CLERICALISM

1. Lucien Fèbvre, *Autour d'une bibliothèque* (*Pages offertes à M. Charles Oursel*) (Dijon, 1942), p. 87.

2. A.D. Vaucluse, V131: Vic. gen. to pref., Dec. 6, 1830, with bill of health (same date) to prefect.

3. A.D. Haute-Garonne, 1M47: Subpref. of St. Gaudens to pref., June 28, 1854, on mayor of Oré (an "intelligent" man). A.D. Cher, 23M103: Subpref. of St. Amand to pref., Oct. 14, 1869; and Jan. 14, 1868, on divisions at La Celle-Bruère; and Jan. 15, 1869 on Oürouer.

4. A.D. Vaucluse, V132: Subpref. of Carpentras to pref., Oct. 9, 1852, pref., Oct.? 1852, to Min. Int.; 1M765: Min. Int. to pref., Feb. 14, 1839, on Le Thor; and 1M765: Min. Int. to pref., June 26, 1877, and prefect's advice written on same letter.

5. A.N. F^{19}4106: pref. Aude to Min. Cults, Sept. 21, 1867.

6. A.D. Yonne, VII: Municipal council complaint, for example, to prefect, Oct. 18, 1834, on mayor; letter from Charmoy to pref., July 1836.

7. A.D. Ille-et-Vilaine, 1V8: Mayor of St. Médard sur Ille, to pref., Aug. 31, 1835, and mayor of Feins to pref., May 15, 1832; A.D. Haute-Vienne, V10: Mayor of St. Léonard to pref., May 13, 1841; V9: Pref. to Min. Cults, May 12, 1868, on riots at Arnac. Weber, *Peasants into Frenchmen*, pp. 358-359.

8. A.D. Haute-Vienne, V9: Subpref. of St. Yrieix to pref., Feb. 10 and July 24, 1836, and archb. of Limoges to pref., June 29, 1836. A.D. Vaucluse, 1M767: Mayor of Lagnes to pref., March 23, 1826, and to subpref. of Avignon, March 5, 1826, as well as anonymous letters of April 10, 1826.

9. Arch. dioc. Bord.: President of *fabrique* at Les Esseintes, to vic. gen., May 15, 1862. The mayor also refused curé's supplemented salary there.

10. A.D. Gironde, O-Queyrac (7): Deliberation of Nov. 20, 1842, and subpref. of Lesparre to mayor, Dec. 1; Arch. dioc. Bord.: Curé of Labarde to vic. gen., July 9, 1861, and archb. to mayor, June 16, 1862; A.D. Cher, 23M89: Mayor of Brécy to pref., Feb. 23, 1862. Cf. A.D. Gironde, 0-Loupiac (71): Mayor complains to pref., July 22, 1859, that the well-treated priest has been painting the church without authorization.

11. A.N. F^{19}5988: Min. Cults to archb., Jan. 21, 1845; several other examples affixed.

12. A.D. Oise, 1V15: pref.'s report, Nov. 9, 1845, on Courcelles.

13. Richard Cobb, *The Police and the People: French Popular Protest, 1789-1820.* (New York, 1976), p. 94.

14. Julien Guigue and Joseph Girard, *La Fontaine de Vaucluse* (Avignon, 1949), pp. 21-22; A.D. Vaucluse, V131: Min. Int. to pref., Oct. 19, 1836, on the affair, and subpref. of Carpentras to pref., Dec. 18, 1836; Corbin, *Archaïsme et modernité*, passim; Silver, "French Peasant Demands", p. 284.

15. A.D. Vaucluse, V131: Subpref. of Orange to pref., May 6, 1839, on affair. In the same year there were several struggles over refusal of burial, as for example at Roussillon: Subpref. of Apt to pref., June 9, 1839.

16. Arch. dioc. Bord. parish file: Curé of Hostens to archb., March 10, 1846; A.D. Haute-Garonne, 1M45: pref.'s report, April 22, 1852, summarizes subpref. on Gradagne.

17. John Merriman minimizes their importance as "radicals" in 1848 and aftermath. Partly due to the thoroughness of quiet repression, relatively few were removed from the profession. After the Falloux Law only about 1200 were considered "dangerous," not 8000, as Michelet had thought. See Merriman, *Agony of the Republic*, p. 121.

18. A.D. Vendée, 5V1: Deliberations of municipal council of St. Germain de Prinçay, Dec. 11, 1832; that rift had gone on seven years (the priest an extreme legitimist); A.D. Haute-Vienne, V10: Subpref. of Rochechouart to pref., March 5, 1842. A.D. Ille-et-Vilaine, 1V13: Petition of Oct. 1837, and subpref. of Fougeres to pref., Oct. 24, 1837; A.D. Saône-et-Loire, V38: Teacher at Mornay to pref., Feb. 3, 1846, with mayor's note scribbled on letter, and pref.'s note, Feb. 7, 1846; Arch. dioc. Bord.: Teacher at Moulis to archb., Jan. 23, 1859. He was also secretary to the mayor and well-supported.

19. For the Yonne see N. Donzeaud, "L'Essor de l'enseignement primaire à la fin du Second Empire," *Bulletin de la société des sciences historiques et naturelles de l'Yonne*, 107 (1957), pp. 189-211, with good data on teachers' adult courses and conquest of illiteracy; Peter Vroom Meyers, "The French Instituteur, 1830-1914: A Study of Professional Formation" (New Brunswick, N.J. Ph.D. diss., Rutgers University, 1972), pp. 81-83.

20. Zeldin, *France, 1848-1945*, I, p. 529; A.D. Yonne, 1M^{12}157: on Chailley. Subpref. of Joigny to pref., June 20, 1853; on Dissangis, subpref. of Avallon to pref., Dec. 23, 1852. A.D. Yonne, VII: Extract from municipal council of Charmoy on burial, Aug. 22, 1836. Here the prefect chastized the mayor for his independent action.

21. A.D. Vendée, 5V1: Subpref. of Sables-d'Olonne to pref., Jan. 21 and Feb. 13, 1834, as well as copies of bishop's letters on La Tenche; A.D. Saône et Loire, V38: Subpref. of Autun to pref., May 13, 1854, on Broye, and for second case, *instituteur* at Montmort, letter of complaint to pref., June 23, 1867. Cf. A.D. Cher, 23M103: Mayor (31 years in post) to pref., July 20, 1867, complains of ex-1848 *instituteur* and wants him sacked.

22. A.D. Yonne, III M268: Anonymous letter from inhabitant of Sens-Surionne on his and five neighboring towns to Min. Int., July 17, 1854.

si le maître décole gene on lui demande sa démission sans motif. . . .sil resiste, si le conseil municipal fait resistence on le suspens sans rien dire et on nomme une commission [council] qui voura tout se qu'on lui demandra on dit que tout sa est fais pour faire hayre le gouvernement.

23. An example: A.D. Saône et Loire, V42: Subpref. of Charolles to pref., Nov. 24, 1859, on teacher at Massy-sous-Dieu driving a mayor "sans énergie" against the priest; Arch. dioc. Bord.: curé of Hourtin to archb., 1872 (n.d.) complains that the teacher uses a weak mayor ("pauvre paysan") against the priest.

24. A.D. Vaucluse, V133: Mayor of St. Hippolyte to pref., April 14, 1862. Statistics on teachers as secretaries in Tudesq, "L'Administration municipale," p. 487; Meyers, "French Instituteur," p. 91.

25. A.D. Vaucluse, 1M765: a clumsy letter from teacher at Blauvac to pref., July 26, 1864; A.D. Haute-Garonne, 1M45: Mayor of Castera to pref., May 2, 1853, with prefect's confirmation scrawled on note, and A.D. Oise, 1V15: Mayor of Eragny, Oct. 26, 1838, to pref. on cure against teacher: "cet Ecclesiastique prétend etre maître et conduire la commune." Many other complaints in file. Arch. dioc. Bord.: Curé of Montbrier to archb., Oct. 20, 1863, mentions this, hopes archb. will influence mayor to get rid of current teacher; Meyers, "French Instituteur," p. 38. In this example and one other given, the mayor was fighting the priest; at the second village, the teacher was transferred for the peace of the commune. Georges Dupeux, *Aspects de l'histoire sociale et politique du Loir-et-Cher, 1848-1914* (Paris, 1962) cites inspector, p. 161; and last letter in Daniel Fabre and Jacques Lacroix, *La Vie quotidienne des paysans de Languedoc au XIXe siècle* (Paris, 1973), p. 377.

26. David H. Pinkney, *The French Revolution of 1830* (Princeton, 1972), passim; René Rémond, *L'Anticléricalisme en France de 1815 à nos jours* (Paris, 1976), p. 64.

27. Georges Weill, "La Révolution de juillet dans les départements," in *1830* (Paris, 1932), p. 144; Albert Dauzat et. al *Nouveau dictionnaire étymologique et historique* (Paris, 1968), p. 172.

28. Adrien Dansette, *Religious History of Modern France*, I (tr. John Dingle; London, 1951), p. 229; F. Pomponi, "Pouvoir et abus de pouvoir des maires corses au XIXe siècle," *Études rurales*, 63-64 (1976), p. 157.

29. J.P. Rocher, "Contribution à l'étude de l'histoire de l'anticléricalisme: Un conflit entre maire et curé à Villeneuve-l'Archevêque sous Louis-Phillipe," *Bulletin de la société des sciences historiques et naturelles de l'Yonne*, 100 (1963-1964), especially pp. 84-87 (quote on pp. 86-87). Henri Forestier, "Le Clergé et l'opinion dans l'Yonne sous la Monarchie de Juillet," *Bulletin de la société des sciences historiques et naturelles de l'Yonne*, 97 (1957-1958), pp. 1-24.

30. A.D. Vaucluse, 1M765: Mayors of Ille-sur-Sorgues and Vedennes to pref., Oct. 13, 1831; and V131: Petition from Oppède to pref., Oct. 26, 1830, and petition from Surriens, 1833 (n.d.) to pref.

31. Déret, *Dompierre-sur-Bèsbres*, pp. 255-258.

32. A.D. Oise, IV24: Subpref. of Clermont to pref., Aug. 21, 1831; A.D. Ille-et-Vilaine, 1V13: Mayor of Tremblay to pref., March 7, 1831; on other places, subpref. of St. Malo to pref., April 18, 1831.

33. A.D. Vaucluse, V131: Mayor of Robion to pref., Aug. 5, 1834, and

archb. to pref., Aug. 19, 1834. Pierre Bailby notes the moral isolation of contemporary priests, by contrast to mayors: "M. le maire est presque toujours un compatriote. Il a ses affaires dans la commune ou dans le quartier. On le recontre ici et là. On plaisante volontiers avec lui. On l'a quelquefois connu à l'école. M. le curé, lui, c'est different. On le salue avec gravité. On l'aborde moins facilement." Pierre Bailby, *Le Curé et sa paroisse* (Paris, 1961), p. 8; next cases: A.D. Ille-et-Vilaine, 1V14: Mayor of St. Méloir-des-Ondes to pref., July 5, 1843; A.D. Haute-Vienne, V10: priest of Nantrat to pref., Nov. 13, 1843.

34. Siegfried, *Tableau politique de la France*, ch. 35; Lynn Case, *French Opinion on War and Diplomacy during the Second Empire* (Philadelphia, 1954), p. 274. A good file on priest's activity, among others: A.D. Oise, 2V241 (*fonds d' évêché*). Pref. of Oise to vic. gen. at election times.

35. See Alfred Cobban, "The Influence of the Clergy and the 'Instituteurs primaires' in the Election of the French Constituent Assembly, April 1848" in his *France Since the Revolution and other Aspects of Modern History* (London, 1970): quote p. 70.

36. Zeldin, *Political System of Napoleon III*, p. 82.

37. Ibid., ch. VI, with many examples. Prefects did not always support mayors: in A.D. Cher, 23M 103, one finds a savage electoral fight between curé and mayor at Sagonne in 1866. Justice of peace to subpref. of St. Amand, Dec. 2, 1866, recommends a new mayor, the assistant mayor who got the position.

38. Such generalizations, of course, must be qualified by area. At conservative Pont-de-Montvert, for example, the Second Empire was a regime of the Left. Patrice L.R. Higonnet, *Pont-de-Montvert: Social Structure and Politics in a French Village, 1700-1914* (Cambridge, Mass., 1971), p. 121.

39. A.N. F^{19}6058 (Vienne): Mayor and inhabitants of Messaie to archb. of Poitiers, May 23, 1847; the Vienne bundle is part of an excellent file on all departments; second case: A.D. Haute-Vienne, V10: *Gendarme*'s report on Montemart disturbances, Feb. 3, 1843; A.D. Oise, 1V15: Mayor of Parnès to pref., April 18, 1841.

40. A.D. Vaucluse, V132: *Commissaire de police* at Apt to subpref. of Apt. on priest at Cadènes, Sept. 3, 1850; *gendarmes* of St. Saturnin to subpref. of Apt, Sept. 8, 1850, on priest at Villars; mayor of Lagnes to pref., Nov. 19, 1864, on André.

41. A.D. Vaucluse, V132: Mayor and assistant Bedoin to *Citoyens Représentants de Vaucluse*, July 14, 1848; *procureur* to pref., Oct. 4, 1848, and archb. to pref., Oct. 4, 1848, on Mormoiron and Vauganis.

42. Magraw in Zeldin, *Conflicts in French Society*, pp. 169-227; pp. 186-190 on this particular village.

43. François Bellon, "Attitude religieuse et option politique à Mazan et Velleron entre 1871 et 1893," *Provence historique*, 13 (1963), pp. 75-90; Cholvy, "Le Diocèse de Montpellier," pp. 225-231.

44. A.D. Saône-et-Loire, V41: subpref. of Louhans to pref., Oct. 13, 1876; and V40: priest to pref., May 18, 1880 (as example), and subpref. of Autun, to pref., June 20, 1880.

45. First quote: A.D. Yonne, ^{III}M^{1}307: Circular signed by mayor of St. Privé,

June 22, 1882; second, III M^{1}307: Municipal council extract at Messangis, May 14, 1905. Guy Lapèrierre has a good section on the banning of processions in Lyon in his *La Séparation à Lyon (1904-1908)* (Lyon, 1973).

46. A.D. Yonne, M^{12}194: Min. Int. and Cults to pref., July 30, 1884, on mayor of Champvallon; A.D. Saône-et-Loire, V15: Min. Int. and Cults to pref., June 11, 1901, asking for reprimand; mayor of a village of Dauphiné who tosses cruicifix in latrine, 1882: in Barral, *Le Département de l'Isère*, p. 298; *Lyon Républicain* (Aug. 7, 1877) reports on a priest who paid sixteen francs for having uttered slightly antirepublican words; A.D. Saône-et-Loire, V15: subpref. of Autun to pref., Sept. 26, 1891, threatens priest with transfer because the priest wanted church bells repaired by "vauriens" in government; last example: A.N. F^{19}6058 (Vienne): Pref. of Vienne to Min. Int., Dec. 10, 1887.

47. A departmental survey is found in Hélène Étienne, "Le Réveil du sentiment national en Ille-et-Vilaine, 1910-1914" (*mémoire, études supérieures d'histoire, faculté* of Rennes, 1967).

48. Laperierre, *La Séparation à Lyon*, p. 39. As an example of clerical patriotism, A.D. Gironde, 1V70: Curé of Cadillac to pref., Sept. 20, 1888, wants new post and his goal is not lucre or gain but is "d'autant plus élevé qu'en dehors de l'amour du bien, il existe, en moi, l'amour du Patriotisme et de la République . . . " And of course for local fetes, strong directives from the prefecture, as in A.D. Puy-de-Dôme, V0321: Instruction for all mayors of department, June 24, 1881. For July 14, prefect demands "un véritable éclat" like the *fêtes fraternelles* of the French Revolution.

49. A.N.F^{19}6005 (Lozère): Pref. of Mende to Min. Int., Aug. 8, 1898, requesting authorization; on ceremony, *La Semaine religieuse* of Mende, July 20, 1898.

50. See J.M. Mayeur, "Géographie de la résistance aux inventaires (février-mars 1906)," *Annales: économies-sociétés-civilisations*, 21 (1966), pp. 1259-1272.

51. Arch. dioc. Bord.: Curé of Hostens to archb., March. 7, 1888; ibid., Curé of Mongauzy to vic. gen., Oct. 7, 1908, and undated petitions from *mères de famille* on his side.

52. A.D. Oise, 1V15: *Procureur de la république, cours d'assises* at Beauvais to pref., Oct. 7, 1902, on village of Parnès; example of dismissal of gravedigger-bell-ringer and arbitrary reduction of new one's salary (eight to five francs) at Flaugnac (Lot) in A.N. F^{19}6002: Bish. of Cahors to pref., March 1, 1890. Pref. to Min. Int., June 2, 1890, backs mayor, who railroaded change through parish council. Several good examples of locksmiths called, in A.D. Puy-de-Dôme, V0321. Local support for mayors: priest, denied repair money, calls mayor of Lagarde and followers "canaille" (1880), but villagers mostly back mayor in A.D. Vaucluse, V132: Mayor of Lagarde to pref., May 1, 1880, and petition of May 26.

53. Claude Mesliand, "Contribution à l'étude de l'anticléricalisme à Pertuis de 1871 à 1913," *Archives de sociologie des religions*, 10 (1960), pp. 49-62.

54. A.D. Vaucluse, V133: Mayor of Saignon to pref., Feb. 27, 1889, and subpref. of Apt to pref., March 5, 1889. We have the card in this file; subpref. of Orange to pref., March 12, 1893 and petition of *pères de famille* at Entrechaux to pref., March 19, 1893; subpref. of Apt to pref., Dec. 13, 1900 and pref. (after consultation with archbishop) to subpref., Jan. 8, 1901, on priest's dismissal from

Mirabeau; mayor of Malaucène to pref., Nov. 2, 1880, and mayor of La
Motte-d'Aigues to pref., Oct. 4, 1880; *pères de famille* at Cairanne, petition to
pref., Oct. 1, 1898, and deputy (Faure of Vaucluse) to pref., Nov. 1, 1898, archb.
to pref., Oct. 25, 1898, and pref.'s note on dismissal; mayor of Méthamis to pref.,
Sept. 24, 1898; *institutrice* of Lagarde-Paréol to pref., Sept. 24, 1898, and mayor to
archb., Oct. 16, 1898.

55. Discussed in my "Church-State Conflict at the Grassroots: Teacher versus
Priest in Brittany, 1880-1914," *Journal of Church and State* (forthcoming).

56. From a document in Louis Trénard ed., *Histoire des Pays-Bas français:
Documents* (Toulouse, 1974), p. 337.

57. A.D. Oise, 1V15: Mayor and *déliberation du conseil* of Courcelles to pref.,
Oct. 23, 1892, and bish. to pref., Oct. 11, 1892, backing curé; A.D. Oise, 1V110,
pref.'s report on *desservant* of Carlepont (and others), Dec. 2, 1885. Prefectoral
character estimates are in this file. A representative electoral catechism for Brittany
is cited in my "Church-State Conflict."

58. See A.N.F¹⁹5971 for this struggle (at Renan's Tréguier, 1904) and many
others. Quote is from pamphlet of *Comité central des Bleus de Bretagne* in
L'Aurore, May 17, 1904. Description also in *La Lanterne*, May 16, 1904.

CHAPTER FIVE. MAYORS VERSUS PRIESTS: THE LID OF REPRESSION

1. In general, see Theodore Zeldin's chapter "The Conflict of Moralities," in
Zeldin, *Conflicts in French Society*.

2. Silver, "French Rural Response," p. 154.

3. Cobb, *The Police and the People*, p. 74; Weber, *Peasants into Frenchmen*,
pp. 455-457.

4. Arch. dioc. Bord. parish files: Archb. of Bordeaux to curé of Reignac, June 3,
1868. There was a strong anticlerical campaign there; ibid: curé of Lacanau to
archb., Aug. 14, 1859, and 1862 (n.d.); and curé of Hourtins to vic. gen. at
Bordeaux, April 7, 1864; Corbin, *Archaïsme et modernité*, passim.

5. See Suzanna Barrows, ch. 10 of Merriman, ed., *Consciousness and Class
Experience*, p. 207; Weber, *Peasants into Frenchmen*, pp. 144-145; Thabault,
Mazières-en-Gâtine, pp. 102-103. Between 1873, when reliable statistics were first
kept, and 1900, the number of *débitants* of alcohol rose by roughly 25 percent,
from 348,599 to 435,379. In *Annuaire Statistique de la France*, 1913, p. 111.
Earlier statistics in Barrows, p. 207. I have also benefitted from conversations with
Patricia Prestwich of the University of Alberta, as well as from her unpublished
work on French alcoholism.

6. Launay, "Les Procès-verbaux de visites pastorales," pp. 183-200.

7. A.D. Ille-et-Vilaine, 2V5-2VII [Visites décanales—Questionnaires et
résponses par les curés et desservants 1883-1907].

8. A.D. Oise, 1V15 (canton de Chaumont 1818-1902): Priest of Vaudancourt to
bish., Feb. 12, 1869; and mayor to pref., Feb. 24. For the café as "contre-église,"
see Judt, *Socialism in Provence*, p. 166. He means it as a forum for rival ideologies,
particularly after 1880. For Leo Loubère, "the café was, above all, a link between

town and country. Their activities [freethinking artisans, pharmacists, etc.] made of the café the counterpart of the parish church where the curé spread legitimist ideals." Leo A. Loubère, *Radicalism in Mediterranean France: Its Rise and Decline, 1848-1914* (Albany, N.Y., 1974), p. 17. Cafés also grew important in the South as replacements for *chambrées* after 1848. At *chambrées*, "a small group of friends met to drink, gamble and talk." Sometimes the talk was political. See Loubère, p. 50.

9. A.D. Haute-Garonne, 1M45: *Arrondissement* of Toulouse. Same 1850-1855: Mayor of Pibrac to pref., Feb. 26, 1855, on carnival; and priest to mayor, Feb. 24.

10. See, for example, Manse, *Mérilheu de mon enfance*, pp. 102-103.

11. Silver, "French Rural Response," p. 155; A. Garric, *L'Histoire de Boussac* (Rodez, 1973) gives self-portrait of priest (there from 1839 to 1886), emphasis added, p. 56.

12. Cholvy, *Le Diocèse de Montpellier*, pp. 211, 210. In 1827 the prefect chided a curé for holding back a naturally happy populace. After 1840, the polka became popular in the Midi.

13. Palanque, *Le Diocèse d'Aix*, p. 211, and p. 183 for example from Le Tholonet, 1827; and A.D. Vaucluse, V131: Mayor of Cabrières to pref., June 15, 1837.

14. Michael Phayer, "Repression of Modern Dancing in France and Germany, 1815-1840" (unpublished paper), passim, quote on p. 17. See also his book *Sexual Liberation and Religion in Nineteenth Century Europe* (New York, 1977).

15. Michael Marrus, "Modernization and Dancing in Rural France: From 'La Bourrée' to 'Le Fox-Trot'," in Edward Gargan et al., eds., *The Wolf and the Lamb: Popular Culture in France: From the Old Regime to the Twentieth Century* (Saratoga, Calif., 1977), p. 149. Professor Marrus, of the University of Toronto, has also been kind enough to send unpublished work to me.

16. In addition to Phayer's paper, "Repression of Modern Dancing," see also Zeldin, *Conflicts in French Society*, p. 49.

17. Marrus, "Modernization and Dancing in Rural France," p. 156.

18. Weber, *Peasants into Frenchmen*, p. 368.

19. A.D. Ille-et-Vilaine, 1V14: Mayor of Poligné to subpref. of Redon, Sept. 26, 1847, confirmed by subpref.

20. Arch. dioc. Bord.: Curé of St. Pierre de Riocaud to vic. gen., Aug. 12, 1868; curé of St. Foy to vic. gen., Aug. 19, 1868; and new curé of Mauriac to archb., 1868 (n.d.), his emphasis.

21. Nègre, *St. Eulalie*, p. 311.

22. Manse, *Merilheu*, pp. 105, 117.

23. Robert Bezucha, "The Moralization of Society: The Enemies of Popular Culture in the Nineteenth Century," in Gargan et al., *The Wolf and the Lamb*, pp. 182-183; Merriman, "The Demoiselles of the Ariège," in Merriman, *1830 in France*, especially pp. 97-100.

24. See, for example, Mme. J. Feltin, "Succès des missions protestantes à Villevallier au milieu du XIXe siècle," *Bulletin de la société des sciences historiques et naturelles de l'Yonne*, 103 (1971-1972), pp. 235-242.

25. A.D. Yonne, III M¹267: Pref. to Min. Int., Feb. 3, 1854, includes copy of the song:

> . . .la faim arrive du village,
> dans la ville, par les faubourgs;
> Alley donc barrer le passage
> avec le bruit de vos tambours. . . .
> que nous font les querelles ruinées
> des cabinets
> faudrait il encor pour ces haines
> armer nos bras cyclopiers?

26. A.D. Yonne, V151: Mayor of Appoigny to pref., March 4, 1846; and justice of peace at Serbonnes to pref., March 30, 1862, on various petitions at St. Maurice. Many other police reports are found in V151.

27. A.D. Yonne, V151: Subpref. of Joigny to pref., July 11, 1856.

28. See René Boudard, "Tentatives de pénétration de la religion réformée en Creuse sous le second Empire," *Mémoires de' la société des sciences naturelles et archéologiques de la Creuse*, 30 (1949), pp. 457-464; my "Minoritarian Religion and the Rise of a Secular School System in France," *Third Republic/Troisième République*, I (1976), p. 229; and A.D. Saône-et-Loire, V263: Min. Int. to pref., March 13, 1835, on surveillance of Protestantism in that department by sub-prefects and mayors.

29. A.D. Yonne, III M261: Mayor of Joigny, *arrêté*, April 10, 1858. (Min. Int. circular to prefs., April 23, 1859, leaves the problem to mayors and local police; second Min. Int. circular in ibid., signed by mayors of Yonne, April 8, 1869.)

30. A.D. Haute-Vienne, 4M114: Mayor of Magnac-Laval to pref., June 28, 1860, pref. to mayor, July 16, and petitions; mayor of Condat to pref., April 21, 1856.

31. Petitions of 1889 (n.d.) to pref. in ibid., and subpref. of Rochechouart to pref., Feb. 20, 1889.

32. A.D. Vaucluse, V131: Report of captain of the *gendarmerie* of department to pref., June 9, 1836; second case: subpref. of Orange to pref., Feb. 18, 1836, on Camaret.

33. A.D. Vendée, 5V1: Mayor of Rochesèvière to pref., Jan. 2, and priest to pref., Jan. 9, 1840; second case: mayor of L'Aiguillon to pref., May 7, 1840, and subpref. of Fontenay, to pref., May 11, including record of priest's sentence. A.D. Ille-et-Vilaine, 1V13: Mayor of Louvigné to subpref. of Fougères, June 22, 1823; subpref. of Montfort to pref., March 3, 1831, on Plélan, where the village was split in opinion.

34. Negre, *St. Eulalie aux Bois*, pp. 298-299. Weber, *Peasants into Frenchmen*, p. 364 and A.D. Vaucluse, 1M739: Mayor's assistant to mayor of Caumont Feb. 1, 1855.

35. Weber, *Peasants into Frenchmen*, pp. 278-99; Michelet cited in Zeldin, *France, 1848-1945*, II, p. 798; Marie Soraye-Racape, *Jadis au pays de Janzé* (St. Hilaire, 1971), pp. 11-21, is good on the ethic of silence in traditional homes.

36. A.D. Vaucluse, V131: Curé of St. Saturnin (les Avignon) to archb., April 28, 1838; second case: A.D. Vaucluse, 1M765: *Commissaire de police* at Le Thor to pref., June 3, 1857; third case: A.D. Vaucluse, V132: Archb. to pref., July 5, 1849, backs curé; while mayor of Gadagne to pref., June 27, backs petitioners. The petitions are in the file.

37. A.D. Vaucluse, 1M765: *Gendarmerie* of Vaucluse to pref., May 28, 1851, and several examples of violence in Magraw, in Zeldin, *Conflicts in French Society*, pp. 169-227. A.D. Puy-de-Dôme, V0323: *Tribunal* of Clermont, *procureur de la République*, May 19, 1900, to pref. on *desservant* of Neuville; other illustrations in Weber, *Peasants into Frenchmen*, passim.

38. Representative folktales in Geneviève Massignon, ed., *Folktales of France* (tr. Jacqueline Hyland; Chicago: 1968). On fin-de-siècle slumming, Hannah Arendt, *The Origins of Totalitarianism* (New York, 1960), chapter on Dreyfus Affair, pp. 89ff.

39. On carnivals, I have checked Jacques Humbert, *Embrun et l'Embrunais* (Gap, 1972), especially, and Claude Macherel and Jacques le Querrec, *Léry, village normand* (Nanterre, 1974), pp. 52-57. The third volume of Van Gennep's master-piece on folklore, *Manuel de folklore français contemporain* (Paris, 1943), and William Graham Sumner, *Folkways* (New York, 1906), are also instructive. Poignant recollections of St. Jean Day especially in Léonce Peyregne, *Les Items d'Abraham de Camy* (Pau, 1976), p. 84: "Et qui donc pourrait, maintenant, ranimer leurs brandons sous la cendre des croyances mortes?" Mont-Guillaume climb described in Humbert, p. 433.

40. Weber, *Peasants into Frenchmen*, p. 403; A.D. Vaucluse, 1M765: *Gendarmerie* of Vaucluse (Avignon) to pref., July 7, 1852, on Lauris; A.D. Yonne, 1M^{12}157: *Gendarmerie* of Yonne, arrest reports, Nov. 30 to Dec. 5, 1853.

41. Weber, *Peasants into Frenchmen*, chapter on charivaris, quote p. 401; A.D. Haute Garonne, 1M47: on mayor at Balma: *tribunal de première instance* of Toulouse, to pref., March 10, 1854; and on mayor at Paussons, subpref. of St. Gaudens to pref., Aug. 25, 1852, including confirmation of revocation scribbled by prefect.

42. A.D. Vaucluse, 1M761: Mayor of Valréas to subpref. of Orange, July 15, 1823; in 1851 a mayor criticized a curé for his "catéchisme patois" (*provençal*), in Cholvy, *Diocèse de Montpellier*, p. 197. On the other hand André Armengaud finds many mayors, teachers, priests using patois in the 1850's. See his *Les Populations de l'Est—Acquitain au début de l'époque contemporaine* (Paris, 1961), p. 328.

43. Frédéric Mistral, *Mémoires et récits* (Paris: Plon, n.d.), p. 9.

44. Arch. dioc. Bord: Curé of Cadillac to archb., Dec. 18, 1834; A.D. Oise, 1V24 (canton de Breteuil 1831-1902): *Commissaire de police* at Breteuil on Vendeuil-Caply (1840s, date illegible).

45. A.D. Cher, 23M89: Council of Veuvy-sur-Barageon to pref., May 15, 1862.

46. Arch. dioc. Bord: Mayor of Rauzan to archb., Feb. 19, 1903; curé of St. Pierre-de-Riocaud to archb. Aug. 18, 1862. On the linkage of cafe-billiard spots and socialism, see the dossier A.D. Yonne: III M 268.

47. A.D. Vaucluse, 1M761: Mayor of Ille-sur-Sorgues to pref., Aug. 8, 1849; anonymous letter to pref., Jan. 9, 1831:

> Comme pères de famille ayant des enfants susceptibles à me ruiner, s'est pourquoi je me permet Mr le prefet de vous écrire ses deux mots pour vous instruire de la Conduite des Caffes de l'Isle, sans doute que monsieur Le préfet ignore de la manière qu'il se joue, he bien Monsieur. J'ose me permettre de vous dire que dans le Caffe. . .il se joue nuit et jour à des jeux prohibés depuis 50 ans.

48. A.D. Vaucluse, 1M761: Mayor of Mondragon to subpref. of Orange, Oct. 7, 1854; subpref. of Apt. to pref., Dec. 22, 1854. Mayor of Camaret to pref., Jan. 7, 1856; A.D. Yonne, III M202 [Loteries non-autorisés]: Confiscated tickets from various lotteries found here. For example, subpref. of Joigny to pref., April 15, 1897, on "Enfants tuberculeux" seizure; and A.D. Vaucluse, 1M765: *Commissaire de police* at Bonnieux to pref., June 2, 1854, on this man.

49. A.D. Vaucluse, 1M765: *Gendarmerie* of Avignon to pref., Dec. 21, 1850, and pref. of Ain to pref. of Vaucluse, Jan. 4, 1851, on this affair.

50. A.D. Vaucluse, V132: Subpref. of Orange to pref., Oct. 18, 1867, and *commissaire de police* at Bollene to subpref. of Orange, Sept. 7; second case: A.D. Vaucluse, V133: *Commissaire de police* at Apt, report of June 19, 1897.

51. Quote cited in Zeldin, *Conflicts in French Society*, p. 17; and Zeldin, *France, 1848-1945*, II, p. 1030.

52. Honoré de Balzac, *Lost Illusions* (tr. Herbert Hunt; Baltimore, 1974), p. 74.

53. Arch. dioc. Bord.: Mayor of Mouliets to archb., 1871 (n.d.), on this situation. He threw his letters into the fire.

54. Van Gennep's term may be too impersonal also for what was a personal, tangible world.

55. The soirée occurs near the beginning of *Lost Illusions*.

56. Zeldin, *France, 1848-1945*, II, passim, sections on writers.

CHAPTER SIX: CLASSIC IN-BETWEENER: THE VILLAGE SCHOOLMASTER OF THE THIRD REPUBLIC, 1880-1914

*Note: This chapter is mostly based on revisions of two articles: my "The Teacher as Notable in Brittany, 1880-1914," *French Historical Studies* (Fall, 1976) and "The Teacher as Outsider," in Gargan, et al., *The Wolf and the Lamb*.

1. The teacher as private for the republican General Staff is a frequently seen metaphor, as in Denis W. Brogan, *The Development of Modern France, 1870-1939*, I (New York, 1966), p. 155. J.P. Azéma and Michel Winock call the teachers "the pillars of the new order" in *La IIIe République (1870-1940)* (Paris, 1970), p. 142. The effect of the Franco-Prussian war on educational thought is perceived in Ernest Renan, *La Réforme intellectuelle et morale de la France* (Paris,

1871). Daniel Halévy, *La République des ducs* (Paris, 1937) is still the best work on the battle for the regime in the 1870s. A superior work on French educational transformations in the modern period is Antoine Prost, *Histoire de l'enseignement en France, 1800-1967* (Paris, 1968). See also Mona Ozouf, *L'École, L'eglise et la République, 1871-1914* (Paris, 1963).

2. Jacques Chastenet, *La France de M. Fallières* (Paris, 1949), p. 198.

3. Georges Duveau, *Les Instituteurs* (Paris, 1966), stresses their ideology; Jacques Ozouf, *Nous les maîtres d'école*, stresses the life of the teacher through reminiscences. See also E. Glay and H. Champeau, *L'Instituteur* (Paris, 1928), and, although more relevant to the post-1918 period, André Glossinde, *Je suis instituteur* (Paris, 1954).

4. One eccentric teacher of Ille-et-Vilaine was reviled by villagers, as he wore "the cuffs of his pants tight around his ankles and sometimes a knitted wool jacket which no one in the region wears any more." A.D. Ille-et-Vilaine, T [*Dossiers individuels des instituteurs*], unclassed: Primary inspector of Redon to insp. acad., Nov. 12, 1905.

5. Thus the head teacher at Brandivy (Morbihan) in 1900, "a good republican devoted, without fanfare, to the Republic, and one who, without distributing ballots or making visits to everyone (which would be beyond the scope of his role), knows how to guide the voter very discreetly in his choice." A.D. Morbihan, T1701: Mayor of Brandivy to prim. insp., Vannes, May 7, 1900. Usually political authorities were more prone to encourage political action on the *instituteur's* part than were educational authorities in the *académie*.

6. I quote from the inspector of the academy of Deux-Sèvres in Maurice Pellisson, "La Situation de l'enseignement primaire en 1898 d'après les rapports des inspecteurs d'académie," *Revue pédagogique*, 1899, pt. 2, p. 117. Other inspectors cited in the article said much the same thing. Jacques Ozouf discusses the political independence of teachers, with examples, in *Nous les maîtres d'école*, pp. 160-163, under the heading "Garder sa liberté."

7. L. Flatrès, *L'Enseignement du français et en particulier de la composition française dans les écoles rurales bretonnes* (Quimper, 1920), p. 29. Flatrès wrote the book prior to the war. Cf. also the description of the teacher written much later by H. Michaud and A. Glossinde in their *Condition et mission de l'instituteur* (Paris, 1945), pp. 71-72. "He is the official receptacle of knowledge, the master of understanding. . . . People consult him on everything and the common people listen to him like an oracle."

8. A.D. Morbihan, T 1687: Mayor of Le Tour du Parc to pref., May 30, 1901. Insp. acad. to pref., June 7, 1901, determined the teacher would stay in the post. We have the villager's letter in the file. When the mayor of La Chapelle-Thourault (Ille-et-Vilaine) needed a new teacher-secretary in 1912, the subprefect of the district specified the requisite qualities for the post's occupant. The teacher-secretary must be "a serious man, *sober*, devoted, *balanced*, although a *firm* republican . . . many qualities for one man to have!" (italics in original). A.D. Ille-Villaine, 2T: Subpref. of Montfort, to pref., July 23, 1912.

9. André Balz' article in *Manuel général de l'instruction primaire* (April 18, 1914), quote p. 342.

10. A.D. Ille-Vilaine, T. [Instituteurs]: Prim. insp. of Redon to insp. acad., April 1, 1913; extract of the deliberation in A.D. Morbihan, T1173.

11. A.D. Ille-et-Vilaine, T [Instituteurs]: Prim. insp. of Fougères to insp. acad., December 30, 1912.

12. Jean Délumeau, et al. *Histoire de la Bretagne*, p. 465; interview with L.L. at Saint-Brieuc, Feb. 24, 1970. I have only used teachers' full names when permission was granted; A.D. Lot-et-Garonne, T72: Pref. to insp. acad., Oct. 25, 1901 on *institutrice* at Duras; on first aid, teacher from Oise in an article in *Manuel général de l'instruction primaire*, May 3, 1913, especially p. 411. See medical map of France in Jacques Léonard, *La France médicale au XIXe siècle* (Paris, 1978), p. 87.

13. Guy Thuillier calls the Third Republic "perhaps" the "Republic of hygiene," but he also finds little evidence of the school's effect in the Nivernais with regard to personal cleanliness. Thuillier, "Pour une Histoire de l'hygiène corporelle: Un exemple régional: Le Nivernais," *Revue d'histoire économique et sociale*, 46 (1968), pp. 232-253. G. Bruno quoted in Léonard, *France médicale*, p. 206.

14. Sample taken from A.D. Finistère, T [Institutrices 1901-1919]: Madame C.L., "grande dame" of Châteaugiron, according to the mayor, was interviewed January 31, 1970. A.D. Puy-de-Dôme: Samples from TO 792, 793, 794; and A.D. Allier, T [Teachers unclassed].

15. Insp. acad. of Ille-et-Vilaine to pref., November 28, 1910, mentioned "foreign candidatures" when rejecting an aspirant from the Gironde. A.D. Ille-et-Vilaine, 2T: Insp. acad. of Loire-Atlantique to pref., February 13, 1899, also noted an aversion to extradepartmental candidates in A.D. Loire-Atlantique, T 113; and the prefect of Basses-Alpes, in a letter of April 9, 1909, to the prefect of Vaucluse, notes a paucity of posts and a preference for his own department's candidates as well. A.D., Vaucluse, T1 [Dossiers des instituteurs et institutrices].

16. A half-dozen monographs for the Loire-Atlantique alone are listed in Alfred Gernoux, "Le Progrès de l'enseignement aux XIXe et XXe siècles," *Annales de Nantes*, no. 106 (1957), p. 13.

17. Some of Pergaud's interesting war letters are found in the seventh edition of his *Les Rustiques: Nouvelles villageoises* (Paris, 1921). See also Jean Hugonnet, "Louis Pergaud, Instituteur," *Europe*, 38 (October 1959), pp. 30-46. Pagnol's biography is *La Gloire de mon père* (Paris, 1957).

18. Interviews L.L. at Saint-Brieuc, February 24, 1970; and Ogès at Quimper, August 9, 1970; teacher's article in *Bulletin de l'instruction primaire*, Jan. 1905; Blanguernon in *Manuel générale de l'instruction primaire*, Dec. 7, 1912.

19. Marcel Faure, *Les Paysans dans la société française* (Paris, 1966), p. 195. Faure calls the peasant a *concret*. A student I taught in the rural Acadian region of Nova Scotia used the term "affaires d'en haut" to dismiss the crisis in Northern Ireland today. The Irish are, if we adopt Faure's term, "hors-groupe;" Marc Bloch, *L'Étrange Défaite* (Paris, 1957), p. 101.

20. Alfred Gernoux, *Les Pionniers de l'enseignement public* (Châteaubriant, 1931), p. 23. He told me substantially the same thing in an interview at Nantes, June 3, 1970. Gernoux was recently made president of the local historical association in Nantes.

21. Interview with L.L. at Saint-Brieuc, February 24, 1970. For the sheer range

of teachers' agricultural activities and their influence in other regions see the handy autobiographical sketches excerpted from the *Manuel général de l'instruction primaire* in Ferdinand Buisson and F.E. Farrington, eds., *French Educational Ideals of Today* (New York, 1919), 202-205. Teacher of Aisne in *Manuel général*, May 9, 1914.

22. A.D. Loire-Atlantique, T 174 [Dossiers individuels des instituteurs] : Teacher to prim. insp. of Saint-Nazaire, on his activities. He and his equally talented wife terminated their careers at a big school in Nantes after the war. Both received several honors; A.D. Ille-et-Vilaine, T [Instituteurs]: Prim. insp. at Redon, inspection report of Nov. 24, 1904. The teacher received an overall grade of 18/20, extremely high. He was "profoundly imbued with laic and republican ideals, a man of action and of vivid faith" and a great influence in the commune (according to the report); A.D. Ille-et-Vilaine, 2T: Circular of insp. acad., October 16, 1906. Teachers in the Côtes-du-Nord and the Morbihan were also connected with this cooperative. On the rise of agrarian syndicalism, see Gordon Wright, *Rural Revolution in France* (Stanford, 1964), pp. 19-25. One of the most illustrious if much maligned figures in the movement was the Breton Abbé Trochu, a very liberal priest and founder of the *Ouest-Éclair* (now *Ouest-France* and one of the largest French dailies). Ibid., pp. 24-25; and A.D. Finistère, T [Instituteurs 1901-1919]. Many speeches in the dossier attest to the last teacher's great reputation in the region.

23. For solidarism, see J.E.S. Hayward, "The Official Philosophy of the French Third Republic: Léon Bourgeois and Solidarism," *International Review of Social History*, 6 (1961), pp. 19-48 and "Educational Pressure Groups and the Indoctrination of the Radical Ideology of Solidarism, 1895-1914," ibid., 8, (1963), pp. 1-17.

24. In Buisson and Farrington, *French Educational Ideals*, p. 205.

25. A.D. Côtes-du-Nord, T. [Dossiers par communes]: Mayor to pref., June 26, 1904; A.D. Ille-et-Vilaine, 2T: Mayor of Montreuil-sur-Ille to pref., June 1912. The inspector located a graduate of the Normal School who played violin (*Académie*, June 1912); A.D. Vaucluse, T1, [Dossier des instituteurs]: Prim. insp. of Orange to insp. acad., December 1, 1901, finds the charge false and the product of the mayor. The societies listed above were the most common.

26. A.D. Allier, T [Instituteurs]: Insp. prim. report, March 4, 1912.

27. A.D. Ille-et-Vilaine, F1768; A.D. Morbihan, T333: (examples taken at random from the file); A.D. Ille-et-Vilaine, 2T [Cours d'adultes]: Letter dated May 26, 1896; A.D. Loire-Atlantique, 64 T4: Extract from the register of deliberations of the municipal council of La Regrippière, November 3, 1895; and Célestin-Marie Godard, "La Crise de la vie rurale," *Bulletin mensuel de la société nationale des conférences populaires* (November 1910), unpaginated.

28. The loss of the teacher's cultural prestige due to urbanization is the main subject of André Bianconi's "Les Instituteurs," *Revue française de science politique*, 9 (1959), pp. 935-950. Charles Péguy called the pre-1914 teachers "ministers of culture," in *Notre Jeunesse* (Paris, 1957), p. 51.

29. Thévenot, *Lhuître*, pp. 261-262 (on early 1900s); A.D. Côtes-du-Nord, T

[Doss. comm.]; Teacher at Maël-Carhaix to prim. insp. of Guingamp, March 20, 1905; A.D. Morbihan, T1683: Subpref. to pref., March 2, 1897; A.D. Puy-de-Dôme, T0794: prim. insp. of Issoire on teacher at Royat, Jan. 22, 1901; A.D. Morbihan, T1690: Prim. insp. of Vannes to insp. acad., Feb. 3, 1896; mayor's pompous "Procès-verbal sur un fait à l'école d' Adultes," Jan. 28, 1896.

30. A.D. Isère, T44: Teachers of Saint-Sorlin-de-Vienne and Les Roches-de-Condrieu to insp. acad., March 14 and March 9, 1899 (respectively). Printed archival documents communicated to me by Professor Jacques Léonard.

31. Duveau, *Les Instituteurs*, pp. 57-63. An example of a teacher reduced to farming is one at Saint-André des Eaux (Loire-Atlantique) whose attic was always full of hay and who built a makeshift barn alongside the school. A.D. Loire-Atlantique, 18T1: Detail in prim. insp. of Nantes to pref., August 17, 1849. Ida Berger and Roger Benjamin also corroborate my thesis: "Industrial expansion, the always growing demand for more and more qualified technicians, has materially diminished the respect people have for someone who only teaches basic elements of culture. . . ." *L'Univers des instituteurs* (Paris, 1964), p. 146. Interestingly, the authors also say industrialization correlates, by department, with feminization of the teaching corps. By the 1960s almost 75 per cent of Parisian teachers were women. *Ibid*, pp. 147-149.

32. Zola's novel is found in *Oeuvres complètes*, VIII (Paris, 1968). This fine edition is part of the series, "Cercle du Livre précieux." Psichari's novel is in *Oeuvres complètes d'Ernest Psichari*, II (Paris, 1948). In Romains' *Men of Good Will* (New York, 1936), see especially I, Chap. 4; Duveau, *Les Instituteurs*, chap. 5. In Louis Pergaud's *La Guerre des boutons* (Paris, 1912), the teacher is a civilizer of wild peasants, but human, at least.

33. An English observer of French schools in 1891 greatly admired this system. Thomas H. Teegan, *Elementary Education in France* (London, 1891), pp. 107-108.

34. See Edmond Blanguernon, "Les Classes-promenades," *L'Éducation*, I (1909), p. 326; Claude Duneton, *Parler Croquant* (Paris, 1973), pp. 174-175.

35. A.D. Ille-et-Vilaine, 2T [Bibliothèques scolaires 1894-1920]: Form filled out by teacher and certified by the mayor; A.D. Allier, T [Instituteurs]. Prim. Insp.'s report from Gannat, Jan. 9, 1911, on teacher of St. Bonnet de Rochefort. On this topic see also the *Bulletin* of the Société Franklin, which since its founding in 1868 had been devoted entirely to school libraries.

36. A.D. Morbihan, T1687: Prim. insp. of Plöermel to insp. acad., January 25, 1904. Another report on a teacher of Ille-et-Vilaine in 1910 mentioned how the odor of the soup, prepared by his wife and the mayor's spouse, made school attractive to children. Prim. insp. of Fougères, report of March 2, 1910, on M.B. in A.D. Ille-et-Vilaine, T [Instituteurs].

37. A.D. Loire-Atlantique, sTi41 [Doss. inds. . . . instituteurs et institutrices]: Prim. insp. of Nantes to insp. acad., October 27, 1908. Again, it should be noted that this was an area of intense Catholic-laic conflict. The *institutrice* used clothes or free sewing courses as propaganda weapons. Guy Thuillier finds this to be true in the Nivernais as well. Thuillier, "Pour une Histoire des travaux ménagers en Niver-

nais au XIXe siècle," *Revue d'histoire économique et sociale*, 50 (1972), pp. 258-259. There, rival Catholic organizations included a Syndicat de l'aiguille and a Cercle des fermières.

38. Jean Orieux, *Souvenirs de campagne* (Paris, 1978), p. 21. For history of the certificate, see Prost, *Enseignement en France*, pp. 123-124 and table pp. 503-506.

39. The composition (with her strike-overs) is found with others in the dossier of the teacher at Trémëheuc in A.D. Ille-et-Vilaine, T [Instituteurs]. Cf. also the splendid evocation of the examination-day atmosphere in Laurence Wylie, *Village in the Vaucluse* (2nd ed.; New York, 1964), pp. 91-93, and Colette's *Claudine à l'école* in *Oeuvres complètes*, I (Paris, 1948). She reminisced in a graceful fashion about the school at Montigny in the 1880s. One girl, after failing an examination, stammered, "Ma foi, voui, que j'aime mieux garder les vaches chez papa. . ." (p. 185).

40. A.D. Finistère, T [Instituteurs 1901-1919]: Extracts of deliberations of the municipal council, July 16, 1898 and March 28, 1908.

41. A.D. Vaucluse, T1 [Instituteurs]: Petition dated August 11, 1889; prim insp. of Orange to insp. acad., September 16, 1889.

42. Adjunct teachers (*instituteurs-adjoints*) were teachers subordinate to the head teacher (*directeur d'école*) in schools where there was more than one class. Teachers who ran the school alone were *chargés d'école*. Most eventually ended up in the last two categories mentioned; A.D. Ille-et-Vilaine, T [Instituteurs]: This sample may underestimate teachers' longevity. For example, a man who came to Baulon as *directeur* probably would have stayed longer had he not died there at forty-nine. When one sees more than a dozen villages on a dossier cover, one can usually infer instability. One man in the sample occupied 14 posts and received two disciplinary sanctions. On the other hand, a teacher who taught at the village of Pacé 36 years received three academic prizes. I would like to thank Professor Jacques Leónard at the Faculté at Rennes for sending me photocopied dossiers for the sample.

43. A. Debray in *Manuel générale de l'instruction primaire*, Feb. 1, 1913, p. 252.

44. A.D. Puy-de-Dôme TO 792: prim. insp. of Clermont, report, Jan. 30, 1896, etc.; A.D. Finistère, T [Instituteurs]: Prim. insp. at Chateaulin, report, February 26, 1913; A.D. Loire-Atlantique, Til97 [Doss. inds. . . . instituteurs et institutrices]: Teacher to prim. insp. at Nantes, June 7, 1893. He married off his daughter—an *institutrice* at the girls' school—to his adjunct. Most likely they continued in that village. Last source is prim. insp. of Nantes to insp. acad., October 5, 1913, which also mentioned the *certificats*.

45. Gustave Ichheiser, *Appearances and Realities: Misunderstandings in Human Relations* (San Francisco, 1970), p. 97; Henri Mendras, *La Fin des paysans: Changements et innovations dans les sociétés rurales françaises* (Paris, 1967), p. 59.

46. Interview with H.L. at Nantes, May 15, 1970; see also the description of the *instituteur* Tafardel in Chevallier, *Clochemerle*, p. 9, and photographs of schoolmasters in Jacques Ozouf, *Nous les maîtres d'école* and Mona Ozouf, *École, église, république*. A film made from Alain Fournier's *Le Grand Meaulnes*, with the same title, skillfully depicted teachers of the *Belle Époque*; Roland Barthès, "Histoire et

sociologie du vêtement: Quelques observations méthodologiques," *Annales: économies-sociétés-civilisations*, 12 (1957), pp. 430-441.

47. A.D. Loire-Atlantique, sTil46: Prim. insp. of Paimboeuf to insp. acad., May 10, 1909. He marvelled at the fact that the playing of the Marseillaise—in front of the schoolhouse bedecked in the national colors—was twice applauded.

48. Interview with Monsieur and Madame Ogès at Quimper, August 28, 1970; also, the speech of the president of the teachers' *amicale* of Ille-et-Vilaine at the death of a highly-rated *institutrice*, at Vieux-Vy from 1880-1907: he mentioned the fact that she was consulted by couples. A large crowd was in attendance. Speech in her dossier, A.D. Ille-et-Vilaine, T [Institutrices]. Detail on hunting permit in J. Garavel, *Les Paysans de Morette: Un Siècle de vie rurale dans une commune du Dauphiné* (Paris, 1948), p. 89; Thabault, *Mon Village*, pp. 205-241.

49. A.D. Ille-et-Vilaine, F1776: [Dossier de Madame Chalmel née Angèle-Joséphine Le Sénéchal. Institutrice publique 1901-1924]. The reference to Jupiter is taken from *Le Montfortais* (Ille-et-Vilaine), Jan. 2, 1898; another good example of this literature is the front-page article entitled "L'Instituteur au pouvoir" in *Le Nouvelliste de Bretagne et de la région de l'Ouest* (Rennes), Oct. 10, 1908.

50. Chastenet, *La France de M. Fallières*, pp. 198-199.

51. François Goguel, *La Politique des partis sous la IIIe République* (3rd ed. Paris, 1958), p. 27.

52. Paul Bois, "Dans l'Ouest: Politique et enseignement primaire," *Annales: économies-sociétés-civilisations*, 9 (July, 1954), pp. 356-367.

53. For the Trégor, see Gabriel Le Bras, *Études de sociologie religieuse*, II, (Paris, 1956), pp. 605-606 (quote p. 606), and Alain de Vulpian, "Physionomie agraire et orientation politique dans le départment des Côtes-du-Nord," *Revue française de science politique*, I (May 1951), pp. 123-126. For the Cornouaille, Le Bras, *Études de sociologie religieuse*, I (Paris, 1955), p. 174. At Plodémét (Cornouaille), teachers helped cement a radical-socialist dynasty from 1877 to 1959. Morin, *The Red and the White*, pp. 26-37. Many other factors were involved in the stability of republicanism there.

54. I have calculated these percentages from statistics in A.D. Loire-Atlantique, 62 T10. For 1913, other random figures can be given here: Dordogne: 6.8 per cent; Meuse: 1.7 per cent; Loire: 1.9 per cent. It is interesting that Brittany had four departements among the eight most heavily conscripted in 1913. The Nord and the Pas-de-Calais were the top two.

55. Morvan Lebesque, *Comment peut-on être Breton: Essai sur la démocratie française* (Paris, 1970), pp. 96-99; M.J. Sydenham, *The French Revolution* (New York, 1966), p. 217; Charles Rearick, "Symbol, Legend, and History: Michelet as Folklorist-Historian," *French Historical Studies*, 7 (Spring 1971), pp. 72-92; report of inspector in A.D. Morbihan, T1049; Hélias, *The Horse of Pride*, p. 149. Children who spoke Provençal were punished, too, under the Third Republic. Laurence Wylie, "Social Change at the Grass Roots" in Stanley Hoffman, et al., *In Search of France* (Cambridge, Mass., 1963), pp. 197-98, and Duneton, *Parler Croquant*, p. 21.

56. Duneton, *Parler Croquant*, pp. 74, 163.

57. A.D. Morbihan, T1943: Inhabitant of Langoëlan to Deputy Brard, July 23,

1908; A.D. Morbihan, T333: M. Le G., *instituteur* at Le Saint, to prim. insp. (of Pontivy?), Jan. 20, 1902, on lecture given by wife in Breton. The subject was China —its government, army, use of torture. There are many examples of sub-prefects demanding a Breton-speaking teacher for a certain area.

The battle against patois still goes on. Note the bellicosity of a contemporary *institutrice* in Manche: "They speak badly in the entire Manche: a *seau* is pronounced 'siaou'. . . . People will never realize to what degree Norman patois still raises its barricades against the teaching of French, and against education generally." "L'École à l'ombre des pommiers," in Jean Planchais, ed., *Les Provinciaux ou la France sans Paris* (Paris, 1970), p. 150.

58. For example, Max Ferré, *Histoire du mouvement syndicaliste révolutionnaire chez les instituteurs des origines à 1922* (Paris, 1955), *passim*.

59. Duveau, *Instituteurs*, pp. 139-42. The urban predominance in *syndicats* is seen in dossiers like A.D. Morbihan, T1937 [Syndicat des instituteurs 1912]; poem in dossier of M. Le N. of Pouldavid, A.D. Finistère T: Instituteurs [1901-1919].

60. Dossier of J.L. of Nantes, in A.D. Loire-Atlantique, sT 178. "Mort sur le champ d'honneur" was often laconically marked on the cover of these dossiers (with date).

61. Extract from Ferry's "Program for Elementary Education" in Buisson and Farrington, *French Educational Ideals*, p. 23. See also, my "Jules Ferry and the Laic Revolution in French Primary Education," *Paedagogica Historica*, 15 (1975), pp. 406-425; see for latter point H. Stuart Hughes, *Consciousness and Society* (New York, 1958). One critic of positivist morality is Henri Bergson, *Les Deux Sources de la morale et de la religion* (58th ed; Paris, 1948).

62. A.D. Fin. T [Instituteurs]: Prim. insp. of Brest, report of December 3, 1925. A.D. Lot-et-Garonne, T133: Prim. insp. of Villeneuve to insp. acad., Nov. 10, 1909.

63. Ferry's rhetoric was conveniently general. In a speech to the teachers in 1881 he said: "You have been freed as citizens by the French Revolution, you are going to be emancipated as *instituteurs* by the Republic of 1800". (*Revue pédagogique* [1881], pt. I, p. 581), table in *Annales . . députés. Documents parlementaires (Session ordinaire)* II (1889, du quatorze mai au quinze juillet), p. 306.

64. For information on salaries I have used Octave Gréard's compendium, *La Législation de l'instruction primaire en France depuis 1789 jusqu' à nos jours*, VI and VIII (Paris, 1898-1900). For the period after 1900, Prost's *Enseignement en France* is a reliable source. I have also used departmental files, such as A.D. Loire-Atlantique 26-T-4, and Peter Sandiford, ed., *Comparative Education* (London, 1918), pp. 324-327. The experienced German teacher's salary cited for 1913 is 3700 marks (4125 francs). The average industrial worker's wage for 1906, according to Jacques Chastenet, was roughly 1350 francs a year. Chastenet, *La France de M. Fallières*, p. 172. A good table comparing teachers' salaries to those of other functionaries for 1907 appears in Ida Berger and Roger Benjamin, *L'Univers des instituteurs* (Paris, 1964), p. 143:

Bank of France	1800-4800 [francs]
Customs clerks	1700-4000

Clerks for indirect taxes	1500-3300
Postal clerks	1500-4000
. . .	. . .
Tenured clerks	1100-2200

65. J. Arren in *L'Éclair*, October 24, 1905, cited by Berger and Benjamin, *Univers des instituteurs*, p. 142.

66. Interview with H.L. at Nantes, May 15, 1970. Because of its price (compounded by a tax), the bicycle was a luxury item for teachers right up to the war. See Eugen Weber, "Gymnastics and Sports in Fin-de-Siècle France: Opium of the Classes," *American Historical Review*, 76 (February 1971), pp. 80-81.

67. In this regard teachers were sometimes models to be emulated. One from the Nièvre wrote: "At Montauban the country folk came to visit my garden and experiment field, and tried afterwards to do better than I. Now there is great competition in the village to see who will have the finest garden." Autobiographical sketch, 1911-1912, in Buisson and Farrington, *French Educational Ideals*, p. 203.

68. A.D. Côtes-du-Nord, T [Dossiers par communes]: Letter, February 16, 1898, about *institutrice* of Saint-Fiacre. Many other letters of this sort are found in the dossiers. Anonymous letter in A.D. Ille-et-Vilaine [instituteurs]. A.D. Lot-et-Garonne, T133: A. Thorinaud of Montluçon to insp. acad., May 10, 1898.

69. Jacques Ozouf, *Nous les maîtres d'écoles*, p. 155. Her term was "le strict nécessaire."

70. A teacher of the Departement of Vienne noted that "since I read late into the night I am judged eccentric." Buisson and Farrington, *French Educational Ideals*, p. 198. H.L. also remembers his teacher's taste for books as abnormal in the village of Guénouvry (Loire-Atlantique). Interview at Nantes, May 15, 1970.

71. Mona Ozouf, *École, église, République*, pp. 151-155; Jacques Ozouf, *Nous les maîtres d'école*, pp. 132-134; Pierre Sorlin, *La Société française, I, 1840-1914* (Paris, 1969), p. 91.

72. Good examples: A. Richard, "Conseils pratiques aux instituteurs," *Revue pédagogique*, 1881, pt. I, pp. 394-407; Cazès (inspector of the Departement of the Aube) "Conseils aux instituteurs sur la conduite à tenir dans la vie," *Revue pédagogique*, 1886, pt. I, pp. 88-94.

73. A.D. Loire-Atlantique, sTi220: Primary inspector of Ancenis to insp. acad., August 7, 1886; A.D. Finistère, T [Instituteurs]: Prim. insp. of Morlaix to insp. acad., Dec. 11, 1893.

74. See Zeldin, *France 1848-1945*, I, pp. 12-22.

75. See Robert Locke, *French Legitimists and the Politics of Moral Order in the Early Third Republic* (Princeton, N.J., 1974), p. 177; in Barrès' *Les Déracinés*, the Kantian professor woos the hero from his native Lorraine; Labat's article is "L'Instruction primaire au point de vue psychologique," *Revue des deux mondes*, 82 (July 1912), pp. 135-172.

76. Félix Pécaut, *Quinze ans d'éducation* (Paris, n.d.), pp. 70-74; also important, G. Tarde, "L'Instituteur et la désertion des campagnes," *Manuel général de l'instruction*, June 17, 1899.

77. Thabault, *Mazières-en-Gâtine*, pp. 207-211.

78. Duneton, *Parler Croquant*, p. 20. Cf. the prophylactic interpretation of the militant Robert Lafont: "On va m'apprendre [in Ferry's school] la langue de la proprété." Lafont, *Lettre ouverte aux Français*, cited in Louis Bayle, *Procès de l'Occitanisme* (Toulon, 1975), p. 127.

79. Teacher at Pont-sur-Madon in *Manuel général de l'instruction primaire*, July 4, 1914; Huguette Bastide, *Institutrice de village* (Paris, 1969), p. 55.

80. A.D. Côtes-du-Nord, T: Prim. insp. of Lannion, to insp. acad., Jan. 6, 1901.

81. Interviews: the F.T.'s at Saint-Anne-La-Palud, August 9, 1970; Mme. C.L. Châteaugiron, Jan. 31, 1970; and L.L. at Saint-Brieuc, Feb. 24, 1970. Jacques Ozouf, *Nous les maîtres d'école*, pp. 7-8. See also Ida Berger, "Contribution à l'étude de la mobilité sociale en France: les instituteurs," *Transactions of the Third World Congress of Sociology* (New York, 1956), pp. 45-50; Gérard Vincent, "Les Professeurs du second degré au début du XXe siècle", *Le Mouvement social*, 7 (1966), pp. 47-73.

82. John Murray Cuddihy, *The Ordeal of Civility: Freud, Marx, Lévi-Strauss, and the Jewish Struggle with Modernity* (New York, 1974), p. 11.

83. Duruy's report quoted in Jean Rohr, *Victor Duruy, Ministre de Napoléon III: Essai sur la politique de l'instruction publique au temps de l'Empire libéral* (Paris, 1967), p. 157; Henry Adams, *The Education of Henry Adams* (New York, 1939), p. 32.

84. Circular in *Revue pédagogique*, 1882, pt. I, p. 223.

85. Ida Berger, ed., *Lettres d'institutrices rurales d'autrefois: Rédigées à la suite de l'enquête de Francisque Sarcey en 1897* (Paris, [1964]), pp. 7-8; A.D. Allier, T [unclassed]: *institutrice* of Nizerolles to insp. acad., March 22, 1895; A.D. Puy-de-Dôme, T0794: *Institutrice* to insp. acad., Nov. 10, 1884.

86. Jean Guéhenno, *Sur le Chemin des hommes* (Paris, 1959), pp. 152-153.

87. Teaching couple, Saône-et-Loire, in Jacques Ozouf, *Nous les maîtres d'école*, pp. 130-131.

88. Quoted in ibid., p. 134.

89. See Mona Ozouf, *École, église, République*, pp. 104-106; Berger, *Lettres d'institutrices rurales*, p. 37.

90. Ibid., p. 55; "Lettres à une institutrice" by A.N., *Manuel général de l'instruction primaire*, Dec. 14, 1912, p. 162.

91. A.D. Allier, T: Prim. insp. of Andrier to insp. acad., Jan. 14, 1911, on teacher at Oludes.

92. See testimony of *institutrice* at Évian-les-Bains, 1897, in Ida Berger, *Lettres d'institutrices rurales*, p. 58: Jacques Ozouf, "Les instituteurs de la Manche et leurs associations au début du XXe siècle," *Revue d'histoire moderne et contemporaine*, 13 (January-March 1966), pp. 98-99; Interview, Madame C.L. of Châteaugiron, Jan. 31, 1970. She married a railway worker; and Pauline Kergomard, "Les Femmes dans l'enseignement primaire", *Manuel général de l'instruction primaire*, May 25, 1889, p. 267.

93. Theodore Zeldin, "The Conflict of Moralities," in Zeldin, *Conflicts in French Society*, pp. 36-45.

94. A.D. Ille-et-Vilaine, T. [Instituteurs]: Prim. insp. of Fougères to insp. acad., Sept. 28, 1911. The anonymous letters are in this dossier. The woman died soon after departing from the commune at age thirty-one, partly from unhealthy conditions there and perhaps also due to the hate campaign. Second case: A.D. Loire-Atlantique, sTi105: Anonymous letter with original punctuation and spelling to academy, March 2, 1907; prim. insp. of Châteaubriant, to insp. acad. March 17, 1907. A film acclaimed in France, *La Fiancée du pirate*, concerns an illegitimate girl growing up in a village. She is continually reminded of her fallen state—like this *institutrice*—but ultimately takes revenge on the whole village by becoming a prostitute, tape-recording compromising words spoken by her clients (including the curé), and playing the tapes from behind a pillar in Church one Sunday. The movie illuminates the worst aspects of village mentality in France.

95. A.D. Lot-et-Garonne, T72: Prim. insp. of Nérac to insp. acad., Nov. 29, 1895.

96. A.D. Loire-Atlantique, sTi144: Prim. insp. of Paimboeuf to insp. acad., Feb. 18, 1897; A.D. Ille-et-Vilaine, T [Instituteurs]: Prim. insp. of Fougères to insp. acad., Oct. 31, 1891; A.D. Loire-Atlantique, sT24: Copies of all the testimonies are in the file and are very precise.

97. A.D. Finistère, T [Instituteurs]: Teacher's letter, August 25, 1907; prim. insp. of Brest to insp. acad., Aug. 28, 1907, and Mar. 2, 1907 (most important reports). The verdict is in the *Dépêche de Brest* of April 4, 1908 (the archives lacked papers of the *Cours d'assises* for 1908). The petition—for which some of the signatures do not appear authentic—is also in this file. If acquitted, the teacher was undoubtedly innocent. According to Professor Jacques Léonard, French judicial authorities then were very stringent in morals affairs and made painstaking investigations of them.

98. For censure of bicycle-riding, see for example A.D. Loire-Atlantique, sTi139: Prim. insp. of Saint-Nazaire to insp. acad., June 14, 1884, on *institutrice* at Saint-Nazaire. A teacher at Scrignac (Finistère) to prim. insp. of Châteaulin, Jan. 1, 1900, told of his adjunct's nights out in Brest. A.D. Finistère, T [Instituteurs 1800-1899].

99. Pagnol, *La Gloire de mon père*, p. 23.

100. A.D. Finistère, T [Instituteurs]: Prim. insp. of Châteaulin to insp. acad., Oct. 24, 1912. In my interview with H.L. at Nantes, May 15, 1970, he also spoke of his teacher at Guénouvry as a teetotaler (by necessity); A.D. Lot-et-Garonne, T133: Prim. insp. of Nérac to insp. acad., Dec. 3, 1887, on teacher at Caubèyre.

101. Foregoing details in my "Pillar of the Republic," pp. 129-130. Generalizing for his district in an unusually sensitive report of 1903, the primary inspector of Vannes noted: "The life of the *laic Institutrice* is often very painful; the unfortunate *Institutrice* is, in most rural areas, often kept apart and I wonder how, in many cases, she does not become totally discouraged." A.D. Morbihan, T1049: "Rapport sur la situation de l'enseignement primaire dans l'arrondissement." Clerical pressure was undoubtedly stronger in Brittany than in most regions, but the Sarcey *enquête* of 1897 shows that *institutrices* were prone to depression in all rural areas (Berger, *Lettres d'institutrices*).

102. My article on the curé-*instituteur* conflict ("Church-State Conflict") covers this problem and contains footnotes to these cases. Interview was with L.L., at St. Brieuc, Feb. 4, 1970.

103. Article by H.M. in *Manuel générale de l'instruction primaire*. (Sept., 1900), p. 239.

104. A.D. Ille-et-Vilaine, T [Institutrice]: *Institutrice* to insp. acad., Feb. 16, 1887. The inspector had mentioned in a report the extreme humidity of her apartment.

105. A.D. Ille-et-Vilaine, T [Institutrices]: Doctor to insp. acad., Oct. 29, 1910, and other letters; A.D. Puy-de-Dôme, T0793: Doctor's certificate, Nov. 13, 1912.

106. A.D. Morbihan, T1941: Prim. insp. of Ploermel to insp. acad., March 7, 1912.

107. The first report is found in *Annales . . . députés. Doc. parls. (sess. ord.)*, 65, 1902, p. 250; the primary inspector of Quimper invoked an obscure law of the Second Empire to turn down the request of a teacher for an extended sick leave with pay. That teacher died very soon afterwards, at age thirty-three. A.D. Finistère, T [Instituteurs]: Prim. insp. of Quimper to teacher at La Fôret-Fouesnant, December 9, 1899.

108. First notes in A.D. Ille-et-Vilaine, T: [Institutrices]; A.D. Lot-et-Garonne, T133: prim. insp. of Nérac to insp. acad., March 24, 1897.

109. Henri Mendras, *Éléments de sociologie* (Paris, 1967), p. 148.

Bibliography of Printed Sources

Ackerman, Evelyn B. "Alternative to Rural Exodus: The Development of the Commune of Bonnières-sur-Seine in the Nineteenth Century," *French Historical Studies*, 10 (1977), pp. 126-148.

——— . *Village on the Seine: Tradition and Change in Bonnières, 1815-1914* (Ithaca, N.Y.: Cornell University Press, 1978).

Adams, Henry. *The Education of Henry Adams* (New York: Random House, 1939).

Agulhon, Maurice. *La République au village* (Paris: Plon, 1972).

Annuaire statistique de la France 1913.

Arendt, Hannah. *The Origins of Totalitarianism* (New York: Meridian Books, 1960).

Armengaud, André. *Les Populations de l'Est—Acquitain au début de l'epoque contemporaine* (Paris: Mouton, 1961).

Aubert, Jacques et al., *Les Préfets en France (1800-1940)* (Geneva: Droz, 1978).

Azema, J.-P. and Michel Winock. *La IIIe République (1870-1940)* (Paris: Calman-Lévy, 1970).

Bailby, Pierre. *Le Curé et sa paroisse* (Paris: Fayard, 1961).

Balz, André. Column in *Manuel général de l'instruction primaire*, (May 1914).

Balzac, Honoré de. *Lost Illusions* (tr. Herbert Hunt; Baltimore: Penguin, 1974).

Barral, Pierre. *Le Département de l'Isère sous la IIIe République, 1870-1940* (Paris: Armand Colin, 1962).

Barthès, Roland. "Histoire et sociologie du vêtement. Quelques observations méthodologiques," *Annales: économies-sociétés-civilisations*, 12 (1957), pp. 430-441.

Bassett, W. and P. Huizinga, eds., *Celibacy in the Church* (New York: Herder and Herder, 1972).

Bastide, Huguette. *Institutrice de village* (Paris: Mercure de France, 1969).

Bayle, Louis. *Procès de l'occitanisme* (Toulon: L'Astrado, 1975).

Bechtel, Guy. *1907: La Grande Révolte du Midi* (Paris: Laffont, 1976).

Bée, Michel et al., *Mentalités religieuses dans la France de l'ouest au XIX^è et XX^è siècles* (Caen: Annales de Normandie, 1976).

Bellon, François. "Attitude religieuse et option politique à Mazan et Velleron entre 1871 et 1893," *Provence historique* 13(1963), pp. 75-90.

Berger, Ida. "Contribution à l'étude de la mobilité sociale en France: les instituteurs," *Transactions of the Third World Congress of Sociology* (New York: Macmillan, 1956).

———, ed. *Lettres d'institutrices rurales d'autrefois: Rédigées à la suite de l'enquête de Francisque Sarcey en 1897.* (Paris: Association des amis du Musée pédagogique, [1964]).

Berger, Ida and Roger Benjamin. *L'Univers des instituteurs* (Paris: Les Editions de Minuit, 1964).

Bergson, Henri. *Les Deux Sources de la morale et de la religion* (58th ed., Paris: Presses universitaires de France, 1948).

Bianconi, André. "Les Instituteurs," *Revue française de science politique*, 9 (1959), pp. 935-950.

Blanguernon, Edmond. Column in *Manuel général de l'instruction primaire*, Dec. 7, 1912.

———. "Les Classes-promenades," *L'Éducation*, I (1909), p. 326.

Bloch, Marc. *L'Étrange défaite* (Paris: André Michel, 1957).

Bois, Paul. "Dans l'ouest: politique et enseignement primaire," *Annales: économies-sociétés-civilisations*, 9 (July 1954), pp. 336-367.

Bouchard, Gérard. *Le Village immobile: Sennely-en-Sologne au XVIIIe siècle* Paris: Plon, 1972).

Boudard, René. "Tentatives de pénétration de la religion réformée en Creuse sous le Second Empire." *Memoires de la société des sciences naturelles et archaéologiques de la Creuse* 30 (1949), pp. 457-464.

Brogan, D. W. *The Development of Modern France, 1870-1939*, 2 vols. (New York: Harper and Row, 1966).

Brogan, Denis. *France under the Republic: The Development of Modern France, 1870-1939* (New York: Harper, 1940).

Brugerette, Joseph. *Le Prêtre français et la société contemporaine*, 2 vols. (Paris: Lethielleux, 1935).

Brun, Abbé Pierre. *Les Églises de Bordeaux* (Bordeaux: Delmas, 1953).

———. *Les Églises de la Gironde* (Bordeaux: Delmas, 1957).

Burguière, André. *Bretons de Plozévet* (Paris: Flammarion, 1975).

Buisson, Ferdinand, and F. E. Farrington, eds. *French Educational Ideals of Today* (New York: World Book, 1919).

Case, Lynn. *French Opinion on War and Diplomacy during the Second Empire* (Philadelphia: University of Pennsylvania Press, 1954).

Cazès, M. "Conseils aux instituteurs sur la conduite à tenir dans la vie," *Revue pédagogique*, 1886, pt. 1, pp. 88-94.

Chalendar, Xavier de. *Les Prêtres* (Paris: Éditions du Seuil, 1963).

Chaline, Nadine-Josette. "Le Recrutement du clergé dans le diocèse de Rouen au XIX^è siècle," *Revue d'histoire économique et sociale*, 49 (1971), pp. 403-425.

Chastenet, Jacques. *La France de M. Fallières* (Paris: Fayard, 1949).

Chesteron, G. K. *The Well and the Shadows* (London: Sheed and Ward, 1935).

Cholvy, Gérard. *Le Diocèse de Montpellier* (Paris: Beauchesne, 1976).

———. *Géographie religieuse de l' Hérault contemporain* (Paris: Presses Universitaires de France, 1968).

———. "Religion et société au 19ᵉ siècle: Le Diocèse de Montpellier," *Information historique*, 35 (1973), pp. 225-231.

Clemenceau, Georges. *Figures de Vendée* (Paris: Plon, 1939).

Cobb, Richard. *The Police and the People: French Popular Protest, 1789-1820* (New York: Oxford University Press, 1976).

Cobban, Alfred. "The Influence of the Clergy and the 'Instituteurs primaires' in the Election of the French Constituent Assembly, April 1848," in Cobban, *France Since the Revolution and Other Aspects of Modern History* (London: Jonathan Cape, 1970).

Colette. *Claudine à l'école* in *Oeuvres complètes* (Paris: Flammarion, 1948).

Corbin, Alain. *Archaïsme et modernité en Limousin au XIXᵉ siècle, 1845-1880*, 2 vols. (Paris: Marcel Rivière, 1975).

Cuddihy, John Murray. *The Ordeal of Civility: Freud, Marx, Lévi-Strauss, and the Jewish Struggle with Modernity* (New York: Basic Books, 1974).

Dansette, Adrien, *Religious History of Modern France*, 2 vols. (tr. John Dingle; London: Thomas Nelson, 1961).

Debray, A. Article in *Manuel général de l'instruction primaire*, Feb. 1, 1913.

Délumeau, Jean et al. *Histoire de la Bretagne* (Toulouse: Privat, 1969).

Délupy, Irène. "Pouvoir municipal et notables à Gruissan, village du littoral languedocien," 65 (Jan.-March 1977), p. 65, *Études rurales*, pp. 71-76.

Déret, Y. *Dompierre-sur-Bèsbres* (Moulins: Édition des cahiers Bourbonnais, 1965).

Devailly, Guy. *Le Diocèse de Bourges* (Paris: Letouzey and Ané, 1973).

Donzeaud, N. "L' Essor de l'enseignement primaire à la fin du Second Empire," *Bulletin de la société des sciences historiques et naturelles de l'Yonne.* 107 (1975), pp. 189-211.

Duclos, France. *L'Opinion publique en Vendée devant la séparation des églises et de l'état* (Nantes: Masters thesis, University of Nantes, 1974-1975).

Duneton, Claude. *Parler croquant* (Paris: Stock, 1973).

Dupeux, Georges. *Aspects de l'histoire sociale et politique du Loir-et-Cher, 1848-1914* (Paris: Imprimerie nationale, 1962).

Duveau, Georges. *Les Instituteurs* (Paris: Editions du Seuil, 1966).

Escoube, François. *Mehun-sur-Yévres: des origines à 1914* (Bourges: Syndicat d' initiative, 1973).

Étienne, Hélène. "Le reveil du sentiment national en Ille-et-Vilaine, 1910-1914" (*Mémoire, études supérieures d'histoire, faculté* of Rennes, 1967).

Fabre, Daniel, and Jacques Lacroix. *La Vie quctidienne des paysans du Languedoc au XIXᵉ siècle* (Paris: Hachette, 1973).

Faure, Marcel. *Les Paysans dans la société française* (Paris: Armand Colin, 1966).

Fèbvre, Lucien. *Autour d'une bibliothèque (Pages offertes à M. Charles Oursel)* (Dijon: Lamarche, 1942).

Feltin, J. "Succès des missions protestantes à Villevallier au milieu du XIXᵉ siècle," *Bulletin de la société des sciences historiques et naturelles de l'Yonne*, 103 (1971-1972), pp. 235-242.

Ferré, Max. *Histoire du mouvement syndicaliste révolutionnaire chez les instituteurs des origines à 1922* (Paris: Société universitaire de librairie, 1955).

Ferry, Jules. Speech to the Teachers in 1881, in *Revue pédagogique*, 1881, pt. 1, p. 581.

Flatrès, L. *L'Enseignement du français et en particulier de la composition française dans les écoles rurales bretonnes* (Quimper: Chavet-Bargain, 1920).

Fonteneau, Jean. *Le Conseil municipal: le maire—les adjoints* (Paris: Éditions ouvrières, 1964).

Forestier, Henri. "Le Clergé et l'opinion dans l'Yonne sous la Monarchie de Juillet," *Bulletin de la société des sciences historiques et naturelles de l'Yonne*, 97 (1957-1958), pp. 1-24.

Franche, Paul. *Le Prêtre dans le roman français* (Paris: Perrin, 1902).

Garavel, J. *Les Paysans de Morette: Un Siècle de vie rurale dans une commune du Dauphiné* (Paris: Armand Colin, 1948).

Gargan, Edward T. "The Priestly Culture in Modern France," *Catholic Historical Review*, 57 (1971), pp. 1-20.

Gargan, Edward T. and Robert A. Hanneman. "Recruitment to the Clergy in Nineteenth Century France: 'Modernization and Decline'?" *Journal of Interdisciplinary History*, 9 (Autumn 1978), pp. 275-295.

Gargan, Edward T. et al., eds. *The Wolf and the Lamb: Popular Culture in France from The Old Régime to the Twentieth Century* (Saratoga, Calif.: Anma Libri, 1977).

Garric, A. *L'Histoire de Boussac*. (Rodez: A. Garric, 1973).

Gernoux, Alfred. *Les Pionniers de l'enseignement public*. (Châteaubriant: no publisher given, 1931).

——. "Le Progrès de l'enseignement aux XIXe et XXe siècles," *Annales de Nantes*, no. 106 (1957), pp. 13-20.

Girard, Louis. "Histoire de l'administration française depuis 1800: Problèmes et méthodes" at Colloquium (Paris, 1975).

Glay, E. and H. Champeau. *L'Instituteur* (Paris: Doin, 1928).

Glossinde, André. *Je suis instituteur* (Paris: Éditions du conquistador, 1954).

Godard, Célestin-Marie. "La Crise de la vie rurale," *Bulletin mensuel de la société nationale des conférences populaires* (Nov. 1910).

Goguel, Fraçois. *La Politique des partis sous la IIIe République* (3rd ed., Paris: Armand Colin, 1958).

Gréard, Octave. *La Législation de l'instruction primaire en France depuis 1789 jusqu'à nos jours*, VI and VII (Paris: Delalain, 1898-1900).

Guéhenno, Jean. *Sur le Chemin des hommes* (Paris: Bernard Grasset, 1959).

Guillemin, Bernard. *Le Diocèse de Bordeaux* (Paris: Beauchesne, 1974).

Guigue, Julien and Joseph Girard. *La Fontaine de Vaucluse* (Avignon: Rullière, 1949).

Halévy, Daniel. *La République des ducs* (Paris: Bernard Grasset, 1937).

Hayward, Jack. *The One and Indivisible French Republic* (New York: Norton, 1973).

Hayward, J.E.S. "Educational Pressure Groups and the Indoctrination of the Radical Ideology of Solidarism, 1895-1914," *International Review of Social History*, 8 (1963), pp. 1-17.

————. "The Official Philosophy of the French Third Republic: Léon Bourgeois and Solidarism," *International Review of Social History*, 6 (1961), pp. 19-48.

Hélias, Pierre-Jakez. *The Horse of Pride: Life in a Breton Village* (tr. June Guicharnaud; New Haven: Yale Univeristy Press, 1978).

Hervieu, Bertrand. "Le Pouvoir au village," *Études rurales*, 63-64 (1976), pp. 15-30.

Higonnet, Patrice L. R. *Pont-de-Montvert: Social Structure and Politics in a French Village, 1700-1914* (Cambridge, Mass.: Harvard University Press, 1971).

Hilaire, Yves-Marie. *Une Chrétienté au XIXe Siècle? La Vie religieuse des populations du diocèse d'Arras, 1840-1941* (Paris: Université de Lille, 1977).

Hughes, H. Stuart. *Consciousness and Society* (New York: Knopf, 1958).

Hugonnet, Jean. "Louis Pergaud, Instituteur," *Europe*, 38 (October 1959), pp. 30-46.

Humbert, Jacques. *Embrun et l'Embrunais* (Gap: Société des études des Hautes-Alpes, 1972).

Ichheiser, Gustave. *Appearances and Realities: Misunderstandings in Human Relations* (San Francisco: Jossey-Bass, 1970).

Judt, Tony. *Socialism in Provence, 1871-1914: A Study in the Origins of the Modern French Left* (Cambridge: Cambridge University Press, 1979).

Julia, Dominique. "La Crise des vocations, essai d'analyse historique," *Les Etudes*, 326 (1967), pp. 250-283.

Karnoouh, Claude. "La Démocratie impossible: Parenté et politique dans un village lorrain," *Études rurales*, 52 (1973), pp. 24-56.

Kent, Sherman. *The Election of 1827 in France* (Cambridge, Mass.: Harvard University Press, 1975).

————. *French Electoral Procedure under the July Monarchy* (New Haven: Yale University Press, 1937).

Kergomard, Pauline. "Les Femmes dans l'enseignement primaire," *Maneul général de l'instruction primaire*, May 25, 1889.

Labat, Emmanuel. "L'Instruction primaire au point de vue psychologique," *Revue des deux mondes*, 82 (July 1912), pp. 135-172.

Langlois, Claude. *Le Diocèse de Vannes au XIXe siècle, 1800-1830* (Paris: Klincksieck, 1974).

Lapèrierre, Guy. *La Séparation à Lyon (1904-1908)* (Lyon: Centre d' histoire du Catholicisme, 1973).

Latty, Gaspard. *Le Clergé français* (Paris: Berche, 1890).

Launay, Marcel. "Les Procès-verbaux de visites pastorales dans le diocèse de Nantes au milieu du XIXe siècle," *Annales de Bretagne*, 82 (1975), pp. 183-200.

Laurent, Marcel. *Deux Communes: Vinzelles et Charnat* (Clermont-Ferrand: Saint-Laure, 1976).

Lebesque, Morvan. *Comment peut-on être Breton: Essai sur la démocratie française* (Paris: Editions du Seuil, 1970).

Le Bras, Gabriel. *Études de sociologie religieuse*, 2 vols. (Paris: Press Universitaires de France, 1956).

Legrand, René. *Historique de la paroisse de Neuves-Maisons* (Nancy: no publisher given, 1974).

Léonard, Jacques. *La France médicale au XIXe siècle* (Paris: Gallimard, 1978).

Leuilliot, Paul. *L'Alsace au début du XIXe siècle* (Paris: S.E.V.P.E.N., 1959).

Locke, Robert. *French Legitimists and the Politics of Moral Order in the Early Third Republic* (Princeton, N.J.: Princeton University Press, 1974).

Loubère, Leo A., *Radicalism in Mediterranean France: Its Rise and Decline, 1848-1914* (Albany, N.Y.: SUNY Press, 1974).

Machérel, Claude, and Jacques le Querrec. *Léry, village normand* (Nanterre: Laboratoire d'éthnologie, 1974).

Manse, Pierre. *Mérilheu de mon enfance: La Vie quotidienne dans un village des Pyrénées au début du siècle* (Pau: Marrimpouey, 1971).

Marc, Henri. *Histoire de Chenôve* (Dijon: Lamarche, 1893).

Marcilhacy, Christiane. *Le Diocèse d'Orléans au milieu du XIXe siècle* (Paris: Sirey, 1964).

Margadant, Ted W., *French Peasants in Revolt: The Insurrection of 1851* (Princeton: Princeton University Press, 1979).

Massignon, Geneviève, ed., *Folktales of France* (tr. Jacqueline Hyland; Chicago: University of Chicago Press, 1968).

Mayeur, Jean-Marie. "Géographie de la résistance aux inventaires (février-mars 1906), pp. 1259-1272.

———. *Un Prêtre démocrate: L'abbé Lémire, 1853-1928* (Paris: Castermann, 1968).

McManners, John. *The French Revolution and the Church* (New York: Harper & Row, 1970).

Mendras, Henri. *Éléments de sociologie* (Paris: Armand Colin, 1967).

———. *La Fin des paysans: Changements et innovations dans les sociétés rurales françaises* (Paris: Armand Colin, 1967).

Merriman, John M. *The Agony of the Republic: The Repression of the Left in Revolutionary France, 1848-1851* (New Haven: Yale University Press, 1978).

———. "The Demoiselles of the Ariège, 1829-1831," in Merriman, ed., *1830 in France* (New York: Franklin Watt, 1975).

———, ed. *Consciousness and Class Experience in Nineteenth Century Europe* (New York: Holmes and Meier, 1979).

Mesliand, Claude. "Contribution à l'étude de l'anticléricalisme à Pertuis de 1871 à 1913," *Archives de sociologie des religions*, 10 (1960), pp. 49-62.

———. "Gauche et droite dans les campagnes provençales sous la IIIe République," *Études rurales*, 63-64 (1976), pp. 207-234.

Meyers, Peter Vroom. "The French Instituteur, 1830-1914: A Study of Professional Formation" (New Brunswick, N.J.: Ph.D. diss., Rutgers, 1972).

Michaud, H. and Glossinde, A. *Condition et mission de l'instituteur* (Paris: Aubier, 1945).

Mistral, Frédéric. *Mémoires et récits* (Paris: Plon, n.d.).

Morel, Alain. "Pouvoirs et idéologies au sein du village Picard hier et aujourd'hui," *Annales: économies-sociétés-civilisations*, 30 (1975), pp. 161-176.

Morin, Edgar. *The Red and White: Report from a French Village* (tr. A. M. Sheridan Smith; New York: Pantheon, 1970).

Moulin, Laure. *Jean Moulin* (Paris: Presses de la Cité, 1969).

Nègre, André. *St. Eulalie aux Bois* (Caen: published by the author, 1970).

Orieux, Jean. *Souvenirs de campagne* (Paris: Flammarion, 1978).

Ozouf, Jacques. "Les Instituteurs de la Manche et leurs associations au début du XXe siècle," *Revue d'histoire moderne et contemporaine*, 13 (Jan.-March 1966), pp. 95-114.

———. *Nous les maîtres d'école: autobiographies d'instituteurs de la Belle Époque* (Paris: Julliard, 1967).

Ozouf, Mona. *L'École, l'église et la République, 1871-1914.* (Paris: Armand Colin, 1963).

Pagnol, Marcel. *La Gloire de mon père* (Monte Carlo: Éditions Pastorelly, 1957).

Palanque, Jean Rémy, ed. *Le Diocèse d'Aix-en-Provence* (Paris: Presses universitaires de France, 1975).

Palmer, Robert. *Catholics and Unbelievers in Eighteenth Century France* (Princeton: Princeton University Press, 1939).

Pastureaud, Françoise. "Alphabétisation, culture, moeurs et croyances populaires: le Marais de monts, Saint-Jean de monts, 1796-1903 (Masters thesis: Ecole pratique des hautes études, 1975).

Paul, Harry W. "In Quest of Kerygma," *American Historical Review*, 75 (1969), pp. 387-423.

Pécaut, Félix. *Quinze ans d'éducation* (Paris: Delagrave, n.d.).

Péguy, Charles. *Notre Jeunesse* (Paris: Gallimard, 1957).

Pellisson, Maurice. "La Situation de l'enseignement primaire en 1898 d'après les rapports des inspecteurs d'académie," *Revue pédagogique*, 1899, pt. 2, pp. 117-119.

Pergaud, Louis. *La Guerre des boutons* (Paris: Mercure de France, 1912).

———. *Les Rustiques: Nouvelles villageoises* (Paris: Mercure de France, 1921).

Péyrègne, Léonce. *Les Items d'Abraham de Camy* (Paul: Marrimpouey, 1976).

Phayer, Michael. "Repression of Modern Dancing in France and Germany, 1815-1840" (unpublished paper).

———. *Sexual Liberation and Religion in Nineteenth Century Europe* (London: Croom Helm, 1977).

Pierrard, Pierre. Juifs et catholiques français (Paris: Fayard, 1970).

———. *Le Prêtre français* (Paris: Bloud et Gay, 1969).

Pierrefeu, Guy de. *Le Clergé fin-de-siècle* (Paris: Delagrave, n.d.).

Pinkney, David. *The French Revolution of 1830* (Princeton: Princeton University Press, 1972).

Planchais, Jean, ed. *Les Provinciaux ou la France sans Paris* (Paris: Éditions du seuil, 1970).

Plongeron, Bernard. *La Vie quotidienne du clergé français au XVIIIe siècle* (Paris: Hachette, 1974).

Pomponi, F. "Pouvoir et abus de pouvoir des maires corses au XIXe siècle," *Études rurales,* 63-64 (1976), pp. 63-64.

Prévost, Jean. *Le Prêtre, ce héros de roman* (Paris: Téqui, 1952).

Prost, Antoine. *Histoire de l'enseignement en France, 1800-1967* (Paris: Armand Colin, 1968).

Psichari, Ernest. *Oeuvres complètes d'Ernest Psichari* (Paris: Conard, 1948).

La Question de l'inamovibilité canonique by L'Abbé*** (Paris: no publisher given, 1873).

Raguin, Yves. *Celibacy for Our Times* (tr. M. H. Kennedy; St. Meinrad, Ind.: Abbey Press, n.d.).

Rearick, Charles. "Symbol, Legend, and History: Michelet as Folklorist-Historian," *French Historical Studies,* 7 (Spring 1971), pp. 72-92.

Rémond, René. *L'Anticléricalisme en France de 1815 à nos jours* (Paris: Fayard, 1976).

Renan, Ernest. *La Réforme intellectuelle et morale de la France* (Paris: Lévy, 1872).

Richard, A. "Conseils pratiques aux instituteurs," *Revue pédagogique,* 1881, pt. I, pp. 394-407.

Rocher, J. P. "Contribution à l'étude de l'histoire de l'anticléricalisme: Un Conflit entre maire et curé à Villeneuve-l'Archevêque sous Louis Phillipe," *Bulletin de la société des sciences historiques et naturelles de l'Yonne,* 100 (1963-1964), pp. 84-99.

Rohr, Jean. *Victor Duruy, Ministre de Napoléon III: Essai sur la politique de l'instruction publique au temps de l'empire libéral* (Paris: Librairie générale de droit et de jurisprudence, 1967).

Romains, Jules. *Men of Good Will* (tr. W. B. Welles; New York: Knopf, 1936).

Sandiford, Peter. *Comparative Education* (London: Dent, 1918).

Schmitt, Charles. *Le Maire de la commune rurale* (Paris: Berger-Levrault, 1959).

Shorter, Edward. *The Making of the Modern Family* (New York: Basic Books, 1975).

Siegfried, André. *Tableau politique de la France de l'Ouest sous la IIIe République.* (Paris: Armand Colin, 1913).

Silver, Judith. "French Rural Response to Modernization: The Vendômois, 1852-1885." (Ann Arbor: Ph.D. diss., University of Michigan, 1973).

————. "French Peasant Demands for Popular Leadership in the Vendômois (Loir-et-Cher), 1952-1890," *Journal of Social History,* 14 (1980), pp. 277-294.

Simon, Jules. *Premières années* (Paris: 1870).

Simoni, Pierre. "Notices nécrologiques et élites locales: l'élite Aptésienne au XIXe siècle," *Annales du Midi,* 87 (1975), pp. 67-95.

Singer, Barnett. "Church-State Conflict at the Grassroots: Teacher versus Priest in Brittany, 1880-1914," *Journal of Church and State,* (forthcoming).

————. "Jules Ferry and the Laic Revolution in French Primary Education," *Paedagogica Historica,* 15 (1975), pp. 406-425.

———. "Minoritarian Religion and the Rise of a Secular School System in France," *Third Republic/Troisième République*, I (1976), pp. 228-254.

Soraye-Racape, Marie. *Jadis au pays de Janzé* (St. Hilaire: published by the author, 1971).

Sorlin, Pierre. *La Société française, I, 1840-1914* (Paris: Arthand, 1969).

Sumner, William Graham. *Folkways* (New York: Ginn, 1906).

Sydenham, M. J. *The French Revolution* (London: Batsford, 1965).

Tackett, Timothy. *Priest and Parish in Eighteenth Century France: A Social and Political Study of the Curés in a Diocese of Dauphiné, 1750-1791* (Princeton: Princeton University Press, 1977).

Tarde, G. "L'instituteur et la désertion des campagnes," *Manuel général de l'instruction primaire*, June 17, 1899.

Teegan, Thomas H. *Elementary Education in France* (London: Simpkin, Marshall, 1891).

Thabault, Roger. *Education and Change in a Village Community: Mazières-en-Gâtine, 1848-1914* (tr. Peter Treagert; Schocken Books: New York, 1971).

Thévenot, Arsène. *Monographie de la commune de Lhuître* (Arcis-sur-Aube: Frémont, 1903).

Thompson, David. *France: Empire and Republic, 1850-1944* (New York: Harper and Row, 1968).

Thuillier, Guy. "Pour une histoire de l'hygiène corporelle: un exemple régional: Le Nivernais," *Revue d'histoire économique et social*, 46 (1968), pp. 232-253.

———. "Pour une histoire des travaux ménagers en Nivernais au XIX^è siècle," *Revue d'histoire économique et sociale*, 50 (1972), pp. 238-264.

Trénard, Louis, ed. *Histoire des Pays-Bas français: Documents* (Toulouse: Privat, 1974).

Tudesq, André-Jean. "L'Administration municipale dans le Sud-Ouest sous la monarchie de juillet," *Annales du Midi*, 84 (1972), pp. 483-492.

———. *Les Grands Notables en France (1840-1849)*, 2 vols. (Paris: Presses universitaires de France, 1964).

Van Gennep, Arnold. *Manuel de folklore français contemporain* (Paris: Pickard, 1943).

Vidal, Abbé B. Article in *La Semaine religieuse de la Lorraine* (Nancy), Sept. 29, 1894.

Vidalenc, Jean. *Le Département de l'Eure sous la monarchie constitutionelle* (Paris: Presses universitaires de France, 1968).

———. *La Société française de 1815 à 1848* (Paris: Marcel Rivière, 1970).

Vigier, Philippe. *La Seconde République dans la région alpine*, 2 vols. (Paris: Presses universitaires de France, 1963).

Vincent, Gérard. "Les Professeurs du second degré au début du XX^è siècle," *Le Mouvement social*, 81 (1966), pp. 49-86.

Vulpian, Alain de. "Physionomie agraire et orientation politique dans le département des Côtes-du-Nord," *Revue française de science politique*, I (May 1951), pp. 123-126.

Weber, Eugen. "Gymnastics and Sports in Fin-de-Siècle France: Opium of the Classes," *American Historical Review*, 76 (Feb. 1971), pp. 70-98.

———. "Comment la Politique vint aux Paysans: A second look at Peasant Politicization," *American Historical Review*, 87 (April, 1982), pp. 357-89.

———. "The Second Republic, Politics, and the Peasant," *French Historical Studies*, 11 (Fall 1980), pp. 521-550.

———. *Peasants into Frenchmen: The Modernization of Rural France, 1870-1914* (Stanford: Stanford University Press, 1976).

Weill, Georges. "La révolution de juillet dans les départments," in *1830* (Paris: Alcan, 1932).

Williams, W. H. "The Priest in History: A Study in Divided Loyalties in the French Lower Clergy from 1776 to 1789" (Ph.D. diss., Duke University, 1965).

Wright, Gordon. *France in Modern Times* (Chicago: Rand McNally, 1974).

———. *Rural Revolution in France* (Stanford: Stanford University Press, 1964).

Wylie, Laurence. "Social Change at the Grass Roots," in Stanley Hoffman, et al., *In Search of France* (Cambridge, Mass.: Harvard University Press, 1963).

———. *Village in the Vaucluse* (2nd ed.; New York: Harper and Row, 1964).

Zeldin, Theodore, ed. *Conflicts in French Society: Anti-clericalism, Education, and Morals in the Nineteenth Century* (London: Allen and Unwin, 1970).

———. *France, 1848-1945*, 2 vols. (Oxford: Oxford University Press, 1977).

———. *The Political System of Napoleon III* (London: Macmillan, 1958).

Zola, Émile, *Oeuvres complètes*, VIII (Paris: Fasquelle, 1968).

II. Unsigned Articles and Entries in the Following Journals or Compendia:

Annales . . . députés. Document parlementaires (session ordinaire).

Annuaire statistique de la France.

L'Aurore.

Bulletin de l'instruction primaire.

L'Indépendance de l' Est.

La Lanterne.

Lyon Républicain.

Manuel général de l'instruction primaire.

Le Montfortais (Ille-et-Vilaine).

La Nouvelle République.

Le Nouvelliste de Bretagne et de la région de l'Ouest (Rennes).

Revue pédagogique.

La Semaine religieuse de Beauvais, Noyon et Senlis.

Le Semaine religieuse (Mende).

La Tribune.

L'Union républicaine (Libourne).

Index

A

Adam, Auguste, 18
Agenais, 56, 129, 138, 141, 144
Agulhon, Maruice, 60, 67, 73, 77, 82
Ain, 15
Aisne, 113
Aix, 32, 94
Allen, Woody, 106
Allier, 63, 101, 112, 113, 115, 118, 135, 136
Allignol, A., 28
Allignol, C., 28
Alsace, 41, 133
Ambert (Puy-de-Dôme), 44
America, 131
Ancenis (Loire-Atlantique), 130
Appoigny (Yonne), 97
Apt (Vaucluse), 13, 103
Ardèche, 31, 100
Ariège, 57
Arnac-La-Poste (Haute-Vienne), 70
Arras (Pas-de-Calais), 20, 27
Arras, Bishop of, 87
Ars (Charen-te), 31
Aube, 116
Aude, 96
Auden, W. H., 132
Aulard, Alphonse, 125
Aurévilly, Barbey d', 136
Autun (Saône-et-Loire), 31
Auvergne, 39, 49
Auxerre, (Yonne), 98

Aveyron, 15
Avignon (Vaucluse), 31, 103

B

Balz, André, 110
Balzac, Honoré de, 14, 21, 30, 72, 90, 104, 118
Barère, Bertrand, 59
Barral, Pierre, 32, 59
Barrès, Maruice, 112, 113, 131
Barthès, Roland, 122
Basque, 102
Basses-Alpes, 50, 75
Bastide, Huguette, 132
Baudrillart, Henri, 137
Bayle, Louis, 126
Bazin, Hervé, 34, 61
Beauce, 35, 116
Beaudéduit (Oise), 46, 55
Beaumont (Dordogne), 22
Beaune (Côte-D' Or), 39
Beauvais, 29, 43, 62
Bécherel (Ille-et-Vilaine), 144
Bédarrides (Vaucluse), 101
Bedoin (Vaucluse), 82
Bellon, François, 73, 83
Béranger, Pierre-Jean de, 30
Bergson, Henri, 144
Bernanos, Georges, 9, 33
Berry, 8
Bert, Paul, 77, 126
Berthier, Curé, 33

193